THE
COMPASSIONATE
ANIMAL

An Interfaith Guide to
The Extended Circle of Compassion

Barbara Gardner

To Debbie

With warm wishes

Barbara

Foreword by Dr Richard D. Ryder

Published by
Animal Books and Media Limited
Ivybridge, Devon, England.

1st edition – 2012
Revised edition - 2014

ISBN – 978-1480155695

For All Sufferers

May they find Peace

CONTENTS

FOREWORD
by
Dr Richard D. Ryder

This book explains why humans need to become compassionate animals by including all conscious entities within their circle of compassion, and suggests why this may be necessary if humans are to survive as a species. Barbara Gardner's argument that there is no moral justification for speciesism, based on the shared evolutionary development of all animals, is compelling. She argues that all animals, including the human animal, share much of their evolutionary history, their DNA, their selfish genes, their physiology, their brain structures, and their consciousness, and should, therefore, all be given respect. Barbara observes that this required emphasis on compassion has been advocated in many of the world's great spiritual traditions for millennia, particularly through the principle of *ahimsa* or non-violence. She examines the outstanding features of these great traditions in the first part of the book, looking at Hinduism, Taoism, Buddhism, Jainism, the ancient Greek philosophies and Monotheism. Finally, she argues for the urgency of the need to revive these values, and to extend them to all sentient beings.

This book is unique in that it brings together ideas that are often kept apart — the mysteries of consciousness, the cosmos, quantum physics and compassion. I believe that these are among the greatest intellectual challenges that face us in the early twenty-first century. Barbara combines her own experience of science, mathematics and applied compassion to effect this synthesis. These qualifications enable her to clarify what is too often clouded and to reveal the essentials in what is frequently concealed. Laser-like, her mind illuminates the salients.

In part three, Barbara looks at the evolution of compassion. Arguing from science, she proposes that sophisticated consciousness probably first emerged on the Earth with the appearance of fish on the 19th December of the metaphorical "year" of our universe so far. She believes that all animals are conscious, perhaps even the insects, and that natural selection has favoured the survival of beings that were both conscious and parentally caring. Hence the evolutionary emergence of inherited compassion, and the continuous battle within all of us between selfishness and altruism. She sees compassion as the power of the conscious brain to override the selfishness of our genes; something we are going to have to do if we are to deal with the great internal and external threats that currently beset our planet.

Barbara believes that consciousness is something that has emerged as the latest stage of evolution. She is almost certainly right. But what then happened before complex brains evolved? Was consciousness waiting in the wings until such 'receptors' as brains came along? Or was the Universe itself, or other parts of it, always conscious? It is possible that if consciousness is a function of complexity itself then a galaxy, for example, might be conscious, but perhaps unable to communicate this fact to its conscious constituents such as ourselves.

Then Barbara deals with the mysteries of quantum physics. These are the counterintuitive rules of thumb that seem to govern events on the sub-microscopic scale, and she describes them with simplicity and clarity. Newtonian and Einsteinian physics apply to large objects (e.g. tables, people and planets) while quantum rules apply to small objects (e.g. electrons, photons and neutrinos). Strangely, these two approaches to physics are largely incompatible.

Interestingly, Barbara also explores the similarities between modern quantum physics and the ancient mystical ideas of Hinduism, Buddhism and Taoism, considering, for example, the state of higher-consciousness or enlightenment — the ancient object of yoga and other meditative practices, tying these in with her knowledge of the brain.

Most importantly, she also re-examines the origins of compassion. I have always felt that there are strong evolutionary reasons why we (and some other animals) should feel compassion. Compassion, after all, must often provide good value in terms of survival. Partly for this reason, I have built my morality of painism around this engine of natural compassion, on which needs to be constructed, so I believe, a sound rational body of moral theory. The erratic dictates of natural compassion need to be universalised and made consistent through reason.

Barbara describes what can go wrong with compassion due to competing impulses, the force of authority (as in Stanley Milgram's experiments), peer group pressures or desensitisation. She looks at the lives of outstanding people who have lived lives of compassion, or who have written movingly on the subject, and then addresses speciesism — the arrogant human prejudice against other species that relentlessly causes us to relegate the other animals to a position of almost total moral insignificance (as if there had been no Darwin).

****

Consciousness has always fascinated me, and I went up to Cambridge as a psychology student determined to find out how it worked. The question I wanted to be answered was "What *causes* consciousness?" So I began to ask this question in lectures but found, to my surprise, that it was met either with ridicule or with downright censure. Behaviourism ruled, and nowhere more sternly than at Cambridge at that time. Only one of my psychology lecturers, Richard Gregory, was prepared to take the question seriously. I remember sitting with him on the grass at Pembroke College in 1962 and asking him the same question: "What causes consciousness? How does it emerge from the neurons of the brain?" He admitted he didn't know but that he thought of it as being like the generation of electricity. "How can something as extraordinary as electricity emerge from rolls of copper wires rotating between magnets?" he asked. The copper wire, the magnets and the act of rotation are all so entirely different from the electricity that its emergence seems almost to be magical. Yet, less than a hundred years after Michael Faraday discovered how to do this, a full explanation in terms of electrons and magnetic fields became available.

For me, this has remained the best analogy for consciousness, as I have waited patiently for an explanation of its causes that has never come.

A short while after this discussion with Richard Gregory I went to a meeting of the Heretics Society that was addressed by the frightening figure of William Sargent, a well-known lobotomising psychiatrist of the period. He was, I think, talking to us on the subject of anxiety — something it was easy to feel in his presence! Afterwards, my friends and I were joined for a drink in a nearby pub by someone who had also been at the lecture, a man with sideburns, colourful waistcoat and cravat.

"You psychologists aren't addressing the fundamental questions", he said. "You are too obsessed with stimuli and responses!"

I saw my chance. "Yes", I agreed. "How about the causes of consciousness? I am not allowed even to raise this question. Some people in the Experimental Psychology Department seem to think that it can't be investigated by science."

"Of course it can", said the man in the waistcoat. "Perhaps one day I will have a chance to do it myself."

It was only later that we discovered that our flamboyant friend was Francis Crick, the co-discoverer of the DNA spiral. At that time, strangely, neither his name nor his discovery, were particularly well known. Years later he went to California where he did indeed do research into consciousness, although never discovering the answer to the question.

Some twenty years later I was having breakfast in a Cambridge college and discussing the vexed question of free will. "I believe that sub-atomic particles have free will", I said, rather rashly. "I agree with you" replied an elderly man sitting opposite me. He was Freeman Dyson the distinguished atomic physicist. "Can you then explain free will?" I asked, "or can you throw any light on the causes of consciousness?" Sadly, he admitted that he couldn't. His attitude, however, encouraged me.

I tell these stories to make it clear that these questions have been thought about by great scientists for a long time, and yet we still have no satisfactory answers.

Over the intervening years I have kept a watching brief on these questions and have, in some of my publications about *speciesism* and *painism*, put forward a few ideas that have particularly appealed to me on the matters relating to both consciousness and free will. (Of course, the two issues are quite separate.) I am prepared to accept that I (whatever "I" means) can have the feelings not only that I am conscious on occasions but that I can make free choices. I am, however, prepared to admit that the latter feeling is probably an illusion.

Of all the experiments that have been conducted on these issues over the last forty years, those of Benjamin Libet stand out. His demonstration that the brain acts about a third of a second *before* we are conscious of making a decision, has usually been accepted as undermining the existence of free will, and I believe it probably does so. Unless we accept a new definition of Time.

So how about Sigmund Freud and the unconscious? He taught us, after all, the value and importance of the unconscious mind. Isn't it possible that we *always* take decisions and make choices unconsciously in the first place, only later allowing them to become conscious and then, rather vainly, proclaiming to the world and to ourselves that "we made a conscious decision"?

I recently attended an interesting evening at Max Velmans' Consciousness Café in Totnes where Anthony Freeman said that the two most important decisions of his life — to become a priest and to marry — were not made consciously. He just seemed to drift into them. Susan Blackmore, supporting this, said we often attribute consciousness to a decision only after the event. Surely, such experiences could be explained in Freudian terms, and *I suspect that many of our decisions, even all of them, are mulled over and decided upon unconsciously*. Only as we act upon them are they illuminated with consciousness.

There are, however, deeper possibilities, that involve the strange world of quantum physics. I once suggested that we may be linking consciousness and quantum theory only because they are both so difficult to understand. I am no longer seriously sure of this. Quantum physics may be impossible to understand but it works! So here are just a few wild possibilities that ought to be considered:-

1) Does the Uncertainty Principle of quantum theory, and the way in which quantum events appear to happen suddenly and for no apparent external cause, in any way resemble so called "free will"? Looking at people and electrons as an observer one may be struck by the similarity in their behaviours. They both seem to do things for their own internal reasons, unpredictably. Perhaps my experience of free will is actually the quantum behaviour of parts of my brain seen, as it were, from the inside!

2) Physicists will tell you that there is incompatibility between the two great theories of physics — that of Newton and

Einstein on one hand (which works brilliantly for big things) and quantum theory on the other (which works extremely well for sub-microscopic things). Personally, I find it almost incredible that something as simple as size (or scale) can really matter so much. But, apparently, it does. So what happens when the scale is transitional? Do both theories operate? No physicist has been able to explain this to me. Yet such transitional size is just about the size of the brain! Possibly, the brain as a whole operates according to Newtonian deterministic rules, while synapses are small enough to be governed by quantum laws which are probabilistic. Neurons may be right on the cusp between the two theories. As consciousness seems to be simultaneously a function of almost the whole brain and of small parts of it at the same time, then maybe there are some transitional effects present. Is this connected in some way with the production of consciousness? Or does it suggest that large areas of brain (operating Newtonially) are in tension with synapses (operating quantumly)? Does this create "the illusion of free will"? Of course, all big things, not only brains, are composed of atoms and sub-atomic particles. So in all big things there must be a scale which is transitional. Does, however, consciousness in some way provide the link between the two approaches to physics?

3) Then there are so-called "field effects" — unseen spheres of influence like magnetism, gravity and, perhaps, time. Yet, once again, scale could play a part. At a sufficient distance even galaxies appear to be particles. Two subatomic particles, previously linked but now separated by, say, a million miles, are still able to influence each other instantaneously. Such action-at-a-distance could explain how distant parts of the brain can operate simultaneously.

4) Another strange phenomenon, according to quantum physics, is the claimed effect that observation has upon the behaviour of particles. It is believed that only when they are *observed* do they go one way or the other. When they are not being observed they are in neither or both states (like Schrödinger's cat, being both dead and alive!). I am not sure I believe this, but, suppose observation is the same thing as consciousness, what then happened billions of years ago before there were any conscious brains? Does this knock the theory on

the head or does it suggest that all sorts of things are conscious and always have been, even from the moment of the big bang?

5) We often think of Newtonian physics as being a matter of informed common sense. The theory seems to accord well with our everyday conscious experiences of reality. On the other hand, quantum theory seems utterly weird — how can particles be in two places at once or act instantly upon each other when a million miles apart? How can they behave unpredictably or be influenced by something as woolly as "observation"? So, in general, we think of Newtonian physics as being "normal" and quantum physics as being "weird". Yet, possibly, it could be the other way around! Total "reality" could be quantumesque while the weirdness could be just that part of it that is filtered by our own conscious experiences. Consciousness might be distorting everything it contacts! So our conscious commonsense everyday experiences (and thus virtually the whole of science) could be the weird and minor exceptions to universal quantum reality.

Is consciousness, then, as fundamental a thing as space, time or mass? Barbara reports that some people believe this. I tend the other way and suspect it is merely a luxury — the froth on an ocean roller, so to speak. It seems to me that consciousness is something that happens when we are aroused by internal or external stimuli that are threatening, novel or otherwise exciting. In other words, consciousness is switched on when there is an emergency. So, when nothing much is happening we are only half-conscious. If everything is a matter of routine we carry on automatically. Actually, we can do quite well without consciousness. Temporal lobe epileptics, like sleep-walkers, for example, can behave automatically like zombies. I have walked for ten minutes with a temporal lobe patient through the streets of Oxford while he was in a seizure! He avoided the traffic but would not respond to questions. Afterwards, he could recall nothing that had happened. Consciousness, in other words, is a fragile flower! It is like a candle flame. It flickers fitfully, and probably has no executive power. As Huxley once said, consciousness is rather like the whistle on a steam train — it appears very important but has no real influence on where the train is going.

Almost certainly, consciousness involves just about the whole brain. We know that, for consciousness to occur, the brainstem reticular formation has to be aroused and so does the thalamus. But these, surely, are merely switches on the way. They are necessary for consciousness but not sufficient. They are like turning on the switch at the wall for the television, and then the power switch on the set. The screen that then lights up is like the cerebral cortex generally, the most vital parts of which, for consciousness, appear to be the frontal lobes. (Susan Blackmore: *Consciousness: an Introduction*, 2nd Edition, Oxford University Press, 2012).

Importantly, Barbara brings all these things together with the issue of compassion. Over the centuries this has variously been called *Mercy* or the *Spirit of Love*. It is based upon empathy — or the awareness of the feelings of others and is, surely, the single most important factor in morality. Compassion is, I would say, the foundation of moral action. Yet, in the wake of two terrible World Wars, I grew up being told that compassion was something unnatural. It had to be learned. Everybody was believed to be basically bad — violent, greedy, power-crazy and sex-mad! So civilisation meant learning to do and feel "unnatural" things such as restraint. This was the only way that human beings could be nice to one another! That is what I was led to believe. It is why people in Puritan times — such as the 1950s — emphasise suppression and self-control. Nevertheless, I found within myself (despite high levels of chronic fear and anger caused by the asceticism of my upbringing) sparks of apparently spontaneous compassion for all suffering creatures. I felt deep concern, for example, for bullied school-friends, frightened children and hunted animals. Yet I found that this compassion seemed to be a gut reaction; I didn't have to learn it! This, I think, is one of the great rediscoveries of the twenty-first century: that compassion is something natural and in all of us.

Of course, compassion has to be protected. Equally natural but negative forces of hatred, cruelty and anger also exist and have to be controlled, otherwise, like weeds, they will strangle our natural feelings of compassion. Fear and anger mask compassion. Also of huge importance, so I believe, is our natural horror at the sight of blood, dismemberment and suffering. This used to be called squeamishness. Yet it is a natural, very powerful and valuable feeling. Nonhumans can also show it. Squeamishness (or horror) can make it difficult for us to kill in war and is, I believe, the basis for post-traumatic stress disorders.

I have built my ethical theory of painism upon these natural feelings of compassion and squeamishness. I consider that the power of these valuable gut reactions needs to be harnessed and utilised as the foundations for a rational and consistent ethical theory. Anger, too, at the sight of injustice and cruelty, needs to be respected. It has, in my case at least, been the source of the large amounts of energy I have needed to campaign effectively. Campaigning is hard work!

Barbara looks at such natural behaviours, as empathy, and links them to the action of mirror cells in our brains and to the issues arising from consciousness. These are important and timely challenges for all of us!

One of the strangest questions raised by consciousness is "Why am I me?" Why is my consciousness stuck in my brain — the cells of which are constantly changing? It is a difficult idea to express. But what anchors my consciousness to my brain? Why doesn't it wander around? If my brain was removed and put in a jar and kept alive, would I still be there? If bits were separated but kept alive, where would I be? If my brain was put in someone else's head would I still be present? Why didn't I exist before, in the millions of almost identical brains that have existed? Why was my me-ness only switched on when this brain came along? What happens if I join up two or more brains? We know that splitting a brain can lead to the feeling of two people being in the same skull. So what happens if several brains are linked by cables? Such questions are all very baffling.

As conscious individuals, we are all certainly parts of a worldwide, even cosmos-wide, community of consciousness. But the strange thing is that our consciousnesses are *not* joined up. Between the consciousness of each individual exists a natural barrier. Each individual consciousness is limited by the boundaries of our bodies. I cannot actually feel your pains or experience your fantasies directly. I can only experience my own internal representations of what you feel. This is why each conscious individual is so important. This separateness of individual consciousnesses is the basis for my ethics of painism (see my *Speciesism, Painism and Happiness*, Imprint Academic, 2011).

Advances in the science of religion are showing that infants distinguish between objects in their environment which are inert and those that are self-motivated (alive). The former only move when acted upon, whereas agents move of their own accord. It has been suggested that this readiness to look for agents is one reason why children are receptive to the idea that the universe is directed by unseen gods. Children also tend to assume that agents are omniscient. Maybe such natural tendencies have had survival value, and it is certainly easy to see why children may, therefore, have a strong natural tendency towards religion. (*New Scientist,* 17 March 2012).

What, then, predisposes children towards an interest in morality? I have suggested that there are four relevant natural tendencies: *to empathise, to feel affection, to hate frustration and to be aware of fairness. All four tendencies appear, untaught, in infancy.* So an infant may show empathy with a wounded animal, for example, affection for a doll or a person, hate restraints and be intensely aware of unfairness (if rewards are withheld from them which are given to others, for instance). It is when these four instincts come together that a child begins to attribute to others her own familiar feelings, and to wish to help. *A sense of morality is born.* These four impulses also feed into the development of natural parental behaviour.

Infants are also, of course, aware of suffering generally. Not just "physical" pains but the sufferings associated with unfairness, fear, loss, frustration and deprivations of liberty. No doubt the experience that many such pains are caused by external agents (including punitive parents or jealous siblings) leads to the general infantile conclusions that all good and bad things are caused by agents. Surely such universal infantile ruminations, predispose us all to take an interest in freedom, justice and morality generally. Our interest in morality is, in other words, quite natural, although sensitive to cultural influences.

I have suggested elsewhere (*Speciesism Painism and Happiness: A Morality for the Twenty-First Century*, Imprint Academic, 2011) that morality is, perhaps, the most important part of any religion. But there are two other crucial psychological functions of religions — first in providing an *explanation* for the universe, its beginnings and how it works, and secondly, in giving us some alleged *power* (through prayer) to control events (such as the outcomes of war, illness and crops). In fact, science has now superceded religion in providing the last two functions but it still does not supply a morality to guide us. That is what this book provides in proposing that our morality should be founded upon compassion — compassion as the awareness of the sufferings of others combined with actions to reduce those sufferings.

There is, of course, a problem if one denies free-will. Without control over our own behaviour how can we be morally responsible for our actions? Indeed, how can we even be praised for showing compassion? The consciousness of decision-making looks increasingly irrelevant. The importance of *viewpoint* itself, however, cannot be overstated. Consciousness may *not* be important in deciding concrete actions from the viewpoint of the outside world, but it is still everything from the viewpoint of the individual who experiences it.

I don't even accept that consciousness has to have a Darwinian advantage. Indeed, it cannot do so unless consciousness actually affects behaviour. We *feel* as though consciousness is important, and particularly in the handling of emergencies and the solving of problems, (that is our *viewpoint*) but it may not be so. Consciousness may simply occur *after* all our decisions are taken.

"Blind sight" (where some blind people can unconsciously "see" using their eyes,) is a striking example of perception that is unconscious, and sleepwalkers, temporal lobe epileptics and most of us when we are doing routine things such as driving our usual way home, manage quite well to get things done even when we are unconscious, or nearly so.

I say "nearly", and this brings out the point that consciousness is a matter of quality. It can be lowered or raised, focused or expanded, clouded or clarified. I believe moods can also affect the quality of consciousness so that it becomes rose-tinted or grey. I am not discussing the *contents* of consciousness (ideas, perceptions, beliefs, fantasies etc.) but its *quality*. (As with photographs where we can distinguish between their contents and their quality.) We can undergo altered states of consciousness as when we experience *sleep* or *light-headedness* or *daze* or *déjà vu* or *dreaming* or *religious experiences* or *depersonalisation* or *derealisation* or *coma* or *stupor*, or *anaesthesia*, or certain forms of *heightened awareness* that include states of manic *ecstacy* or *super-realism*. Dissociative conditions, too, such as *amnesia* or *trance* affect the quality of consciousness. Even the precursors of psychotic delusions, sometimes called *delusional moods* (when consciousness is bathed in an aura of mystery or significance or strangeness or threat) can be regarded as forms of altered quality of consciousness. So can the effects of many neurological conditions, not least *epileptic aura*. Similar are the effects of some *psycho-active drugs*. None of these are thoroughly understood and need far more study. But will any provide an answer to our basic question; what *causes* consciousness itself? Perhaps we should not be so amazed that consciousness somehow emerges from the pink porridge of our brains. Is it any more extraordinary than the way radio and television images emerge from silicon and plastic, or indeed, electricity from wires rotating in a magnetic field?

Are consciousness and compassion restricted to life on planet Earth? I doubt it. I suspect the cosmos is seeped through with such mysteries. However froth-like consciousness may be in *causal* terms, it is, surely, the most important thing there is for all conscious beings.

****

This book goes far further, however, than a mere discussion of the mysteries of 'normal' consciousness. It is about raising consciousness to a higher state – one of enlightenment. Barbara carefully analyses what the various spiritual traditions say about this process. Using mindfulness or meditation the connections between higher consciousness and compassion can be revealed.

I suspect that the grains of compassion are within all of us from birth but that certain experiences, such as meditation, can liberate them and encourage them to grow. This is the book's crucial assertion: that higher consciousness and compassion walk together, and that enlightenment is achieved by practising compassion towards all living and suffering things.

Dr Richard Ryder invented the terms 'speciesism' and 'painism' and is a past RSPCA Chairman, and Mellon Professor at Tulane University. He is a Patron of the Animal Interfaith Alliance.

REVIEWS

'Barbara has made an outstanding contribution to our understanding of the human-animal relationship. Her book, "The Compassionate Animal" explores the age-old religious traditions which have given us a profound guidance in developing empathy towards all sentient beings. The book is immediately informative, educative, challenging and inspiring. It has been an honour and a privilege to know Barbara who has dedicated her life to the wellbeing of all humans as well as non-human creatures. Her book is a testimony to her intellectual, emotional, and spiritual commitment to serve the cause of animal welfare. I hope that "The Compassionate Animal" will be on the shelves of all school, university and public libraries and politicians, policy makers and opinion formers will read it so that they can comprehend the significance of the subject'.
Satish Kumar - Editor-In-Chief, Resurgence Magazine

'The guidebook for anyone searching for their soul, for peace of mind, for a point to living at all. Barbara Gardner's mesmerizing book shows how spiritual teachings from long ago are wholly applicable today and can help us bring out the best in ourselves, allowing us to escape the thoughtless conduct and rudderless trek through life that bring unhappiness to ourselves and those around us. In Jain terms, this is a 'right' book.'
Ingrid Newkirk – Founder & President PETA

'A book so long overdue has arrived. At a time when scientists are at last concluding that non-human animals are conscious, the onus is surely on us all to treat other species as considerately and compassionately as we treat our own. Barbara Gardner creates a compelling argument towards accelerating this path of kindness, and understanding our role in more urgently releasing animals from their physical and psychological pain - until the cruelty ends.'
Jill Robinson MBE, Dr.med.vet. h.c. - Founder & CEO Animals Asia Foundation

'Barbara Gardner's words ooze with compassion – the very spirit she is trying to convey to us through this panoramic book of multi-cultural wisdom. It clearly demonstrates that this world is not about Us and Them, but about Us and Us, and we must include all living beings in our love and kindness. Read these words and feel the inner depths of kindness, and your spirit will glow from within.'

Dr Atul K. Shah - CEO Diverse Ethics and author of 'Celebrating Diversity'

'A Wonderful book...and a most important contribution to the humane debate...it is a real widener.'

Jon Wynne-Tyson, Author of 'The Extended Circle' and founder of Centaur Press

ACKNOWLEDGEMENTS

I would like to thank Dr Richard D. Ryder for all the support he has given me in writing this book, for proof reading the various drafts, for advising me and for his kind contribution to the foreword. I would also like to thank Jon Wynne-Tyson, author of *The Extended Circle,* for his constructive advice and encouragement and for being the source of many of the quotations drawn upon in this book. I am grateful to Christina Tomlinson for proof reading and advising on the style and to all those who encouraged me and provided moral support, including Satish Kumar, Dr Atul Shah, Ingrid Newkirk, Jill Robinson MBE and Heidi Stephenson. I would also like to thank all my family and friends for their love and support.

INTRODUCTION

'Why is compassion not part of our established curriculum,
an inherent part of our education?
Compassion, awe, wonder, curiosity, exaltation, humility –
these are the very foundation of any real civilisation,
no longer the prerogatives, the preserves of any one church,
but belonging to everyone, every child,
in every home, in every school.'

Yehudi Menuhin – Just For Animals

This book is called *the Compassionate Animal*, but what is compassion and who is the compassionate animal? Compassion is the emotional response to empathy, which leads to the desire to alleviate the suffering of others, where empathy is the capacity to recognise and share the feelings of others. *The Compassionate Animal* is who we could become in the next stage of the evolution of the Cosmos. Wouldn't it be wonderful if we could live in a peaceful world where everyone shared the same perennial philosophy of wisdom and compassion and showed that compassion to all living things? Why should this dream not become a reality?

Compassion is the basis of all of the world's spiritual traditions. It is a common theme in Hinduism, Confucianism, Taoism, Buddhism, Jainism, Ancient Greek Philosophy, Judaism, Christianity, Islam, Zoroastrianism, Sikhism and others. The common thread in all these spiritual traditions is *'The Golden Rule'* which says *'Treat others as you would wish to be treated yourself.'* So why do these different traditions, which vary in many respects, having grown up at different times and in different parts of the world, all have compassion as their common theme and the source of their teachings? I argue that the founders of all these spiritual traditions had awakened to the spirit of compassion that was evolving in the Universe through the consciousnesses of all living beings.

Who are the *others* who, according to the Golden Rule, we should treat as we would wish to be treated ourselves? I demonstrate that these *others* include, not just humans, but all conscious, sentient beings that are capable of suffering and feeling pain, wherever they have evolved in the Universe.

Pluralism and an Interfaith Approach

This book takes an interfaith approach, acknowledging that every spiritual tradition has something valuable to offer. It is important to recognise that, despite their differences, they are all part of a single truth. The Hindus and the Jains celebrate pluralism and recognise that all faiths view this single truth from different perspectives and that we all know part of the truth, but not necessarily the whole truth. This is beautifully illustrated by the Jain story of four blind men and an elephant.

In the story, the four blind men have never seen an elephant before and they are asked to feel one and explain what they feel. The first blind man feels the trunk and says that it's a snake, the second blind man feels an ear and says that it's a piece of cloth, the third blind man feels the tail and says that it's a rope and the fourth blind man feels a leg and says that it's a tree. They all argue amongst themselves. None of them are right, but they all think that what they had felt was the whole elephant, so they cannot agree with each other. If they had their sight restored and could comprehend the whole elephant, how amazed would they be? Then they could all see the same whole and share a single truth and be in agreement with each other.

In 1893 the Hindu monk Swami Vivekananda, known as 'the monk who changed the world', travelled from India to Chicago to talk at the World Parliament of Religion. There he inspired the world with his views on pluralism. He said,

> *'As the different streams have their sources in different paths, which men take through different tendencies, various though they appear, crooked or straight, all lead to Thee'.*

He then went on to quote from the Bhagavad Gita which said,

'Whosoever comes to Me, through whatsoever form, I reach him; all men are struggling through paths which in the end lead to me'.

In the first part of this book we examine these different spiritual traditions, their roots and their attitudes towards compassion. It is interesting to note that, although each tradition acknowledges compassion, they all currently practise it to varying degrees, recognising different breadths in their circles of compassion. Some traditions currently include only humans in this circle, while others include all sentient beings. This book aims to show that, at the root of all faiths, compassion was extended to all those who can suffer and feel pain, animals as well as humans. The founders of *all* the traditions recognised our interrelatedness with the whole of the natural world and acknowledged our interconnectedness. But for many faiths, this relationship, beyond the boundaries of the human species, is currently being overlooked.

Another interesting observation is the way in which spirituality can be cyclical over time. There are periods of great wisdom in some societies, often inspired by a great reformer, when there is a deep understanding of compassion and the golden rule, and there are later periods of ignorance when the true meaning of the original *spirituality* is forgotten. At such times the original teachings descend into *religions* that are based on rituals, supported by priests and their hierarchies. These often result in great spiritual reformers, such as Mahavira, Buddha, Isaiah, Jesus and Muhammad, coming forward and restoring the concept of compassion in order to return to the original *spirituality*.

The Perennial Philosophy and People of Compassion
In part two we look at examples of great people of the past who have built on the teachings of these great founders and have demonstrated compassion to all sentient beings. In particular we look at the saints and mystics who discovered *the Perennial Philosophy*.

We look at how the phenomenon of speciesism resulted in the fall of compassion for animals in some faith traditions and their societies. We then look at the revival of the extended circle of compassion made by the philanthropists and the humane movement of the past few centuries and the enormous difference they have made to society today.

The Evolution of Compassion

Why are empathy and compassion so important to us and why do we have a potential for empathy and compassion at all? Was this potential necessary for our individual survival and the survival of our communities? Was it necessary for our individual happiness and the cohesiveness of our societies?

In the third part of the book we examine the evolutionary development of consciousness and compassion, starting with the evolution of the Universe, then of life, animals and finally the animal brain, and we demonstrate how closely linked the physiology and minds of animals are to our own. We also ask if compassion has been important in evolutionary terms and look at the compassion shown by non-human animals.

One of the most significant and important questions we ask is where is the Universe, which has been in a constant state of evolution and emergence, evolving to? Is the current conscious mind the ultimate evolutionary development or are there higher states of consciousness which we are in the process of developing? Does that higher state of consciousness lie in *the compassionate mind*?

Consciousness

In the fourth part, we examine consciousness and its relationship to compassion. Many of the spiritual traditions have devoted a considerable amount of time enquiring into the mystery of consciousness and much effort has been devoted to prayer, quiet contemplation and meditation, as a means of experiencing and understanding the different levels of conscious existence. Some traditions believe in a universal, cosmic consciousness that pervades the whole of the Universe whilst, at the same time, transcending it. This universal spirit has been named many things including Brahman, the Tao and God. The followers of these spiritual traditions believe that, in the depths of meditation, contemplation or prayer and on death, the individual consciousness can become united with the universal consciousness in a great expansion of the mind that cannot be explained but can only be experienced.

There has, to date, been no conclusive scientific explanation of consciousness, but some scientists believe that its workings are inextricably linked to the world of quantum physics. We examine quantum physics and try to understand how it may be connected to consciousness and enquire into whether consciousness may be inextricably linked to the Universe at the quantum level.

Whilst many spiritual practitioners believe that it is possible to achieve higher levels of consciousness and enlightenment through meditative practices, contemplation and prayer, others go further and believe that enlightenment can be achieved through the practice of *compassion to all living beings*.

The Extended Circle of Compassion

Throughout the book we ask 'Who should be included in our circle of compassion?' Is it only humans? Should it include all highly evolved animals? Or should it include all sentient beings? Some spiritual traditions, such as Jainism and Buddhism, believe that all living beings are included within our circle of compassion. They believe that they have the right to be included because they are able to experience consciousness, pain and suffering, and also because they can experience compassion themselves. The Buddhists believe that all sentient beings have the potential to attain *Buddhahood* or enlightenment. The Jains believe that *ahimsa,* or non-violence, should be extended to all living beings. In Judaism, the principle of *tsa'ar ba'alei chayim* requires that no harm is done to any creature.

We investigate how these traditions, particularly the Buddhist tradition, analyses the mind and studies the phenomenon of suffering. We look at how, in Buddhist philosophy, such states of suffering can be overcome through meditative practices and by developing a mind of compassion for all living beings.

The Future

If compassion is fundamental to our happiness or to our spiritual development, are we behaving in a way that extends compassion to all those living beings who deserve it? Are we living by the Golden Rule and treating others as we would wish to be treated ourselves? If not, why not? And what are the consequences?

In part five we enquire into the future. What is to become of us, our planet and our environment and of all other sentient beings if we do not behave with compassion? What legacy will we leave behind us, both for this world and for those we share the planet with?

The Scientific Method

I should like to be clear that I am fully committed to the scientific method of investigating the world. Science is a very powerful and reliable tool for helping us to understand the Universe in which we live. It has proved itself to be highly successful and indispensable for explaining everything around us. The scientific method is also very rigorous, as every new theory has to be tested and proved by experiment. Most things in the physical Universe can be explained through science. However, I agree with many scientists, such as Paul Davies and Roger Penrose, that scientific theory is limited to the boundaries of the Universe. Questions such as 'what was there before the beginning of the Universe?' if indeed the concept of before has any meaning here, indicate a limit to the laws of physics that operate within the Universe, as we know them. What initiated the Universe? Why did it happen at all? Are there boundaries at which science, logic and common sense can go no further? Is this where the Perennial Philosophy of mysticism is to be found?

Therefore, is it not reasonable at least to be open-minded towards other methods of understanding existence? This does not mean accepting things on blind faith or believing in anything without evidence. Everything should be rigorously scrutinised. But does it mean that we should be open-minded to the possibility that our current experience of the four dimensions of space and time may not be all there is? As the astrophysicist Arthur Stanley Eddington (1882 – 1944) once famously said,

> *'The Universe is not only stranger than we imagine, it is stranger than we <u>can</u> imagine.'*

For millennia sages have fathomed the mysteries of consciousness and compassion, just as scientists have explored science and mathematics. And just as theoretical physicists have conducted thought experiments into the wonders of the Cosmos, so too have these sages explored consciousness in the laboratory of the mind, through the medium of meditation, contemplation and prayer. For thousands of years they explored the deep ravines of the mind and reported back on their discoveries in great texts such as *the Upanishads*. They said that what they had discovered could not be explained in words or mathematics. Nor could it be imagined. It could only be experienced. And what they experienced was deeply linked to the cultivation of *compassion*, a treasure that is available to all sentient beings that are endowed with the gift of consciousness and who share a place with us in this Cosmos.

PART 1

COMPASSION
IN THE
SPIRITUAL TRADITIONS

1

THE
COMPASSIONATE ENLIGHTENMENT

'A human being is part of the whole,
called by us the 'Universe',
a part limited in time and space.
He experiences himself, his thoughts and
feelings, as something separate from the rest
– a kind of optical delusion of his consciousness.
This delusion is a kind of prison for us,
restricting us to our personal desires and
to affection for a few persons nearest to us.
Our task must be to free ourselves from this prison
by widening our circle of compassion
to embrace all living creatures and
the whole of nature in its beauty.'

Albert Einstein – The New York Post

Over the millennia humans generally have demonstrated a considerable amount of aggressive behaviour towards their fellow humans and to other sentient beings, which has caused tremendous suffering in the world. Many very destructive wars have been fought and humans have exploited others through commerce and politics, where their ultimate goal has been the accumulation of power and wealth. Humans have also been guilty of neglect, allowing many to live in extreme hardship while others live in comparative luxury. Most spiritual philosophies suggest that such behaviour results from negative human emotions, such as greed, hate and envy that are driven by the ego. This weakness in human nature has changed little over time and is still prevalent today. The only difference now lies in the methods humans use to control and exploit others. The underlying human emotions remain the same.

Throughout these troubled times, however, there have been other humans who have not been driven by negative emotions or by their egos. Such individuals have taught that there is a better way and have practised a more compassionate style of life. Some of these people were naturally attuned to this understanding, while others trained themselves rigorously in order to transform their minds through meditative practices and prayer. Throughout history inspiring people have arisen and started a spiritual revolution based on compassion that has been endorsed by a large number of followers.

But all too often the understanding of their original teachings had become lost over time and their following turned into a formal religion with doctrines and priestly hierarchies, and the original principle of compassion had become lost. Other reformers have then arisen to re-establish the compassionate philosophy. As a result, there have been cycles of periods of compassionate enlightenment and periods of spiritual separation. Where are we today in such a cycle and can we learn anything from the wisdom of these compassionate people of the past that will improve the world we live in today?

The Fall from the Golden Age

Many of the current spiritual philosophies teach of a 'great separation', or a 'fall of man' in the dim and distant past following some 'golden age'. They teach that during this golden age humans, along with all the other animals, were innocent and had no ego. They, therefore, experienced no negative emotions such as hate, greed or envy. During this time they lived in harmony with nature. But then their egos started to develop and the human species went through a 'great separation' that divorced them from the environment with which they were inextricably interwoven. Could the separation, described in such stories, be associated with the latest development of the neocortex of the human brain, during our evolutionary history? Could these stories have referred to the period when humans slowly evolved from their animal ancestors to that creature we define as distinctly 'human'?

The Taoists, for example, believe that during a golden age, humans had lived in harmony with the *Tao*, the 'Way of the Universe', but had since turned their back on it. Their egos had created a separation between them and the rest of nature. According to Taoist philosophy, once humans started to work against the Tao, they found that everything in life was difficult and this resulted in unhappiness. In order to try to regain their happiness, humans attempted to possess and accumulate material things, but this brought stress into their lives. Any happiness they gained from the things they strived for was temporary and this made them dissatisfied. They lost touch with the Way and everything in it and they no longer understood it. They stopped co-operating with nature and began to manipulate and control it for their own benefit. But they found that they could not control nature. Plants died and the land became deforested and turned into deserts. Humans couldn't grow sufficient food so they started to kill and eat the animals, which had once been their friends, until the animals grew to fear them. When humans realised that they couldn't get what they desired from nature and the other animals, they turned on themselves and fought each other, resulting in bloody battles and eventually wars.[1]

A similar tale is told in the Bible in the story of Adam and Eve, a beautiful allegory about humankind who had once lived innocently in the *Garden of Eden*, in harmony with nature and naked like the other animals. They had named the animals and could communicate with them. Then the evil serpent tricked Eve into tempting Adam to bite into the fruit of the tree of knowledge of good and evil, which God had forbidden them to do. This was the end of their innocence and they discovered their egos. They then understood the difference between good and evil, they felt shame and had to clothe their naked bodies. God banished them from the Garden of Eden and they were no longer able to communicate with the other animals or live in harmony with nature.[2]

In the creation stories of the indigenous people of Australia, there is a sacred era called the *Dreamtime*, when the spirit beings created the material world. In Dreamtime mythology every living being in this world lived eternally as a spirit-child in the 'Dreaming' before being born into this world. When they died they returned to the Dreaming. The aboriginal people believe that the world is land-centred, not human-centred, so humans should not exploit the land, but should remain interconnected with it and with the rest of creation. They should include in their perception of the world those who have gone before them, the ancestors, and those who are yet to come. According to the mythology, certain sites on the land hold special feelings that can be sensed, but not explained, by people who are in tune with nature, with whom such sites resonate. However, many people have lost this connection.[3]

In Jain cosmology, the Universe goes around in vast cycles of happiness and unhappiness. There is a half cycle of ascending happiness and another half cycle of descending happiness, each divided into six epochs. Long ago there was a peak of happiness, when humans were strong and lived long, healthy lives, in harmony with nature and the other animals. But according to Jain cosmology, we have passed through four epochs of descending happiness since then, as humans have become more and more separated from the natural world and from their spirituality. The further the decline the greater the selfishness, greed, hate, anger and pride of humans and the more destruction they inflict on the natural world. In Jain cosmology, we are currently in the early stages of the fifth epoch of the descending cycle, which will last around 21,000 years.[4]

The Axial Age of Enlightenment

Such spiritual traditions all suggest that after the time of the golden age most humans experienced a separation from the natural world, during which time they became increasingly unhappy. But they also report stories of spiritual leaders who arose and taught about happiness, wisdom and compassion. A peak of this compassionate thinking occurred around 500 BCE, at a time that the German philosopher Karl Jaspers called '*The Axial Age*' in his book *Vom Ursprung und Ziel der Geschichte (The Origin and Goal of History)*. He claimed that this was a time of enlightenment and spiritual revolution, which occurred separately and spontaneously in different parts of the world. China, India, Greece and Israel and Judah, all had their great spiritual thinkers at that time. These included Confucius and Laotse in China, Buddha and Mahavira in India, Pythagoras, Socrates and Plato in Greece and the prophets, such as Isaiah in Israel and Judah. Whilst there were some differences in their teachings, there was a common underlying principle. This principle was 'Compassion'. From compassion they developed the *'Golden Rule' – 'do to others as you would have them do to you'*. They trained their minds through meditative practices, contemplation and prayer to remove negative emotions such as greed, envy and hate and to develop positive emotions such as love, humility and kindness. Most important of all, they trained their minds to suppress the ego, as they perceived the ego to be the root of all their troubles. They believed that such practices would not only lead to happiness and equanimity in the practitioner, but would also permeate the society around them, making it stable and peaceful.[5]

Confucius, who lived in China between 551 BCE and 479 BCE, first developed the Golden Rule. He extended the long-existing practice of the 'Li', or the rites of the court, to include genuine concern for others. The Li required everyone to treat others with respect and dignity, starting with the family and then extending out to friends and neighbours. However, Confucius believed that this had stagnated into a system of complex rituals which lacked underlying meaning, so he sought to put the meaning back into those rituals. He advocated that not only should you treat others as you would wish to be treated yourself, but you should also help to 'establish others'. By this he meant that if you wanted to achieve anything for yourself, you should first help others to achieve it.[6]

Also in China, at about the same time, Laotse recorded the long established philosophy of the Tao in his book *The Tao Te Ching*. By 'Tao' he meant the 'Way of the Universe' where everything in the material world is part of the heavenly world and has its own inner nature. The Taoists believe that going with the flow of nature will result in successful outcomes and in peace and harmony, whilst to fight against nature will result in hardship and struggle. To this day the Taoists practise a peaceful life, living simply in harmony with nature and without interference from the ego. They also believe in extending compassion to all natural things.[7]

At a similar time in northern India, the Buddha is said to have discovered enlightenment whilst sitting under the Bodhi tree, meditating on the morning star. Frustrated that the wisdom of the early Hindu philosophies had been lost to ordinary people and had become restricted to the secret knowledge of the Brahmin priests, he sought a spirituality that could be experienced directly by everyone. After experiencing both luxury and asceticism in his life, he realised, in that moment, that the way to happiness was the middle way, a path that lies between indulgence and hardship. He also discovered that enlightenment could be achieved by the extension of compassion to all living things[8].

But Buddha's discovery was not new. Mahavira, a Jain, had been preaching a similar philosophy in northern India at much the same time. Like Taoism in China, Jainism had been in existence for millennia and Mahavira is believed to be the twenty-fourth and final Thirthankar of the current age. The Jains believe that the first Thirthankar was Adinath, also known as Rishabhadev, who could have lived around 10,000 BCE. The word *Jain* means a 'Conqueror of the Spirit' and *Thirthankar* means a 'ford maker' or one who helps other beings to cross the river of human misery to reach enlightenment on the other side. The basic philosophy of Jainism is the principle of *ahimsa* or 'non-violence', which advocates that violence should never be enacted on another living being in thought, word or deed. Fundamental to Jainism is the belief that non-violence and compassion should be extended to all living things, including all animals, plants and the environment. In no other religion is the extension of compassion to all sentient beings so strongly emphasised. As a result the Jains will not eat animals or exploit them in any way. It is a truly beautiful spirituality, brimming with compassion.[9]

Around the same time in the West, the Pythagoreans were also practising non-violence, which included non-meat-eating. They were a group founded by the philosopher, scientist and mathematician Pythagoras. The Orphic Sect, who were contemporaries of the Pythagoreans, practised non-violence and non-meat-eating at that time too. Later, Socrates and Plato based their philosophies on the ethical values of these groups and taught of a 'Platonic Realm', separate from the material world, where the soul or 'psyche', the 'Good' and the 'forms', such as the mathematical truths, existed.[10]

In Israel, the Prophets Isaiah, Hosea and Ezekiel were prophesising about a *Peaceable Kingdom*, like the Garden of Eden, to which man would one day return and which he would share with the other animals. Here the lion would lie down with the lamb and everything would be at one with the Creation and eat a plant based diet.

Revivals of the Spirit of Enlightenment

Ever since the axial age a number of religions developed out of the original teachings on compassion that had lost touch with the insights of their founders. Hierarchies of priests and religious doctrines grew up. Then, many sages, prophets and bodhisattvas are reported to have revived the earlier teachings on compassion and the golden rule, rebelling against the institutionalised religions that had developed from the former spiritual philosophies.

Prior to the first millennium, for example, the Jewish leader, Hillel re-introduced the spirit of compassion and the golden rule to the Abrahamic religion. Living in Jerusalem, he was the spiritual head of the Jewish people and believed that 'love of man' was the core of the Jewish teaching. One day a Gentile asked Hillel to explain the Torah whilst standing on one foot. Hillel took up the challenge, stood on one foot and said 'What is hateful to you, do not do to your fellow: this is the whole Torah; the rest is the explanation; go and learn'[11]. Hillel was saying that the golden rule was the fundamental teaching and the rest was just the detail. Knowledge of the scriptures is fine, but one had to understand and live by the golden rule.

A short time later, a major reformer called Jesus, who was very likely to have been influenced by the teachings of Hillel, reiterated the golden rule[12]. Jesus believed that he was the Messiah that had been foretold by the prophets in the Old Testament and that the Holy Spirit had sent him to save mankind. The religious leaders of the time had made people believe that by buying animals to sacrifice in the temples they could also buy a place in heaven. Jesus, sickened by the animal sacrifices, angrily turned the tables over in the blood-soaked temple in Jerusalem, disgusted that the house of God had become no more than a market for greedy traders. He accused them of turning the house of God into a den of thieves[13]. From the teachings and the example of this great reformer, the religion of Christianity was founded.

Then, six hundred years after Jesus, Muhammad, another great reformer, taught of compassion once again. He felt strongly that the worship of Jesus as the Son of God, which had grown up over the intervening period, detracted from the original belief that it was only God who should be worshipped. He believed that Jesus was just another prophet in the line of prophets from the Abrahamic faith and he also believed that he himself was another prophet. Muhammad was also concerned that the Jews had divided into separate sects and had drifted from the true religion, as preached by Abraham. In 610 AD, called by what he felt was divine inspiration revealed through the Archangel Gabriel, he wrote the holy book *The Qur'an* (meaning 'the recitation') in order to bring the faith back to its true origins. When he started preaching in public the Meccan priests persecuted him for his controversial views, but from his teachings the religion of Islam was founded.

The Dark Ages
But after that came the Dark Ages. Again, the spiritual teachings disintegrated into formal religions with their doctrines and priestly hierarchies, as many people failed to grasp the true meaning of compassion and the golden rule. People were killed and tortured in the name of religion. Heretics and witches were burned. Again, the religions split into sects and sub-divisions and people fought holy wars in the name of their religion. Christians fought Muslims in the crusades of the Middle Ages, Catholics fought wars with Protestants during the reformation and, more recently, Muslims fought Hindus in twentieth century India, splitting the state into India and Pakistan. But the people who waged these wars had lost touch with the meaning of the foundation of their religions, which were all originally based on the concept of compassion and loving one's enemies. During these times saints and great leaders arose who, once again, attempted to re-establish the concept of compassion and the golden rule. Among these were many early saints like St Francis of Assisi and, more recently, great political reformers like Martin Luther King and Mahatma Gandhi, who both practised non-violent resistance.

Not only have many humans fought against and enslaved each other, but many have fought with nature itself, failing to recognise their interrelatedness to the natural world and the interconnection between all living things. In the blind arrogance of anthropocentrism, some humans have treated themselves as separate from the rest of nature and superior to everything in it. They have exploited and damaged the environment and cruelly persecuted other sentient beings in the greatest separation of them all. Many humans have succumbed to their egos and their negative emotions of greed, envy and hate and in the process caused themselves and many others to suffer. They have sought to resolve their unhappiness by accumulating power and possessions, but this has only led to dissatisfaction and further suffering. With so much technology and power in the hands of today's humans, where will their unchecked egos and negative emotions lead? What future is there for humans, for all other sentient beings and indeed for the planet Earth?

2

BRAHMAN

'Life is Brahman.
From life is born all creatures,
By life they grow, and to life they return.'
The Taittirya Upanishad III 3.1

'The highest truth is this:
God is present in all living beings.
They are his multiple form...
The first of all worships is the worship of those around us.
He alone serves God who serves all other beings.'
Swami Vivekananda[1]

About 5,000 years ago, it is believed that the Aryan people migrated to northern India from the Russian Steppes bringing with them the oldest known teachings on spirituality. Their traditions were merged with those of the people already living in the Indus Valley and this formed the Hindu tradition[2]. The first written records discovered were the *Vedic texts* which date back to around 1,500 BCE and it is assumed that they are based on a knowledge that had been passed down verbally for many centuries. These were written in Sanskrit and incorporated a body of texts which spanned more than three millennia[3]. The earliest texts are the Samhita collection of Vedas, which were written before 1,200 BCE and included the *Rig-Veda*, the *Sama-Veda*, the *Yajur-Veda* and the *Atharva-Veda*.

Veda means 'revealed knowledge'. *Vedanta*, which means 'perfect knowledge', is the ultimate goal of the Vedas, which is claimed to be enlightenment. The main text of Vedanta philosophy is *The Upanishads* which is the final Vedic text and incorporates the philosophies of the earlier Vedic texts. Upanishad means 'sitting down near' and refers to sitting down at the feet of a great teacher in an intimate session of spiritual instruction. There are 200 known Upanishads, the earliest twelve being written during the Vedic, pre-Buddhist era, which date back to around 1,000 BCE. These are known as the main 'mukhya' Upanishads. Later Upanishads span the post-Buddhist era from around 500 BCE onwards into the middle ages, with the latest one being written in 1926 AD. These later Upanishads are heavily influenced by Buddhist philosophy. Their main theme is the union of the universal spirit, the Brahman, with the individual spirit, the Atman, through meditation[4]. It is in the Upanishads that the divine symbol Aum is identified as the cosmic vibration that underlies all existence.

Another major Vedic text is the *Bhagavad Gita*, which was written between 500 BCE and 200 BCE. It comprises a dialogue between Lord Krishna and the prince Arjuna during the battle at Kurukshetra. When Arjuna expresses his doubts about going into battle and the harm that he would be doing, Krishna advises him that he has to do his duty, but that he should do it without attachment to any reward[5]. In Vedic philosophy, working in the world with no expectation of profit, status or other reward and remaining unattached to the output of your work is one of the pre-requisites for freeing the spirit. There is, however, some debate as to whether the battle was a real battle or an allegory of the struggle within the human soul.

Brahman and Atman

The followers of the Vedas, the Hindus, believe in a universal spirit, which they called Brahman. They believe that in its perfect spirit form everything was unified and was one with the universal spirit. But the universe had cooled and condensed into matter and in the process the spirit had separated into individual parts. Everything in nature is believed to be a condensed form of Brahman, every animal, plant and inanimate object. But the Hindus believe that they all have an individual soul or 'Atman', which can potentially be reunited with the universal soul of Brahman.

> *'The Cosmos comes forth from Brahman and moves*
> *In him. With his power it reverberates,*
> *Like thunder crashing in the sky. Those who*
> *Realise him pass beyond the sway of death.'*
> (The Katha Upanishad 3.2)

Vedanta is the philosophical tradition that is concerned with self-realisation by which the individual soul, the Atman, finds union with the cosmic consciousness, the Brahman, through control of the mind during meditation. Indeed it is claimed that the goal of evolution is to attain this unitive state:

> *'Entering into the unitive state,*
> *He attains the goal of evolution.'*
> (The Paramahamsa Upanishad 4)

The Upanishads

The Upanishads are a collection of writings by many anonymous contributors over many centuries. These writers were explorers of the mind who were reporting back on their experiences of journeying through the various layers of consciousness to discover the ultimate state where the individual mind becomes one with the universal spirit of Brahman. They explored the states of being awake, dream sleep and dreamless sleep and noticed the separation of the observer from the sense of self in the state of dreamless sleep. By delving deeper into further layers of consciousness they could create a state of fully conscious awareness in the state of dreamless sleep where they could be a detached watcher or seer, separate from the body and the mind. In this state the finite became infinite. They discovered and reported in the Upanishads that every level of consciousness has a deeper level of reality. When we wake up into conscious awareness we discover that the reality experienced during dream sleep was an illusion, although it appeared to be very real during the dream. But the authors of the Upanishads suggested that the reality experienced during conscious awareness is only slightly more real than the dream, and not so real when compared to the reality experienced when the Atman is merged with the Brahman. As the nineteenth century psychologist

Havelock Ellis observed,

'Dreams are real as long as they last. Can we say more of life?'

   In this final level of absorption, the writers reported, there is no time or space or causality. The ultimate realisation was *Tat tvam asi* or 'You are That', where 'That' is the reality that you are searching for and 'You' is not you as the finite person in mind and body, but you in your pure conscious state. The message of the Upanishads is that 'There is no joy in the finite, there is joy only in the infinite.' This is our native state, to which we seek to return[6].
   The Upanishads give hope that whatever anyone has done, everyone has a divine self within them to which they can return:

> *'As the sun, who is the eye of the world,*
> *Cannot be tainted by the defects in our eyes*
> *Nor by the objects it looks on,*
> *So the one Self, dwelling in all, cannot*
> *Be tainted by the evils of the world.*
> *For this Self transcends all.'*
> *(Katha Upanishad 11.2.11)*

This native state, they suggested, provides eternal life:

> *'In the city of Brahman is a secret dwelling, the lotus of the heart. Within this dwelling is a space, and within that space is the fulfilment of our desires.... Never fear that old age will invade that city; never fear that this inner treasure of all reality will wither and decay. This knows no ageing when the body ages; this knows no dying when the body dies.'*
> *(Chandogya Upanishad viii.1.1.5)*

> *'When all desires that surge in the heart*
> *Are renounced, the mortal becomes immortal.*
> *When all the knots that strangle the heart*
> *Are loosened, the mortal becomes immortal.*
> *This sums up the teaching of the scriptures.'*
> *(Katha Upanishad 11.3.14-15)*

Over time the Hindus developed many gods, such as Shiva, the destroyer and Vishnu, the preserver and a pantheon of inferior gods, but the main god was always Brahman, the creator god and universal spirit. In other religions, such as the Abrahamic religions of Judaism, Christianity and Islam, the creator spirit became a personified individual, separate from the individuals in his creation. He became Jahweh, God or Allah, developing into an individual being with his own distinct personality. Other religions had a pantheon of gods, which always had one senior god. The Greeks had Zeus, the Egyptians Ra, the Romans Jove and the Nordic people had Odin. Not only did the God of these religions become separate from his creation, but the place where he existed became separate from the world of his creation. Humans and animals lived on Earth and the gods lived in Heaven, a place that existed in a different dimension. This separation of Earth from Heaven, of the material world from the spirit world, of humans from the gods, became known as dualism.

But the followers of the Upanishads and the other Eastern traditions, saw this separation as illusory. In the Indian Vedic traditions, as recorded in the Upanishads, the individual self, the Atman, could be reunited with the universal spirit, the Brahman. In order to achieve this the individual had to eliminate the ego, which binds humans to an unhappy material existence and let go of all attachments to material things. They had to eliminate all negative emotions and cultivate positive ones. By developing infinite wisdom the individual could achieve enlightenment, a transcendental state of complete unity with the universal spirit of Brahman. This state, they believed, could be achieved in this life through meditation and could liberate the individual from his karma, the actions that kept him bound to the endless cycle of birth, death and rebirth in this world. Thus, on death, he could be reunited with the universal spirit forever.

According to the Vedic tradition, the Universe has its own energy, known as 'prana'. This energy flows through everything. Animals have their own energy systems that flow through their bodies, through a system of 'nadis', rather like blood flowing through the body in the system of veins and arteries. It was believed that working with this energy would lead to harmony with the cosmic energy, leading to good health. To work with this energy could also provide healing, whereas to block it could lead to sickness.

Brahman Dwells in All Creatures

In the Upanishads the experience of the Brahman is not limited to humans or to any class of human. The Brahman exists within all creatures in the Cosmos:

> *'The Self is in all...*
> *All creatures,*
> *Great or small, born of eggs, of wombs, of heat,*
> *Of shoots, horses, cows, elephants, men and women;*
> *All beings that walk, all beings that fly,*
> *And all that neither walk, nor fly.'*
> *(The Aitareya Upanishad III.1.3)*

> *'Life is Brahman.*
> *From life is born all creatures,*
> *By life they grow, and to life they return.'*
> *(The Taittirya Upanishad III 3.1)*

> *'O Lord of Love, revealed in the scriptures,*
> *Who has assumed the forms of all creatures...'*
> *(The Taittirya Upanishad I 4.1)*

> *'The Lord dwells in the womb of the Cosmos,*
> *The Creator who is in all creatures,*
> *He is that which is born and to be born;*
> *His face is everywhere.'*
> *(The Shvetashvatara Upanishad II 11.16)*

> *'All creatures, dear one, have their source in him.'*
> *(The Chandogya Upanishad VI 8.4)*

Compassion to All Life

Although the main theme throughout the Upanishads is the union of the Atman with the Brahman through the inward looking practice of meditation, there is also reference to the outward looking practice of compassion or altruism. *The Paramahamsa*

Upanishad 1 asks, 'What is the state of the illumined one?' and answers:

> *'He has renounced all selfish attachments*
> *And observes no rites and ceremonies.*
> *He has only minimal possessions,*
> *And lives his life **for the welfare of all**.'*

Later with the coming of the Jain Tirthankars and Buddha there is a considerable extension of the Hindu inward spiritual practice of meditation to the outward spiritual practice of showing compassion towards others and undertaking altruistic behaviour.

Despite the fact that the sages who wrote the Upanishads had wanted to share their experiences of the exploration of the mind with everyone, their wisdom eventually became the knowledge of only a privileged few. These were the Brahmin priests who kept the knowledge to themselves in order to maintain their position in the social hierarchy. The original spiritual wisdom was reduced to a religious cult with meaningless rituals. It was not until the coming of Buddha and Mahavira that there was a revolution of thinking that challenged the religious hierarchy and proposed the idea that wisdom was something that could be attained by anyone who had the determination to discover it for themselves. This wisdom was not learned through study or by the practice of rituals, but was experienced. It was practice and self-development that led to enlightenment and anyone could access this if they really tried. According to Buddha and Mahavira it was through the development of feelings of empathy to others and extending compassion to all living things, that this ultimate state of enlightenment could be achieved.

Hindu Attitudes towards Animals Today

There are over 900 million Hindus today and strict Hindus still practice a diet free from animal products. In 1966 the International Society for Krishna Consciousness (ISKCON), also known as the Hare Krishna movement, was founded by A.C. Bhaktivedanta Swami Prabhupada and is now a worldwide movement. Its beliefs are based on the traditional Hindu scriptures, particularly the *Bhagavad Gita*, and the practice of bhakti yoga (devotional service). Famous for chanting the *Hare Krishna Mantra* or *Maha Mantra*, they are strict non-meat-eaters, who avoid the use of all animal products. More details are available at *www.iskcon.org.*

3

THE TAO

'There is a thing confusedly formed,
Born before Heaven and Earth,
Silent and Void,
It stands alone and does not change,
Goes round and does not weary,
It is capable of being the mother of the world.
I know not its name
So I style it 'The Way.''

Laotse – Tao Te Ching (chapter 25)

Taoism (or Daoism) is the ancient Chinese philosophy based on the *Tao* (or *Dao*), which means the 'Way of Heaven'. It can be traced back to pre-historic folk religions in China, but is traditionally regarded as being founded by Laotse (Lao Tzu) in around 600 BCE when he recorded the existing Tao philosophies in his book, the *Tao Te Ching* (or *Dao De Jing*). Tao Te Ching means the Tao Book of Virtue. Laotse, who received imperial recognition as a divinity in around 200 BCE, was not the first Taoist. The semi-legendary Yellow Emperor, who ruled around 2,500 BCE, is also noted as a major Taoist teacher. After Laotse, Chuang-tse (Zhuangzi), also known as Master Chuang, who lived around 300 BCE, was also recognised as a Taoist teacher.

Laotse described the Tao as an all-pervading essence that came before Heaven and Earth that shaped them and yet exists within them.

'Man takes his law from the Earth;
the Earth takes its law from Heaven;
Heaven takes its law from the Tao.
The law of the Tao is its being what it is.'
(Tao Te Ching - chapter 25)

Taoists believe that the Tao is in this world, within the Universe and all around us in nature. To be truly happy the individual has to move with nature and go with the flow of natural things. If they do this they will find peace and harmony, but if they try to work against nature they will find conflict and discord. Unlike the Buddhists, they do not believe that all of life is suffering and filled with attachments and desires that lead to misery. This is only the case if you try to work against nature. Nor do they believe that life needs to be transcended to reach nirvana. Instead, life is there to be enjoyed, by living in harmony with nature. The world is not a setter of traps, but a teacher of valuable lessons. If life's lessons are learned and nature's way is followed, people will live happy lives filled with peace and serenity[1].

Chi

Taoists recognise *chi* (or *qi*) energy, which flows through everything in the Universe and is essential to the Way of Heaven. It lives in animals, plants and rocks. All things in nature are born, live and die and when they are born they take in chi energy and when they die it leaves them. But the chi energy continues, constantly moving and changing and flowing through nature. The Taoists believe that to flow with the Way of Heaven it is important to align one's own chi energy with that of the natural world. To do this one has to be relaxed and spontaneous. This chi energy is like the prana energy described in the Indian Upanishads.

The Age of Perfect Virtue

The Taoists believe that there had once been a Golden Age, when humans had lived in harmony with nature and the other animals. It was a time when they had been happy. But their egos had developed, causing a separation between humans and the rest of nature. This caused them to work against the Tao and everything became a struggle, resulting in misery and the loss of their equanimity. To try to regain their lost happiness, humans started trying to possess and accumulate material things. But this created stress. The pleasure they gained from the material things they had accumulated was temporary and this made them dissatisfied. The more humans lost touch with the Way, the less they understood it. They stopped co-operating with nature and started to manipulate and control it for their own ends. But humans could not control nature. Plants died and the land became deforested and turned into deserts. Crops failed, so humans began to kill and eat the animals, which had once been their companions. When humans had plundered nature and the other animals, they turned on themselves, waging wars. Humans enslaved, tortured and murdered each other. The Taoists believe that humans' only solution to their unhappy predicament is to return to the Way and live in harmony with nature[2]. Zhuangzi called this golden age the 'Age of Perfect Virtue' and wrote:

> *'In the Age of Perfect Virtue, men lived among the animals and birds as members of one large family. There were no distinctions between 'superior' and 'inferior' to separate one man or species from another. All retained their natural virtue and lived in the state of pure simplicity...'*

Taoist Objections to Confucianism
The Confucianists, who were contemporaries of the Taoists in China, believed in practising the rituals of the court, the *Li*. Confucius believed that the virtues of the past had been lost and that the government of people on Earth was no longer synchronised with the government of Heaven. He advocated reverence for the ancestors and for their ancient rituals and ceremonies, where the Emperor, who was believed to be the Son of Heaven, acted as an intermediary between Heaven and Earth. There were rules for every detail of life and the rituals had to be religiously followed. The Taoists at that time saw these rituals as unnatural and complicated and not conducive to harmony with the Way[3]. They believed that the rigid rituals and ceremonies of the Confucian Li were an impediment to the flow of chi. They believed in simple living, which would lead to peace and equanimity. The Li was also confined to the relationship of humans to their fellow humans and to social and political life. Taoism, on the other hand, was concerned with the individual's relationship to the rest of nature, including Heaven and Earth and all other species.

P'u (The Uncarved Block)

Central to Taoist philosophy is the concept of the *P'u*, the 'uncarved block', which means that everything is best in its natural form and not interfered with,

'Unpretentious like wood that has not been fashioned into anything'[4].

Taoists believe that things in their original simplicity contain their own natural power. This requires us to be aware of both our inner nature and the inner nature of all other things. In Taoism, when a person is aware of their inner nature, they can ensure that they are in the right place, doing the right thing. They know and accept their limitations. This does not mean that they should not try to aim for improvement, but it does mean that they can work with their weaknesses rather than against them. Weaknesses in one situation may be strengths in another situation. Being aware of one's inner nature gives one the confidence not to be persuaded by others to do something that is not in one's own nature. This is what Taoism calls 'the Way of self-reliance'. It gives the individual the power to believe in himself and in his abilities. Instead of trying to eliminate one's negative afflictions, one can turn them into something positive, that can be worked with.

Wu Wei (Effortless Effort)

The Taoists believe that to live in harmony with nature, one has to be able to yield to things, like water in a river yields when it comes up against a hard rock. The water cannot break through the rock, instead it gives way to it and passes effortlessly around the rock.

'The soft overcomes the hard and the weak the strong.'
(Tao Te Ching, chapter 36)

'The softest thing in the world dashes against and overcomes the hardest.' (Tao Te Ching, chapter 43)

In the same way, instead of fighting against nature, we should yield to it and move around it. This principle is known as *Wu Wei*, which means 'effortless effort', or effort without force or ego, or not going against things. In the martial art *T'ai Chi Chu'an*, the T'ai Chi master defeats his opponent by yielding to their blows. The opponent's energy is expended in hitting out at the yielding master, rather like hitting a cork in water. The harder the opponent hits, the more energy is expended. Eventually the opponent is exhausted and defeated, while the T'ai Chi master, having expended minimal effort, has preserved his energies. Such yielding is not only practised in combative situations but in daily life. According to Taoism, if someone tries to provoke you, it is better to yield to them, rather than to argue back. Eventually the effort will become too much for them and they will give in.

Laotse observed that people were so caught up in *Yu Wei*, 'keeping busy', that they had lost their connection with the Way and this was causing disharmony and unhappiness. They were living by their ego and running round, expending energy and achieving very little. The Taoists believe in working in the world through Wu Wei, with total detachment from the results of that work and with no expectation of reward.

> *'Therefore the sage manages affairs without doing anything,*
> *and conveys his instructions without the use of speech.*
> *All things spring up and there is not one which declines to show itself;*
> *They grow, and there is no claim made for their ownership;*
> *They go through their processes and there is no expectation of reward.*
> *The work is accomplished and there is no resting in its achievements.*
> *The work is done, but how no one can see;*
> *'Tis this that makes the power not cease to be.'*
> *(Tao Te Ching – chapter 2)*

> *'When the work is done and one's name is becoming distinguished,*
> *to withdraw into obscurity is the way of Heaven.'*
> *(Tao Te Ching – chapter 9)*

Te (The Virtue of the Small)

The Taoists also believe in the *Te*, meaning the 'virtue of the small', whereby being humble is seen as a good thing. Trying to be clever is not a virtue and is in conflict with wisdom. A clear mind sees things as they really are and can analyse them objectively and come to the truth, whereas a clever mind, which is stuffed full of knowledge and arrogance, cannot see clearly or form objective views. Laotse wrote,

> *'The wise are not learned; the learned are not wise'*

> *'The perception of what is small is the secret of clear-sightedeness;*
> *the guarding of what is soft and tender is the secret of strength'*
>
> *(Tao Te Ching, chapter 52)*

Whilst the intellect may be useful for analysing things, it does not help with broader and deeper matters, which are beyond its limitations. Zhuangzi said,

> *'A well-frog cannot imagine the ocean, nor can a summer insect conceive of ice. How then can a scholar understand the Tao? He is restricted by his own learning.'*

T'ai Hsu (The Great Emptiness)

Taoists believe wisdom to be superior to knowledge, although knowledge gained through experience of life is far more valuable than knowledge gained through scholarly activities. To have wisdom one requires an empty mind or *T'ai Hsu* which means the 'Great Emptiness'. Laotse wrote,

> *'To attain knowledge, add things every day. To attain wisdom, remove things every day.'*

The value of a clear mind is beyond description. When we have brilliant ideas, or when the answers to problems we have been grappling with suddenly come to us, they come from nothing, spontaneously and when we least expect it. It is a result of us being completely awake, like a clear-minded, all seeing child. The Tao Te Ching says,

'Return to the beginning, become a child again.'

An enlightened person is like a child whose mind has been emptied of the minutiae and filled with the wisdom of the *Great Nothing*, which is the Way of the Universe. Taoists believe that, to be like a child again, we need to be open-minded and spontaneous. We need to use Wu Wei and respond to circumstances, using our intuition and just be sensitive to the things around us and respond appropriately. When we do this, they argue, we find that things just seem to go right, but when we try to force alternatives, things go wrong and we struggle. An advantage of using Wu Wei is that you don't have to make difficult decisions. Taoists believe that masters who follow the Way listen to the voice of wisdom and simplicity within them and do not concentrate on learning and knowledge. Everybody has that inner voice, but few choose to listen to it. Taoists believe that such an approach to life is beneficial for health and vitality and increases life span.

Laotse said that the Way was indescribable with words. It had to be experienced and could not be explained. One had to let go of rational thinking and enter a dimension that existed beyond language and concepts. The Way was nameless and unseen. One had to eliminate the ego and desire from the mind to obtain this understanding.

'The Tao that can be described is not the enduring and unchanging Tao.
The name that can be named is not the enduring and unchanging name.
Having no name, it is the Originator of heaven and earth;
having a name, it is the Mother of all things.

Always without desire we must be found,
If its deep mystery we would sound;
But if desire always within us be,
Its outer fringe is all that we shall see.'
(Tao Te Ching – chapter 1)

'With no desire, at rest and still,
All things go right as of their will.'
(Tao Te Ching – chapter 37)

One had to access the emptiness, by entering deeper and deeper layers, starting from the manifest, going to the unseen and then arriving at *the Dark*. The Chinese had a form of yoga called *Zuo-wang* which taught them to shut out the outside world and close down their ordinary modes of perception. In the trance of the meditation the emptiness could be experienced. It was also called the 'Womb of all being' as it was believed to bring forth new life. In the emptiness one could return to one's true nature, a nature that people had enjoyed before the great separation, which had brought false artifice into peoples' lives and had separated them from the Way. In this state one could attain perfect wisdom and impartiality. This was similar to the meditation techniques practised in India, as described in *the Upanishads*, which led to the union of the Atman with the Brahman and the experience of the Absolute.

Zhuangzi

The Taoist writer Zhuangzi, who lived around 300 BCE, had undergone a transformative experience when he had trespassed into a game park to poach some fowl. He noticed a magpie and thought that it would notice him and fly off. But the magpie was so engrossed in hunting a cicada that it didn't spot Zhuangzi. Suddenly a preying mantis appeared and was so engrossed in hunting the cicada that it didn't spot the magpie, which swooped down and ate them both, but was still oblivious to Zhuangzi and his cross bow. Instead of shooting the Magpie, Zhuangzi sighed with compassion and realised that life was one danger after another. All life was caught up in a chain of mutual destruction. Zhaungzi was so caught up with the magpie that he didn't notice the game-keeper appear, who chased him out of the park. For three months Zhuangzi was deeply depressed and realised that, until one becomes reconciled to the endless process of death and destruction, one can have no peace. Everything is in flux and constantly changing and is in the process of becoming something else. But we are always trying to freeze our experiences to make them permanent. He realised that this was not the Way of Heaven and that trying to fight it was the cause of suffering. The solution was to move with the Way of Heaven and accept the constant change. Once he realised this he felt exhilarated. He realised that, once one had given up thinking of oneself as a unique and precious individual, whose life must preserved at all costs, a person could observe their predicament with detachment and serenity, and become reconciled with the Way of Heaven and be at peace.

Tz'u (Compassion – A Community of Feeling with All Things)
There are three treasures of the Tao: humility, moderation and compassion. Most of all the Taoists value compassion, *Tz'u*, which Laotse described as 'the first treasure'. From compassion, they believe, follows wisdom and courage and those who have no compassion, have no wisdom. Through compassion Taoists always value the sufferer and recognise 'a community of feeling with all things'.

> *'All things alike go through their processes of activity,*
> *and then we see them return to their original state.*
> *Where vegetables have displayed luxuriant growth,*
> *We see each of them return to its root.*
> *This returning to their root is what we call the state of stillness;*
> *And that stillness confirms that they have fulfilled their appointed end.*
> *The confirmation of that fulfilment is the regular unchanging rule.*
> *To know that unchanging rule is to be intelligent;*
> *Not to know it leads to wild movements and evil issues.*
> *The knowledge of that unchanging rule produces a grand capacity for forebearance,*
> *And **that capacity for forebearance leads to a community of feeling with all things**.*
> *From this community of feeling comes a kingliness of character;*
> *And he who is king-like goes on to be heaven-like.*
> *In that likeness to heaven he possesses the Tao.*

Possessed of the Tao, he endures long; and to the end of his
bodily life,
Is exempt from all danger of decay.'
                    (Tao Te Ching – chapter 16)

Here Laotse says that '*a community of feeling with all things*' leads to 'a kingliness of character' which, in turn, leads to possession of the Tao.

4

BUDDHA

'All your fellow creatures are like you.
They want to be happy.
Never harm them and when you leave this life
you too will find happiness. '
Buddha – Dhammapada

'In Buddhism the highest spiritual ideal
is to cultivate compassion for all sentient beings and
to work for their welfare to the greatest possible extent. '
Tenzin Gyatso – 14ᵗʰ Dalai Lama

Buddhism is a philosophy that was founded in northern India during the axial age around 500 BCE, based on the life and teachings of the Buddha. It has probably been the most significant spiritual philosophy in history in terms of its time-span and geographical spread. It spread quickly throughout India, north into Nepal, the Bhutan and Tibet, north-east into China and Japan and south-east into Burma, Thailand, Cambodia, Malaysia and Indonesia. Today it is widespread in the West, mainly due to the popularity of the Dalai Lama, following his exile from Tibet in 1959.

Siddhartha Gautama (Buddha)

The Buddha was born in 463 BCE as a prince called Siddhartha Gautama in Lumbini, an area that was then in northern India, but is now in Nepal. While his mother, Queen Mahamaya, was carrying him she had a dream that foretold that he would either be a great king or a sadhu, a holy man who renounced worldly things. His father wanted him to become a king and was so worried that he would choose the other path that he kept him within the boundaries of the palace. Here he lived in luxury, was trained for his future as the king and had a beautiful wife and son. But at the age of twenty-nine Siddhartha grew restless and wanted to know what lay beyond the palace boundaries, so he ordered his charioteer to secretly take him outside one day so that he could see what lay beyond the palace walls. It was on this excursion that he saw four sights that shocked him so much that they changed his life.

The first sight was of an old man. Siddhartha had never seen old age before. He asked his charioteer why the man was so frail and bent and the charioteer explained that this was old age, which happened to everyone eventually. Siddhartha was horrified and wondered what the point of his youth and beauty was if it was going to fade and he was destined to spend the rest of his days in old age in this terrible state.

The second sight was of a sick man. Siddhartha had never seen sickness before and he questioned his charioteer about this. When he realised that anyone could be struck down with illness at any time, he was shocked again and wondered what the point of having health and vitality was if he could be struck down at any time by sickness.

The third sight was of a corpse being carried on a stretcher to be cremated. Siddhartha had never seen death before. When the charioteer explained that this was the fate of everyone, he was again horrified and wondered what the point of life was if you died at the end of it.

Saddened by the first three sights of old age, sickness and death and wondering what the meaning of life was if it could be blighted by these afflictions, Siddhartha was struck by the realisation that all of life was suffering and that it could not be avoided. Then he saw the fourth and final sight, which was of a sadhu, or holy man, walking along the road with his alms bowl. When he asked his charioteer about the holy man, the charioteer explained that the sadhu had renounced all material things in order to pursue a holy life, because a normal life in the material world could only lead to suffering. Siddhartha decided that he must do the same and discover enlightenment.

So, that night, he left the palace and went to live the life of a sadhu. For six years he lived an existence of self-mortification and fasting, divesting himself of his clothes and gaining a reputation amongst other sadhus as a great renunciant. He practised various forms of yoga and achieved trance-like states, during which he experienced some sort of spiritual awakening. But when he came out of the trances he returned to his usual ordinary self, afflicted by negative emotions and his sense of ego. He did not feel that he had achieved anything. He sought various teachers and followed them, but he still did not feel that he had discovered a real, lasting sense of enlightenment. All he had achieved, as a result of his extreme asceticism, was to become skeletally thin and ill, almost to the point of death.

Eventually he became so disillusioned that he decided to stop following the teachings and practices of others and, instead, he tried to work out a way forward for himself. This was a fundamental change in attitude and it lies at the heart of Buddhist philosophy. Siddhartha realised that you should not rely on the teachings of others but that you should test those teachings and experience them for yourself. There is no faith in Buddhism, just experience. Later in life, when Siddhartha was teaching, he advised his followers not to accept the things he told them, but to try them for themselves and, if they didn't work, to discard them and try something else.

Buddha's Enlightenment

Siddhartha wondered what it was that could give him the experience of enlightenment that he sought, when he recalled a time while he was a boy sitting under a tree watching the fields being ploughed. He had noticed that the plough had torn up young grass shoots and killed many insects. He had suddenly experienced great empathy towards the insects and felt sorry for their suffering. In that moment of selfless empathy, his ego and his personal concerns had disappeared and he experienced the great joy of compassion welling up inside him. Although he had known nothing of yoga in those days, he sat automatically in the yogic position and entered a trance-like state.

So he decided to try to repeat this experience and headed into the forest and found a Bodhi tree by a river and sat under it. He resolved not to leave that place until he had repeated the experience of his childhood and achieved enlightenment. And so he sat in meditation all through the night and, in the morning, as he meditated on the morning star, he at last entered the state of true enlightenment. At that point he realised that neither extravagance nor asceticism were helpful, but that there was a middle way between the two. His mind became clear. The answer had always been there. Suddenly he had a moment of realisation and saw the truth clearly for what it was. He had discovered an elimination of the ego, the removal of all negative emotions and a state of full and infinite compassion for all living things.

When Siddhartha had finished his meditation he found that he could remain in his compassionate and enlightened state of mind, unlike the empty trances he had previously experienced, the effects of which wore off after the meditation had been completed. He gave up the ascetic lifestyle and started to eat normally again and to return to health and live the middle way of being neither extravagant nor deprived. His former friends were at first disappointed in him for leaving the life of the ascetic and they turned their backs on him. But eventually they could see the change that Siddhartha had achieved and they wanted to learn from his experience. Siddhartha explained it to them and emphasised that they should not simply take his word for it, but they should practice it for themselves and experience it. As they did this, his friends gradually came to understand his methods and became his followers. At this stage some of them began to call him *The Buddha* meaning 'The Enlightened One' and suggested that he should share his wisdom with others. At first Buddha was reluctant and wanted to rest and enjoy the happiness and equanimity he had discovered, but gradually he realised that his compassion required him to go and make a positive effort to share this happiness and equanimity with others and help relieve them of their suffering. So he and his followers commenced a new life of travelling and teaching the enlightenment of compassion.[1]

The Four Noble Truths
The first of the Buddhist teachings was the *Four Noble Truths*. *The first noble truth* stated that everywhere there is suffering. This was the observation that Buddha had made when he left the palace. During his time in the palace he had been living an illusion of luxury, unable to see the suffering in the real world. This is still the experience of many people who live a life of relative comfort.

Today we are vaccinated against disease and rarely see sickness before old age. Even old age and death are kept behind closed doors for a large part of our lives. But when we do eventually see these things, we are smitten with sorrow and we suffer because of it.

The second noble truth defines the causes of suffering. These are not only the physical sufferings of sickness, old age and death, but also our mental sufferings. According to the Buddha, the root of our mental suffering is the ego, the sense of self which believes that it must fight for itself in the world. The ego creates negative emotions such as greed, envy and hate. The ego tries to possess and accumulate things and, in turn, becomes dissatisfied. When we try to resolve our discontent by accumulating material things such as wealth, a nice house, a bigger car or a better job, we find that the more we achieve, the more we want to achieve and the more dissatisfied we become. The ego also makes us competitive. For example, when we have a nice house we achieve short-term satisfaction, but when we see our friends acquiring an even nicer house, we can become envious, dissatisfied and unhappy. We can initially be thrilled when the boss awards us with a pay rise, but when we discover that our colleague was awarded a greater pay rise, we can become disappointed, jealous and angry.

The third noble truth states that there is a cure for suffering. Although you cannot prevent physical suffering (such as sickness, old age or death), and you cannot always find cures to your physical situation (such as being poor or not being in the right marital or employment situation, or being mistreated by others), you can nevertheless cure or manage your mental suffering as you live through these situations.

The fourth noble truth explains that cure. This involves two things. The first is the suppression of the ego, which Buddhists regard as the root of all negative emotions and mental sufferings. The second is the cultivation of positive emotions, such as loving kindness and compassion. In order to do this we must practice *mindfulness*.

Mindfulness and Skilfulness

The Buddha taught that we must always be *mindful* of our situation. Instead of reacting to a situation, we should take time to stop and consider our emotions. We should observe our response to events. Are we reacting with negative emotions such as anger or jealousy? Are we about to do or say something that we might regret? What is the cause of that anger or jealousy? It almost always has its roots in the ego. But that is not to say that there are times when an angry response is not justified. If we see an injustice being inflicted on a fellow sentient being, it is right to be angry and initiate a response that will defend it. But how do we respond? We may have to act quickly and not have time to stop and analyse our emotions.[2]

Along with the practice of *mindfulness*, Buddha taught the practice of *skilfulness*. By training the mind in mindfulness during meditation we can develop a state of mind that enables us to respond quickly in a skilful manner during the course of our everyday lives. During a meditation Buddha would observe his thoughts and emotions and try to understand them and to deal with negative emotions. But this wasn't enough for Buddha. He went on to cultivate the positive emotion of empathy and turned this empathy into the positive action of compassion. *Empathy* is the capacity to recognise and share the feelings of others. *Compassion* is the response to empathy, which leads to the desire to alleviate the suffering of others. Through this practice he systematically altered his mind from one that was dominated by selfishness, craving and greed, into a mind that was dominated by selflessness and compassion. He removed all hate and envy from his mind and replaced it with loving-kindness. With this new mind, he was able to deal with life's situations in a skilful manner.

The Immeasurables
Buddha also practised a meditation called *The Immeasurables*, during which he would go deeper and deeper into a yogic journey of the mind, evoking ever deepening feelings of benevolence and love. There were four stages. The first stage involved developing a feeling of *friendship* with everyone and everything. The second stage involved recognising their suffering and developing a feeling of *empathy* with them. The third stage involved feeling *sympathetic joy* at their happiness, without envy or sense of damage to his ego. The fourth and final stage involved developing a feeling of *total compassion* towards them, without feelings of

attraction or antipathy. This brought him to the transcendent state of infinite wisdom and compassion, where the whole of nature, the whole of the Universe and everything in it was encompassed by his compassion. In this state he experienced complete happiness and equanimity.[3] This was *Nirvana*. It was the Peace of Brahman or *Shanti*, the peace that transcends all understanding.

Bodhisattvas

Many Buddhists believe that by achieving this state of enlightenment we can be freed from our *karma*, the 'actions' that keep us bound to *samsara*, the endless cycle of birth, death and rebirth. They believe that when we depart this life, having achieved this state, we will be eternally united with Brahman and will never be reborn again into this life of suffering. All living things have this potential, however small. But there are those who achieve this state and stay on Earth to help others to achieve their potential. Such people are called Bodhisattvas. There are two schools of Buddhism. The first is the *Theravada school* of Buddhism, which means 'the narrow vehicle'. People who follow this school of thought focus on their own development to achieve enlightenment in order to be liberated. The second is the *Mahayana school* of Buddhism, which means 'the great vehicle'. People who follow this school aim to develop themselves and also to help others to achieve their potential. Their compassion ensures that they work not only for themselves, but also for the benefit of all living things.[4]

Compassion for *All* Beings

Buddhists do not confine their compassion and altruism only to other human beings. Buddha's discovery that enlightenment came from the experience of compassion occurred when he remembered the time in his childhood when he had felt empathy and compassion towards the insects that were being killed by the plough. Buddhist compassion is extended to 'all sentient beings' as described in this beautiful Buddhist prayer which is regularly recited by the Dalai Lama and quoted in his book *The Many Ways to Nirvana*:

'With a wish to free all beings
I shall always go for refuge
To the Buddha, Dharma and Sangha
Until I reach full enlightenment.

Enthused by wisdom and compassion
Today in the Buddha's presence
I generate the mind for full awakening
For the benefit of all sentient beings.

As long as space remains,
As long as sentient beings remain,
Until then, may I too, remain
And dispel the miseries of the world.'[5]

The Emperor Ashoka

The spread of Buddhism owes much to the influence of the exceptional Indian Emperor Ashoka (304 BCE – 232 BCE). During the period between the life of Buddha and the time of Christ a number of empires were created through bloody conquest. Julius Caesar (100 BCE – 44 BCE) was largely responsible for building the Roman Empire, Alexander the Great (356 BCE – 323 BCE) conquered most of the lands between the Ionian Sea and India, while the Chinese Emperor Qin (259 BCE – 210 BCE) united the many states of China into one state. All these emperors conquered and then ruled with tyranny. Ashoka, on the other hand, after ruthlessly conquering the whole of India, converted to Buddhism.

Ashoka was the son of a Mauryan emperor and was a trained warrior who hunted and was reputed to have killed a lion with only a rod. But after witnessing the mass deaths of the Kalinga War, which he had led in 260 BCE, he was so horrified by the suffering it had caused that he decided never to wage war again and to rule India according to the values of *ahimsa* (non-violence). He became a non-meat-eater and banned sacrifices and hunting and taught of compassion for all living beings, encouraging non-meat-eating amongst his subjects. He built hospitals for humans and animals and had banyan trees planted and wells dug along the roads of his empire for the use of travellers, both human and animal. He drew up edicts for non-violent behaviour, which he had carved on pillars and rocks throughout his empire. He sent representatives out into the world to teach Buddhism, but also tolerated other religions. Ashoka was largely responsible for the spread of Buddhism throughout the world. Although his successors did not follow his example, his leadership had a profound effect on generations of Indians thereafter. Today around forty percent of Indians are non-meat-eaters compared to around two to five percent in other parts of the world.

Buddhist Attitudes towards Animals Today

Today there are around 376 million Buddhists worldwide, but do they still base their practice on the Buddha's teaching of showing compassion to all sentient beings? Buddhist writer, Norm Phelps, is highly critical of his fellow Buddhists in his book *The Great Compassion* for limiting their circle of compassion to humans, contrary to the teachings of the Buddha. Phelps says,

> *'Buddhism ought to be an animal rights religion <u>par excellence</u>. It teaches the unity of all life; it holds kindness and compassion to be the highest virtues; and it explicitly includes animals in its moral universe.'*

But he criticises his fellow Buddhists for eating meat, as this is based on a flawed argument which allows Buddhists to consume animals as long as they have not been responsible for killing them. Phelps argues that, by eating an animal, there is still an indirect responsibility for the harm caused to a fellow sentient being. By eating meat not only is harm caused to the other sentient being, but bad karma is created by the meat eater.

5

THE JAIN TIRTHANKARS

'Unless we live with non-violence and reverence
for all living beings in our heart,
all our humaneness and acts of goodness,
all our vows, virtues and knowledge,
all our practices to give up greed and acquisitiveness
are meaningless and useless.'
Mahavira - Agamas

'Love is not love
if it does not include love of animals.'
Satish Kumar – You Are Therefore, I Am

Although Buddha had discovered enlightenment for himself, independently from any contemporary teachings, there were other people living in northern India at that time, to whom the techniques of enlightenment had been known for many generations. These people were the Jains. One of these was Mahavira who was born in 599 BCE and was a contemporary of Buddha. He is known as the twenty-fourth Jain Tirthankar. A *Jain*, or *Jina*, is a 'spiritual conqueror' and a *Tirthankar* is a 'ford maker' or one who guides others across the river of suffering to enlightenment on the other side. The concept of the Jain Tirthankar is similar to that of the Buddhist Boddhisattva, however the Tirthankars had existed long before Buddha and the Boddhisattvas. The first Tirthankar was Adinath, also known as Rishabhadev, who some believe could have lived as early as 10,000 BCE.

There is no historical evidence for the first twenty two Tirthankars, but seals have been discovered in the Indus Valley that date back to the stone age, which depict pictures of people in yogic positions, and in particular the standing yogic position, which has been associated with the Jains. However, historical evidence exists for the last two Tirthankars, Mahavira and his predecessor Parshvanath, who lived between 877 BCE and 777 BCE and achieved nirvana 250 years before Mahavira. Modern Jainism is based on the teachings of all of the twenty-four Tirthankars, but primarily on the teachings of the last Tirthankar, Mahavira.

Mahavira

In the same way as Siddhartha Gautama was given the name *Buddha* meaning 'Enlightened One', Vardhamana Jnatrputra was given the name *Mahavira* which meant 'Great Hero'. Mahavira had been the son of a chieftain and was said to have had a magnificent physique. However, at the age of thirty he decided to abandon his existing life and renounce his worldly attachments. Renouncers were common at the time and Mahavira joined them in the forest, living naked and practising the usual austerities. The existing Vedic tradition had deteriorated into rituals and animal sacrifices in order to appease the gods and, by the age of forty two, Mahavira had realised that this life was not the way to *moksha* or 'enlightenment'. For Mahavira the only way to enlightenment was through non-violence to all living things. He believed that everything in nature had a life force, which shared in the life-force of the Universe. This was the individual spirit, the Atman, which was part of the universal spirit, the Brahman. To harm any living thing was to harm that life-force and, therefore, to cause harm to yourself, as you were a part of that life-force. Therefore enlightenment was to be achieved through 'non-violence', which was known as *ahimsa*. All the ethical principles that followed were based on this one primary principle of ahimsa[1].

Every human being, every animal, every plant and every rock had a *Jiva* or 'soul' with a life-force and everything had the potential to develop into something better and eventually achieve enlightenment. All living things shared the same nature and should therefore be treated with the same respect as we would expect to be treated ourselves. Mahavira had realised the *Golden Rule*. In order to achieve enlightenment you had to take three steps. First you must understand that everything shares the same sacred life-force and is linked to the universal spirit of Brahman. Then you have to treat everything with ahimsa, or non-violence, and finally you have to show compassion for every living thing. To Mahavira this was simple and didn't require the great effort of yoga or its austerities. You simply had to understand that everything shares the same life force, do no harm to anything and treat everything with respect and loving-kindness. Mahavira said,

> *'All beings are fond of life, hate pain, like pleasure, shun destruction, like life, long to live. To life all life is dear.'*
> *(Acaranga Sutra)*

> *'All breathing, living creatures should not be slain or treated with violence, abused or tormented. This is the supreme unchangeable law.' (Sutrakritanga)*

> *'Unless we live with non-violence and reverence for all living beings in our heart, all our humaneness and acts of goodness, all our vows, virtues and knowledge, all our practices to give up greed and acquisitiveness are meaningless and useless.' (Agamas)*

During the axial age, around 500 BCE, both Buddhism and Jainism responded to the Vedic tradition in the same way as Jesus later responded to the practices of the orthodox Jewish tradition and the Protestants responded to the Roman Catholic Church in the Middle Ages. They were all reformers who believed that the original traditions and true spiritual values had been lost and had been replaced by worldly hierarchies which were preoccupied with meaningless rituals. Both Buddhism and Jainism sought to return to the core of their spirituality, which was non-violence and compassion. Like Buddha, Mahavira had left a life of relative comfort to practise a life of austerities, only to realise that neither excess comfort nor austerity could lead to the liberation of the spirit. There had to be a *middle way*, which involved the practice of non-violence and compassion.

The Five Ethical Values

The Jains have five ethical values:

> *non-violence,*
> *honesty,*
> *chastity,*
> *not stealing, and*
> *not coveting.*[2]

The final four ethical values all stem from the first principle of non-violence (ahimsa). This was not limited to physical violence but also included violence of speech or action or even neglect. They thought that, at all times, one should be mindful about one's behaviour and ensure that no action or lack of action could cause harm to another living being.

The Jains have this beautiful prayer:

> *I ask pardon from all living creatures.*
> *May all creatures pardon me.*
> *May I have friendship for all creatures*
> *and enmity towards none.*

Jains also believe that there are three components to the spiritual path: *right faith, right knowledge* and *right conduct.* Three is an important number for the Jains because of the significance of the three components. Nine is also an important number, as it is three times three. Therefore the number nine and multiples of nine frequently appear in Jain tradition[3].

Jain Cosmology

According to Jain cosmology, life goes round in great cycles of happiness and misery. There is a half cycle of ascending happiness, which is divided into six epochs and another half cycle of descending happiness, which is also divided into six epochs. Currently we are in the early stages of the fifth epoch of the descending cycle, which will last around 21,000 years. So we are in pretty unhappy times. This fifth descending half cycle started 2,500 years ago, around the time of the Axial Age, which the Jains see as the last of the ages of great transformation, when Mahavira, the last of Tirthankars lived. The previous twenty-three Tirthankars lived during the fourth and previous epoch of the descending half cycle. According to Jain cosmology, the further the decline, the greater the selfishness, greed, hate, anger and pride of humans and the more destruction they will inflict on the natural world. Because of this the Jains believe that the Thirthankars are sent to help mankind[4].

Like the Buddhists, the Jains also believe in karma and that by practising non-violence and compassion one can work out old bad karma and develop new good karma. They believe that all living things on this Earth are caught up in the endless cycle of birth, death and rebirth (samsara), trapped by the bad karma from the actions of their current and previous lives and destined to be stuck in a mortal existence for as long as they carry that bad karma. But through the practice of non-violence and compassion, man and the animals can shed bad karma, develop good karma and achieve enlightenment. After death, following the achievement of enlightenment, one is freed from all karmic bonds and the individual spirit can be reunited with the universal spirit. Like the Boddhisattva, the Tirthankar, although liberated from the world, can return to help other beings work through their suffering and become spiritual conquerors.

Jain Pluralism

An aspect of Jainism which has held it true to its vision of non-harming is its *pluralism*, whereby the Jains will always look at other points of view and never assume that their point of view is the only one that is correct. As a result the Jains have been very tolerant and there have been no wars in the name of Jainism. They have a story of four blind men who are introduced to an elephant and are asked to describe it. The first blind man feels its leg and experiences a tree, the second blind man feels its trunk and experiences a snake, the third blind man feels its tail and experiences a rope, while the fourth blind man feels its ear and experiences a cloth. However, none of them have experienced the whole elephant or understood what they had felt. The Jains are mindful that, like the blind people feeling only a part of the elephant, their views may be based on only part of the truth and that they should be aware that there may be more to a situation than meets the eye. That does not mean that their view is wrong, it is just not the whole truth.

In the same way, Jains do not believe that other religions are wrong. In the end they are all partly true. They may not represent the whole truth, but they are all on different paths, coming from different directions, and heading to the same destination, like many rivers heading from different sources to the same ocean, or many paths heading up a mountain to the same peak. Thus the Jains have been very tolerant of other religions and have co-existed peacefully with them. In many western countries, where facilities are limited, Jains, Sikhs and Hindus share the same temples and worship together at each other's festivals[5].

Svetambaras and Digambaras

Many westerners are apprehensive about Jainism because its austerities are seen to be too severe. The concept of non-violence to all living things often appears too extreme for most western tastes, where people consider themselves not to be violent people, but still find the idea of not hurting an insect or a micro-organism unachievable. The images of Jains wearing facemasks to ensure that they do not inhale flies, or sweeping the path in front of them with a broom to ensure that they do not tread on insects, seem extreme. So too does the idea of going naked or *sky clad* and pulling out your hair. But like all religions, Jainism has divided into many sub-divisions over time. The two main sub-divisions are the *Svetambaras*, who make up the majority of the Jains and the *Digambaras* or 'sky clad' Jains, which are a minority.

The Digambaras are more extreme than the other Jains, believing that any concern for hair and clothing is a form of attachment to the body and therefore the hair should be plucked out and clothes should not be worn. They believe that this is the way to achieve the highest form of detachment from the material world and hence to achieve *moksha* or 'enlightenment' in this life. People who do not practise these things can, however, come back in a future life to do so. They further believe that women should not go naked and therefore cannot practise the highest form of detachment, so are therefore unable to achieve moksha in their female form. They will have to come back as a man in a future life to achieve liberation.

But not all Jains agree with this and there has been much debate and literature on the subject. By far the majority of Jains are family lay people who dress in the contemporary style of the community in which they live. They believe that it is your attitude towards detachment from material things, rather than going naked that matters. They also believe that women can attain moksha. They still observe the non-harming of living things, however, and leave a positive green footprint.

All Jains strictly practise non-meat-eating, as to eat meat would require the harming of sentient beings. Some Jains however keep livestock for dairy purposes, but treat those animals with the utmost respect and consideration for their good welfare[6].

Scholars have identified three forms of Jainism today, which they call orthodox, heterodox and neo-orthodox. The *Orthodox* Jains are the traditional followers of Jainism in India, who stick to the rituals that have developed over the years and live exclusively amongst themselves. They tend to be strict ascetics who renounce the world. They believe that the way to achieve enlightenment is not to live in the world and be part of it, but to be separate from it. A minority even starve themselves to death, when the time is right, in order to separate the spirit from the material world. They are atheists and believe that whilst individuals have souls, there is no God or universal spirit of Brahman to join with.

The *Heterodox* Jains, on the other hand, focus not so much on renouncing the world, but on the way they live and work in it. They are theistic and believe that we are all part of the universal spirit of Brahman. They have no problem with Hindu gods, whom they see as all being descended from the one original spirit. These Jains tend to interact more with Hindus and other religious groups. The *Neo-orthodox* Jains see themselves as the most modern and progressive Jains and often live in the western world. They are frequently astute business people and develop considerable wealth[7].

The difference between the orthodox Jains and the other types of Jains is similar to the difference between the Theravada Buddhists and the Mahayana Buddhists. The *Theravada* (narrow vehicle) Buddhists focus on their own internal transformation through meditation and ascetic practice, while the *Mahayana* (great vehicle) Buddhists go out into the world and behave altruistically.

Neminath

Although the Jains have also developed a highly complex cosmology, which is in itself very interesting, the fundamental requirement of Jain living is not to be knowledgeable but to live a peaceful life and practise ahimsa. To live a life of non-violence, they believe, is to understand everything. Although all the Indian religions - Hindu, Buddhist, Sikh and Jain - advocate non-violence, the Jains have the greatest advocate of compassion towards animals in their twenty-second Tirthankar, *Neminath*.

Neminath believed that humans had no more rights than any other species, but that humans had extra obligations to practise non-violence. His attitude towards animals is highlighted in the story of his wedding day and the incidences that led to his life as the twenty-second Tirthankar.

At the time of his wedding Neminath was a prince. Whilst he was heading towards the house of his bride, he saw an enclosure full of animals, tightly packed and waiting to be slaughtered. He was shocked by the crying of the animals and asked his aides why the animals were being kept in such cruel conditions. They explained to him that the animals were waiting to be slaughtered for the feast of his wedding party. Overwhelmed with compassion, Neminath went to his future father-in-law and asked that the animals be immediately set free. His father-in-law asked,

'Why? The lives of animals are there for human use. They are our slaves and meat. How can there be a feast without flesh?'

Prince Neminath was dismayed. 'Animals have souls' he explained, 'they have consciousness, they are our kin and our ancestors. They wish to live as much as we do, they have feelings and emotions. They have love and passion. They fear death as much as we do. Their instinct for life is no less than our own. Their right to live is as fundamental as our own.'

The prince explained to his future father-in-law that he could not marry or love his daughter if it meant that animals had to be enslaved and killed. So he abandoned the wedding and left. He also abandoned the life of a prince and responded to his inner calling to go out and awaken the sleepy masses, who had been conditioned into thinking selfishly and who killed animals for their comfort and pleasure. The animal kingdom welcomed Neminath as the prophet of the weak and wild. They gathered round him.

Many thousands of people were moved by the teachings of Neminath and renounced meat and took up the work of animal welfare. Even the princess whom Neminath was going to marry was so inspired by him that she decided to remain unmarried and dedicate herself to the care of animals. Her father, too, underwent a transformation and announced that all animals in his kingdom were to be respected and he banned hunting, shooting, caging and the keeping of pets[8].

Adinath

All of the twenty-four Tirthankars have an animal associated with them to symbolise the central place of animals in Jain teaching. The first Tirthankar, Adinath, who was renowned for bringing agriculture to his people, also taught compassion to animals. He taught farmers that they should always sow more seed than they needed so that there was enough for the birds and mice and insects as well. There should be enough seed to harvest for food, to sow for the following year and to leave on the ground for the wild animals[9].

Jain Attitudes towards Animals Today

There are around five million Jains in the world today, who still practice ahimsa towards all living beings, which includes not exploiting or eating animals or using animal products. The popular Jain philosopher and writer, Satish Kumar, has written,

> *'Love is not love if it does not include love of animals. What kind of compassion is it which adores human life, but ignores the slaughter of animals? Division between humans and animals and putting human interests before animal interests is the beginning of sectionalism, racism, nationalism, class and caste discrimination, and of course speciesism. The same mindset, which enslaves animals, goes on to enslave humans in the name of self-interest, national interest and umpteen other narrow interests. Therefore, we, the Jains, advocate an unconditional and unequivocal reverence for all life.'*[10].

6

THE GREEK PHILOSOPHERS

'As long as man continues to be the destroyer of
lower, living beings,
he will never know health or peace.
For as long as men massacre animals,
they will kill each other.
Indeed, he who sows the seed of murder and pain
cannot reap joy and love.'
Pythagoras[1]

'Animals share with us the privilege of having a soul.'
Pythagoras[1]

At the same time as philosophies were being developed in India that linked the individual spirit with the universal spirit, and in China which linked the individual soul to the Way of Heaven, a similar philosophy was being developed in the area around the Mediterranean. This was based on Socrates' concept that *The Good* and the 'soul', or 'psyche' lived in a spiritual realm. Later his student Plato extended this concept and proposed that the *Forms*, which were concepts found in mathematics, science and music were inextricably linked to the way of the Universe through a medium known as the *Platonic Realm*. These, he believed, represented eternal and esoteric truths that existed independently of the material world in which they manifested themselves. These *truths* had always existed and were discovered, not designed by man. When man discovered these truths, he became connected to the Universe in a mystical and transcendental way[2]. Plato was born in 369 BCE and lived in Athens. He was influenced by both Pythagoras and his teacher Socrates.

Pythagoras

Pythagoras had been born on the Aegean island of Samos around 570 BCE, although the records of his life and teachings are sketchy. During his life he had travelled extensively, learning from the greatest teachers of his time, visiting places such as Egypt, Babylon, Arabia and Phoenicia. He is best known for the mathematical theory that was named after him, which states that the square of the hypotenuse of a right angled triangle is equal to the sum of the squares of the other two sides. However, it is clear that this theory was known to the Egyptians and Babylonians at least 2,000 years earlier, as it was used in architecture, most significantly in the building of the pyramids.

Pythagoras was also the founder of esoteric teachings and had founded a sect known as the *Pythagoreans*, which attracted highly intelligent men and women as its members. As well as discussing and developing theories on mathematics, science and music, the Pythagoreans also undertook spiritual practices, which included the ethics of non-violence to all living things. They were non-meat-eaters and refused to take part in the sacrifice of animals. They also practised a form of yoga and believed in karma and reincarnation. They were peaceful and tolerant people. Part of their way of 'being one with the universal spirit' was to see the divine in nature through the beauty of mathematics, geometry, science, astronomy and music. However, they kept the knowledge of their secret society largely to themselves, so we have little knowledge of the details of what they discovered and taught. Sadly, the secrecy of the cult also led to distrust by the people around them, who later destroyed it, killing many of its members.

The Orphic Sect

Plato would also have been influenced by the *Orphic Sect*, which was similar to the Pythagoreans and had existed in Greece at around the same time. They modelled themselves on Orpheus, a mythical hero from Thrace, who was a man of peace, who made men forget their quarrels and tamed wild animals. The Orphic Sect also adhered to the principle of non-violence, were non-meat-eaters and refused to participate in animal sacrifices[3].

Socrates and the Good

The person who influenced Plato most, however, was his teacher Socrates. At around 420 BCE, Socrates rose to fame as a philosopher in Athens. He was the son of a stone-cutter and was a poor, ragged and unattractive looking man who had no interest in making money and never charged his students for his teachings, unlike most of his contemporaries. Despite his humility, he attracted large crowds who were fascinated by his philosophical discussions. Socrates' method was not to follow lines of reasoning that resulted in answers, but to question everything, challenging people's views of the world. He revealed to those who debated with him that the things they thought they understood were misconceptions. He challenged people's deepest held views and left them realising that they did not really understand anything.

Socrates was the founder of *dialectic*, a rigorous dialogue designed to expose false beliefs and elicit truth. By rigorous questioning Socrates managed to uncover the inherent flaws and inconsistencies in every point of view, thereby revealing the prejudices and false assumptions on which people based their understandings and belief systems. He was a genius at it. Many Greeks at the time believed that courage was a noble virtue, for example, but during a discussion with an army general called Laches, who was a strong proponent of this view, Socrates pulled this belief apart. By bombarding Laches with example after example, he persuaded him that courage was in fact foolish and dangerous and was not a virtue at all. He also argued that other 'virtues', such as temperance, wisdom and justice were equally not true virtues. They just stemmed from something absolute and transcendent which he called *The Good*.

For Socrates, philosophy was about understanding how we should live well, and he believed that this was based on the abstract concept of *The Good*. He described what he called the *Psyche*, which was the soul, resembling the Indian 'Atman'. The Psyche, he believed, was eternal and existed independently of the body, having existed before the birth of the body and carrying on after its death. The Psyche enabled living beings to reason and to seek the Good, and it was the purpose of man's life on earth, not to work for material achievements, but to cultivate the Psyche. This could be done by interrogating one's fundamental assumptions, to see things as they truly are, going beyond false assumptions, and arriving at a perfect intuition that would make one behave well at all times. Compassion and altruism were fundamental to the development of the Good in the Psyche.

For many people who listened to and debated with Socrates, the realisation that their deeply held beliefs and understandings were in fact dubious or uncertain, was like a moment of enlightenment when they experienced bliss. The truth was not something new that they discovered, but was something that had been there all the time, something eternal that they already unconsciously knew, but had been hidden from them by the assumptions and prejudices that had been built up in their minds. It was the purpose of the dialectic to break down these misconceptions and reveal the truth. According to Socrates, the Good was something that was already out there just waiting to be discovered. It was in another realm that was perfect and eternal.

Socrates' Allegory of the Cave

In his book *The Republic*, Plato relates Socrates' *Allegory of the Cave*, which describes how the Good is withheld from our understanding and how things could be if we were to discover it. In the allegory, a group of men are chained up all their lives in a cave. They are kept turned away from the sunlight and can only see the shadows of things from the outside world reflected on the walls of the cave. These men represented the unenlightened human condition, in which it is impossible to see the Good directly. Yet we are so conditioned by our deprived circumstances that we take these shadows to be reality. If the prisoners were set free they would be dazzled and bewildered by the bright sunlight, the colours and the three-dimensional forms of the things that had cast the shadows. They would probably find it too much to bear and would have to go back into the cave to the security of the life they understood. This is what Socrates thought such an awakening would be like for us.

Sadly, Socrates lived in dangerous times during the peak of the Peloponnesian wars, when Athens was facing defeat. Many Greeks saw this state of affairs as the result of the gods' revenge for the irreligious culture of the times. Socrates' teachings were perceived as blasphemous and he was targeted as being a cause of this divine retribution. In 399 BCE Socrates was arrested and accused of not recognising the state gods and of corrupting the people. His honest explanation that he was only talking about the truth did little to save him and he was sentenced to death by drinking hemlock. Even when death was imminent Socrates maintained a humble equanimity and thought of others. He washed himself so as to save others the trouble after his death, thanked his jailer for his kindness and joked about his predicament. Accepting his death with a serenity that transcended his suffering and, drinking the hemlock, he peacefully passed away[4].

Plato and the Platonic Realm

His pupil Plato, who was thirty at the time, was outraged. The execution of Socrates made him realise that the whole system of government was corrupt and that the murder of his teacher was a travesty of justice. Although he was the son of an aristocratic family who had planned for him to attain high political office, Plato's anger at this event made him change his mind. Deciding that he would work with the philosophies of Socrates and become a political reformer, he dedicated the rest of his life to writing about good governance. Plato's book *The Republic*, describes a utopia of what he regarded as the successful state. He set up a school of mathematics and philosophy called *The Academy* in a sacred grove on the outskirts of Athens. It was dedicated to the hero Academius and the teaching was conducted by discussion in the Socratic manner[5].

Combining Socrates' concept of the Good as being eternal and transcendent with the Pythagorean description of mathematics and science, Plato developed the concept of the *Forms*. He proposed that the Forms were things that existed in another realm, independently of the material world in which they manifested themselves. For example, there were many things in nature that were round, but the perfect circle was a concept that existed independently of circular objects in nature, but which manifested itself in those objects. A circle was a concept, not one that had been invented by man, but one that had always existed in its own right and that man had discovered. Beauty was another example. You could look at a beautiful object, but the object only took the form of beauty, which was an eternal and independent thing.

People could be beautiful, but their beauty was ephemeral and would fade and die. But the concept of beauty was eternal.

Plato believed that mathematical truths were also forms. Mathematical forms manifested themselves everywhere, particularly in geometry. No-one ever invented mathematics, they only discovered it. Even though Pythagoras discovered Pythagoras' Theorem, it was an eternal form which had already made itself known to the Egyptians 2,000 years earlier, when they had utilised it in the building of the pyramids. Pythagoras' theorem would apply in any part of the Universe at any time, whether it was discovered or not.

Another example of a mathematical curiosity is one based on the cubes of integers. If you add together the cubes of a series of integers, starting at one, their sum is the same as the square of the sum of those same integers. For instance, take the integers one, two and three. If you find their cubes (one cubed is one, two cubed is eight and three cubed is twenty-seven) and then you add these together (one plus eight plus twenty-seven) you get thirty-six. Now, if you add those integers together (one plus two plus three) you get six and six squared is also thirty-six. Try this for a longer set of integers, say one, two, three, four and five and you will find that the rule will always apply. But where does this rule exist? Plato argued that, although the rule manifests itself when you write it down or even think the method through, the mathematical truth exists out there somewhere and has done for all eternity. That 'out there somewhere' is, Plato suggested, the *Platonic Realm.*

Another interesting mathematical truth is Pi. This is the ratio that relates the radius of a circle with its circumference ($2\pi r$) or with its area (πr^2), where $\pi = 3.142$ etc. etc. The interesting thing is that this is not a finite number and the etc. etc. goes on forever. The same is true about Newton's laws, Kepler's laws and Einstein's $E=MC^2$. They can be applied to so many different situations in the Universe, but they have a unique and eternal existence of their own. It is, Plato suggested, almost like mathematics is a message from this other dimension, giving us a glimpse of this eternal realm, rather like the shadows in Socrates' cave.

The realm of the forms became known as the *Platonic Realm* after Plato who had proposed it. Plato also believed that the spirit was part of the Platonic Realm and that by opening oneself up to an understanding of the eternal truths of the forms, one could access this realm and transcend the material world of suffering. According to Plato, the Cosmos existed on two levels. One was the eternal spiritual world where the perfect forms existed. The other was the material world where the forms manifested themselves and where the psyches of all living things lived in worldly, ephemeral bodies. The material world was impermanent and our lives in it were also impermanent. According to Plato, it is our goal on Earth to cultivate the Psyche and develop it for life in the eternal world of the forms. We are not on Earth to accumulate material wealth, but to study and understand the Cosmos and to develop the Good in us, he believed.

Eureka Moments and the Mystical Experiences

According to Plato, when the mind perceives a mathematical idea it makes contact with the Platonic Realm and consciousness breaks through into the realm of ideas. He believed that when we communicate with each other through mathematics we are communicating at the level of the Platonic Realm and transcending other forms of communication. Many mathematicians have reported experiences of inspiration, when they feel that they have suddenly broken through into this Platonic Realm. These are sometimes called *Eureka Moments*. They may have been puzzling over a difficult mathematical problem for ages, working with pen and paper and trying to think the problem through without success. Then, one day, when they are doing something quite different, the answer breaks through in a moment of inspiration. Such moments of inspiration are reported to be experienced in many fields, not just mathematics, such as music, art and poetry.

Such phenomenon have been studied in contemporary times by the French mathematician Jacques Hadamard, who cites many examples of mathematicians suddenly realising the answer to some mathematical problem they have been puzzling over for ages. These are often accompanied by experiences of euphoria, as if they have broken into that higher level of expansive consciousness that typifies the enlightened state.

Indeed, when Archimedes had his Eureka moment (when he stepped into a bath of water and suddenly realised the solution to a problem that had been troubling him for a long time) he is said to have been so ecstatic that he jumped out of the bath and ran naked down the street to tell his colleagues the answer. The problem that he had been working on was how to measure the volume of irregular objects with precision. As he stepped into the bath he realised that the volume of his body must be equal to the volume of water that he displaced, which was clearly measurable if the bath was a regularly shaped object.

Today there are some scientists who believe that understanding truths about the Universe can only ultimately be achieved through mystical experience and that there is a point beyond which science and logic cannot go. In his book *The Mind of God*, Paul Davies, for example, explores the beauty of mathematics and its relationship to the Platonic Realm. He says,

'Scientific method should be explored as far as it can possibly go. Mysticism is no substitute for scientific enquiry and logical reasoning as long as this approach can be consistently applied. It is only dealing with the ultimate questions that science and logic may fail us. I am not saying that science and logic are likely to provide the wrong answers, but they may be incapable of addressing the sort of 'why?' as opposed to 'how?' questions we want to ask.'

He uses the example of 'turtle trouble', which was described by Stephen Hawking in *A Brief History of Time*, to explain what he means when he says that science and logic fails to address the 'why?' questions. During a lecture on cosmology a woman in the audience stood up and declared that it was all nonsense and that the Earth was a flat plate that rested on a turtle. When asked what the turtle was resting on, she answered that it was resting on another turtle. Then came the debate about how far down the turtles went. Were there an infinite number of turtles or was there a final turtle? If there was a final turtle, what held it up? And this is the problem that science discovers when trying to explain the intricacies of the Cosmos. Is it finite or is it infinite? If it is finite, what lies beyond the boundary and if it is infinite, how do we understand this? Scientists have also tried to go down to the small (the atomic realm) and the very small (sub-atomic particles and strings). They have a number of theories of the Universe, including Einstein's theories, quantum mechanics and string theory, but they do not yet have a Grand Unifying Theory that unifies them. Some scientists are, however, positive that such a theory will be found in the not too distant future.

Paul Davies argues that where science comes up against the limitations of our understanding of the Cosmos, the mystical experience can take us to that final step. He explains that mystics achieve an understanding of ultimate reality in a single experience, which is very different from going through the tortuous effort of the scientific approach. They describe an overwhelming sense of being at one with the Universe or with God, of glimpsing a holistic vision of reality, or being in the presence of a powerful and loving influence. Sometimes the mystical path involves an inner sense of peace, a compassionate, joyful stillness that lies beyond the activity of busy minds. Albert Einstein spoke of a 'cosmic religious feeling' that inspired his thought experiments on the Universe and the mathematician Roger Penrose has described his experiences of mathematical inspiration as a sudden 'breaking through' into the Platonic Realm. The mathematician Kurt Godel describes his experiences of being able to directly perceive mathematical objects such as infinity by adopting meditative practices. The astronomer Fred Hoyle described an inspiration that happened to him while he was driving over Bowes Moor as a revelation like the one that occurred to Paul on the road to Damascus. Others talk about an enormous sense of euphoria, which lasts for days after the revelation[6].

The zoologist Konrad Lorenz described this moment of inspiration as experienced by a chimpanzee in his work during 1972, noting that animals, as well as humans, were capable of experiencing eureka moments. He put a chimpanzee in a room with a box and a banana, which was suspended out of reach. The chimpanzee was agonising about how he could reach the banana. Lorenz wrote, 'The matter had given him no peace and he returned to it again. Then suddenly – and there is no other way to describe it – his previously gloomy face 'lit up'. His eyes now moved from the banana to the empty space beneath it on the ground, from this to the box, then back to the space, and from there to the banana. The next moment he gave a cry of joy, and somersaulted over to the box in sheer high spirits. Completely assured of his success, he pushed the box below the banana. No man watching him could doubt the existence of a genuine 'Aha' experience in anthropoid apes.'[7]

The American mathematician, computer scientist and philosopher, Rudy Rucker describes the experience saying, 'No door in the labyrinthine castle of science opens directly onto the Absolute. But if one understands the maze well enough, it is possible to jump out of the system and experience the Absolute for oneself... But ultimately mystical knowledge is attained all at once or not at all. There is no gradual path.'

Aristotle and Anthropocentrism
The great insights of Pythagoras and Socrates led to Plato's ideas about the Platonic Realm. Sadly, Plato went on to grow stale after this and he lost touch with the ethical teachings of his predecessors. So keen was he to develop a model of the perfect political system that he forgot about compassion. In his book *The Republic* he created a utopia with a plan for an efficient and ruthless state. His system was intolerant and punitive and, despite his previous revulsion of the execution of his teacher Socrates, he even advocated the death penalty. The decline in ethical values and moral understanding that commenced with Plato continued further with his student Aristotle.

At the age of eighteen Aristotle left his birthplace of Chalcidice and went to Athens to study at the Academy as a student of Plato. He stayed there for twenty-four years, during which time he was loyal to Plato and accepted the theory of the Forms. He became more and more critical, however, of the view that the Forms existed in another realm and he doubted the existence of this realm. He was a materialist. After Plato died in 347 BCE, Aristotle left Athens and was invited by King Philip to take up residence in Macedonia in order to educate his son Alexander. In 336 BCE the King was assassinated, and in the following year, Aristotle returned to Athens and set up his own school known as *The Lyceum*, near the temple of Apollo Lyceus[8].

Aristotle became a biologist and a rationalist. He emphasised man's faculty of reason and believed that man was superior to the other animals because of his ability to think rationally, something he assumed that other animals could not do. He perverted Socrates' concept of the Good by saying that it lay in man's ability to live a life of reason. He perceived women to be inferior to men and to be a defective form of human being. Man, on the other hand, had intelligence, which was immortal and this linked him to the gods. Full of the sorts of prejudices which Socrates would have challenged with his dialectic debate, Aristotle went on to become a respected philosopher of the time and his philosophy laid the foundation for future western prejudices. In the twelfth century AD the Europeans discovered his writings and were enamoured by his rational proofs of man's relationship with the divine. His philosophies were introduced into the teachings of the Church by Thomas Aquinas, where they diverted the course of western Christianity, introducing human arrogance, prejudice, sexism, racism and speciesism into the Church. Much later the French philosopher Descartes would base his work on the teachings of Aristotle to equally bad effect[9].

Aristotle's pupil Alexander went on to become Alexander the Great and brutally conquered most of Persia and Asia. Aristotle went on to postulate that the sun and the planets orbited the earth! His geocentric theory of the Cosmos was as misguided as his anthropocentric theory of life.

There was certainly a gulf between the minds of Socrates and Aristotle. But was this a gulf that has been apparent in human beings throughout time? Even though Aristotle spent twenty-four years as a student of Plato who had, in turn, been a student of Socrates, Aristotle was a rationalist who couldn't grasp the insights of Socrates. How could a student who had received so much exposure to the workings of such a great mind fail to grasp these insights? What Aristotle lacked, perhaps, was the *experience* of the realm of the Good. You could calculate and think and rationalise all you liked, but that would never lead you to an understanding of the realm of the Good. This had to be experienced in the mystical sense. This is what Buddha, Mahavira and the mathematicians described above claimed they had experienced. It was the moment of enlightenment, the Eureka moment, the infinite expansion of the consciousness to grasp the 'All' that is, the feeling of infinite compassion and the experience of bliss.

Could it be that there are very clever rationalists who can never experience this state of being, but that there are geniuses who can? Could the geniuses have something that the rationalists don't have? A better brain perhaps? Or is there something else going on? Perhaps it isn't so much that there is something *missing*, but that there is something *blocking* genius. Perhaps that something is, the ego. According to the Eastern philosophies, it is only when we suppress the ego and eliminate negative emotions that we can see clearly and make that break into Socrates' realm of the Good or experience the realm of Brahman, as described in the Upanishads, or achieve Buddha's enlightenment. It is then, perhaps, that we can share the great compassion experienced by Buddha, Mahavira and Socrates.

7

THE PEACEABLE KINGDOM OF MONOTHEISM

'Behold, I have given you every herb bearing seed,
which is upon the face of all of the earth,
and every tree, in which is the fruit of a tree yielding seed;
to you it shall be for meat. '
Genesis 1: 29

'All the beasts that roam the earth
and all the birds that soar on high
are communities like your own.
We have left nothing out in the Book.
Before their Lord they shall be gathered all.'
Muhammad - The Qur'an 6.38

Monotheism includes the three Abrahamic faiths of Judaism, Christianity and Islam and also the faiths of Zoroastrianism and Sikhism. The history of the Abrahamic religions is described in the Bible and is the foundation of Judaism, Christianity and Islam. The Bible is divided into the Old Testament and the New Testament, with the Old Testament beginning with the Creation and the story of Adam and Eve, followed by the story of Noah and then, after many generations, with the account of the life of Abraham, who lived around 1,700 –1,800 BCE, and of his sons. The earliest parts of the Old Testament were first written down around 800 BCE and added to throughout the lives of the sons of Abraham, up until the time of Christ, which is reported in the New Testament. Judaism is based on the Old Testament and the Torah, Christianity is based on the Old and the New Testament and Islam is based on the Qur'an.

The Biblical Creation and the Fall

The Old Testament starts with the Creation, in which God created the Universe in six stages or 'days', which culminated in a seventh stage, or day of rest, or Sabbath (Genesis 1). On the sixth day, God created living creatures, creeping things, beasts of the earth and man in his image to have dominion over the earth. Significantly, he gives both man and the animals a vegetarian diet:

> *'And God said, "Behold, I have given you every herb bearing seed, which is upon the face of all of the earth, and every tree, in which is the fruit of a tree yielding seed; to you it shall be for meat. And to every beast of the earth, and to every fowl of the air, and to everything that creepeth upon the earth, wherein there is life, I have given every green herb for meat"; and it was so.' (Genesis 1: 29-30).*

Then the Bible goes on to say that God saw that *everything* he had made was good, not just man as is often taught. God saw that his whole creation was good:

> *'And God saw <u>everything</u> that he had made and, behold, it was very good.' (Genesis 1:31).*

The next part tells the story of the Garden of Eden, which describes a perfect world where humans lived at one with nature before the Fall (Genesis 2-3). God creates the first man, Adam and brings the animals to him, whom he lives with and names. God tells Adam that he can freely eat of any tree in the garden, but not the tree of knowledge of good or evil, as he would surely die. God then creates Eve from one of Adam's ribs and they live happily in Eden in innocence, unaware and unashamed of their nakedness. But then the serpent tempts Eve to eat the fruit of the tree of knowledge and Eve tempts Adam to also eat of it. As a result, they lose their innocence and become aware of and ashamed of their nakedness and try to cover themselves up with fig leaves. God is angry and banishes them from the Garden of Eden, telling them of the misery that their deed will bring them. Significantly again, he orders them to eat a vegetarian diet:

'...Thou shalt eat the herb of the field: in the sweat of thy face shalt thou eat bread, till thou return unto the ground...' (Genesis 3: 18-19).

But, after the Fall, in a post lapsarian age, man begins to eat meat.

The Covenant between Noah and Every Living Creature

Many generations after Adam and Eve, came Noah. At this time man had become corrupt and wicked in God's eyes and God chose to destroy all living things. However, Noah found favour with God and God decided to protect Noah and his family and two of each type of animal, so that they may be fruitful and replenish the earth. God warned Noah that he was going to cause a mighty flood and he instructed him to build an ark, giving him the plans, and to collect his family and two of each type of animal to go into the ark to be saved. This Noah did, and the flood came and washed away every living thing off the face of the earth, but Noah and those in his ark were saved. After the flood God blessed Noah and his sons and said 'Be fruitful and multiply and replenish the earth'.

He then said something that showed that he gave man complete dominion over animals, as he had given Adam dominion over the Garden of Eden and everything in it. God says,

'And the fear of you and the dread of you shall be upon every beast of the earth, and upon every fowl of the air, upon all that moves upon the earth, and upon all the fishes of the sea; into your hand are they delivered' (Genesis 9:2).

This would seem to imply a tyrannical rule, rather than the implied stewardship given to Adam. Furthermore, God no longer expected man to be vegetarian, as he did for Adam and Eve, and he says,

'Every moving thing that lives shall be meat for you; even as the green herb I have given you all things' (Genesis 9:3).

That this was a concession and a compromise is emphasised in the next sentence, when God prohibits the eating of meat with the blood in it, as this still holds the life-blood or soul of the animal. He says,

> *'But flesh with the life thereof, which is the blood thereof, shall ye not eat' (Genesis 9:4).*

This quote is frequently used by those who want to condone meat-eating by Jews, Christians and others. But it was the sign that God recognised man's fallibility since the Fall, after he had tasted the fruit of the tree of knowledge of good and evil. (It may also be significant that man was living in a desert environment where there were insufficient 'green herbs' to sustain him). But, significantly, God says that he makes his covenant with both man and animals. He says,

> *'This is the token of the Covenant which I make between me and you and every living creature that is with you, for perpetual generations' (Genesis 9:12).*

Dominion or Stewardship?

There has been much theological debate over whether man has been given dominion or stewardship over animals, dominion implying domination and stewardship implying responsibility. The common interpretation is that man can use animals for his needs, providing he treats them with respect and care and does not cause them unnecessary suffering. Animals are part of God's creation and should be used wisely and respectfully.

The Peaceable Kingdom

But after God had given man this concession, recognising his weakness, he made it man's duty to return to the Garden of Eden and to find a new *Peaceable Kingdom*. From then on, the prophets prophesised about this Kingdom and about the coming of the Son of God, one who would redeem mankind and give them eternal life. In Isaiah's prophecy of the coming of Christ, he says,

> *'And there shall come forth a rod out of the stem of Jesse, and a branch shall grow out of his roots. And the spirit of the Lord shall rest upon him, the spirit of wisdom and understanding, the spirit of counsel and might, the spirit of knowledge and of the fear of the Lord. And shall make him of quick understanding in the fear of the Lord: and he shall*

*not judge after the sight of his eyes, neither reprove after
the hearing of his ears. But with righteousness shall he
judge the poor, and reprove with equity for the meek of the
earth, and he shall smite the earth with the rod of his mouth
and with the breath of his lips shall he slay the wicked. And
righteousness shall be his loins, and faithfulness the girdle
of his reins.' (Isaiah 11: 1-5).*

Isaiah has a vision of the Peaceable Kingdom, where there is a
return to non-meat-eating, not just for man, but also for the
animals. He goes on to say,

*'The wolf also shall dwell with the lamb, and the leopard
will lie down with the kid; and the calf and the young lion
and the fatling together; and a little child shall lead them.
And the cow and the bear shall feed; their young ones shall
lie down together; and the lion shall eat straw like the ox.
And the suckling child shall play on the hole of the asp, and
the weaned child shall put his hand on the cockatrice's den.
They shall not hurt or destroy in all my holy mountain: for
the earth shall be full of the glory of God, as the waters
cover the sea.' (Isaiah 11: 6-9).*

There are two messages here. First, that animals share in the
Peaceable Kingdom and second, that all beings shall live in peace
together there. Hosea has the same vision,

*'And in that day I make a covenant for them with the beasts
of the field, and with the fowls of heaven, and with the
creeping things of the ground: and I will break the bow and
the sword and the battle out of the earth, and will make
them to lie down safely.' (Hosea 2:18)*

Ezekiel makes a similar prophecy by foreseeing an
eschatological river where every living thing shall live (Ezekiel
47:9) and on whose banks will grow trees that will be meat for all
those living creatures (Ezekiel 47:12).

Also in Isaiah, God has become tired of animal sacrifices
from a people who do not understand his ways. He says,

'What to me is the multitude of your sacrifices? I have had enough of burnt offerings of rams and the fat of fed animals. I do not delight in the blood of bulls, or of lambs, or of he-goats. Bring no more vain offerings. When you spread forth your hands, I will hide my eyes from you, even though you make many prayers, I will not listen; your hands are full of blood.' (Isaiah 1: 11-16).

Hosea reiterates this,

'For I desire Love not sacrifice, the knowledge of God, rather than burnt offerings.' (Hosea 6: 6).

Isaiah also said,

'He that kills an ox is as if he slew a man; he that sacrifices a lamb, as if he cut off a dog's neck'. (Isaiah 66.3)

In the book of Proverbs it is recognised that,

'A righteous man regardeth the life of his beast' (Proverbs 12:10).

In Ecclesiasticus it says that,

'A man has no pre-eminence above a beast: for all is vanity' (Ecclesiasticus 3:19).

The Ten Commandments

According to the Old Testament, Abraham's God promised the land of Canaan to Abraham and his descendants so that they could found the mighty nation of Israel. At God's command Abraham left Ur in Mesopotamia and settled in Canaan in around 1,750 BCE, where both his son Isaac and his grandson Jacob settled. But when they were hit by famine, Jacob and his twelve sons, the founders of the twelve tribes of Israel, migrated to Egypt where they initially prospered. But then the Egyptians turned on them and held them as slaves in Egypt for four hundred years, until around 1,250 BCE when God took pity on them and liberated them under the leadership of Moses. The Israelites fled Egypt and were pursued by the Pharaoh and the Egyptian army until Moses miraculously parted the Sea of Reeds, allowing the Israelites to pass to safety. The parted sea then closed, drowning the Pharaoh and his army and allowing Moses and the Israelites to escape to the Promised Land.

The Old Testament describes how, later on in the journey, God made a covenant with Moses and his people on Mount Sinai and gave them the law that would make them his holy people. The law consisted of the Ten Commandments, which were recorded on two stone tablets and placed in a chest called 'the Ark of the Covenant'. In Judaism, God also gave Moses the Torah on Mount Sinai. The Torah is the first part of the Jewish Bible and includes the first five books of the Old Testament - Genesis, Exodus, Leviticus, Numbers and Deuteronomy. It also includes 613 commandments. The ark and the covenant it contained were carried by the Israelites on to the promised land of Canaan, but Moses died before entering the Promised Land, leaving Joshua to lead the Israelites for the remainder of their journey.[1]

The Ten Commandments form the basic law of all the Abrahamic religions, which include Judaism, Christianity and Islam. They are as follows:

> *You shall have no other gods but me.*
> *You shall not worship any idol.*
> *You shall not misuse the name of the Lord, your God.*
> *You shall keep the Sabbath holy.*
> *You shall respect your father and mother.*
> *You must not kill.*
> *You must not commit adultery.*
> *You must not steal.*
> *You must not give false evidence against your neighbour.*
> *You must not covet your neighbour's possessions.*

Commandments six to ten may look familiar. They are virtually the same as the Jain's five ethical principles: non-violence, chastity, not stealing, truthfulness and not coveting. Is this similarity merely a coincidence, or have the Jain and Jewish religions been founded on the same source, or have they influenced each other? Did these five ethical principles date back to shared ancestors, which some, such as Karen Armstrong, suggest were the Aryan tribes of the Russian Steppes, who migrated south to India to become the Hindus and the Jains, and south-west through Persia to the Middle East to become the sons of Abraham?[2] If the Jain principle of non-violence (ahimsa), which includes all living things, corresponds to the sixth commandment, 'You must not kill', surely at one time, the sixth commandment too, would have applied to all living beings, not just human beings?

Tsa'ar ba'alei chayim

There is an ethical precept in Jewish tradition from the Talmud of *tsa'ar ba'alei chayim*, the mandate 'not to cause pain to any living creature', which strikes a strong accord with ahimsa. In the third century, Rabbi Levi teaches the importance of tsa'ar ba'alei chayim, insisting that the inflicting of suffering on animals must be avoided.[3]

In the Old Testament killing for food was allowed, but only if it was necessary and the killing was undertaken mercifully. At that time, people were living in a desert environment, where a vegetarian diet would have been limited. The instructions for the method of the slaughter of animals, by a clean cut to the throat with a sharp knife, were given because this was the most humane method of slaughter available at the time, not because it was a strict rule which had to be obeyed whatever the circumstances. The fundamental principle was to do the most humane thing, not to obey a rule.

Jewish Attitudes towards Animals Today

Although there are many Jews who do not currently extend their moral circle to include all sentient beings, there are a number of Jews that do, and there are a number of Jewish animal welfare organisations which promote non-meat-eating, such as:

The Jewish Vegetarian Society (JVS) (*www.jvs.org.uk*);
The Jewish Vegetarians of North America (*www.jewishveg.com*);
and Micah Publications (*www.micahbooks.com*), the publisher of Jewish animal rights books.

Jesus' Early Life '*With*' the Animals

The New Testament describes the life of Jesus, the Christ who was foretold by the prophets in the Old Testament. It starts with the story of his birth in a stable in Bethlehem and describes his humble beginnings, where he was put in a manger and was surrounded by animals. Those who were invited to visit him included, not only wise men, but humble shepherds, protectors of sheep, an analogy that is frequently used to describe Jesus himself, who is seen as 'The Good Shepherd'.

Jesus began life as an apprentice carpenter, following his father's trade. During his early life we are told that he debated in the temples and could hold his own against priests and scholars. Not much is known about what Jesus did with his life between the time when he was an apprentice carpenter, from about the age of twelve, to the time when he started to teach in his mid to late twenties. Some question whether he went away and spent time with spiritual ascetics? At the time of writing, we have no information on this and can only speculate. We do know, however, that at the beginning of his time as a preacher, after his baptism in water by John the Baptist, he spent forty days fasting in the wilderness *with wild animals* and angels. Mark 1: 13 says,

> *'Jesus was in the wilderness forty days, tempted by Satan; and he was with wild animals; and the angels ministered to him.'*

The word for 'with' is *meta* which means 'being at peace with' or 'being in companionship with' and suggests that Jesus was in the wilderness in the companionship of wild animals. This heralds the peace between animals and humans described in Isaiah 11: 6-9 and reflects the text in Hosea 2:18,

> *'In that day I will make a covenant for them with the beasts of the field and with the fowls of the air and with the creeping things of the ground'.*

Jesus Extends the Circle of Compassion

Although one of Jesus' main teachings was the Golden Rule, '*Do to others as you would wish others would do to you*[4]', this was not new, as it had already been taught five centuries earlier, during the axial age, by Confucius, Laotse Mahavira, Buddha and, later, by Socrates. It had also been taught by the Jewish Rabbi, Hillel, who had lived in Jerusalem prior to the first millennium and who would have influenced the young Jesus. Hillel had cheekily been asked by a Gentile to explain the Torah whilst standing on one leg. He stood on one leg, recited the golden rule and said,

> *'This is the whole Torah, the rest is the explanation, go and learn' (Shab. 31a).*

But Jesus had not just come to reiterate the golden rule and repeat what had been said before in the Old Testament. He was a major reformer and a firebrand. Although Jesus said that he had come to fulfil what was written in the Old Testament, he also frequently says, *'You have heard that it was said that ... but I say to you...'* so he was actually expanding on what had been written before. Jesus had come to extend the circle of compassion and to lead his flock to the Peaceable Kingdom. Jesus taught some revolutionary ideas about compassion, humility and forgiveness. He extended the Old Testament principle of *'Love your neighbour, hate your enemy'* to *'Love your enemy'*. He discarded the long-standing Old Testament principle of *'An eye for an eye and a tooth for a tooth'* and suggested turning the other cheek. He said,

> *'Love your enemy, bless those that curse you, do good to those that hate you and pray for those that use you and persecute you' (Matthew 5:43-44).*

This is expressed in the parable of the Good Samaritan and forms an extension of forgiveness and compassion beyond the inner circle of family and friends to one's enemies. Jesus had started to extend the circle of compassion! He blesses the poor, the meek, the hungry, the merciful, the pure in heart and the peacemakers, describing them as 'the salt of the earth' and 'the light of the world'[7]. He then says,

> *'You have heard that it was said, "You shall not kill or you shall be in danger of judgement", but I say to you, whoever*

is angry with his brother without cause shall be in danger of judgement' (Matthew 5:21-22).

Here he extends the sixth commandment *'You shall not kill'* to the full meaning of *tsa'ar ba'alei chayim*, which means, not only not killing, but also not harming by thought, word or deed.

Jesus also advocates not worrying about material requirements. He says,

> *'Do not lay up for yourselves treasures on earth, where moth and rust corrupts and where thieves break through and steal. But lay up for yourselves treasures in heaven, where neither moth nor rust corrupts and where thieves do not break through and steal. For where your treasure is, there your heart will also be' (Matthew 6:19-21)* and

> *'Take no thought for your life, what you shall eat, what you shall drink, what you shall wear. Is life not more important than food and the body more important than clothing? Behold the birds of the air. They do not sow, or reap or gather, yet God feeds them. How much more will he feed you?' (Matthew 6:25-26)* and

> *'Seek first the Kingdom of God and his righteousness and all these things shall be given to you.' (Matthew 6:33).*

He also teaches the importance of living in the 'Now' and not worrying about the future, when he says,

> *'Take no thought for tomorrow, for tomorrow will look after itself' (Matthew 6:34).*

The Ultimate Sacrifice

Jesus' ultimate expression of compassion was shown during the crucifixion when he sacrificed his life so that others could be saved. His last words demonstrated compassion for the very people who had tortured him and hung him there and, as if that wasn't bad enough, had even mocked him. He says,

'Forgive them Father, for they do not understand what they are doing' (Luke 23:34).

No Mention of Animals

No-one can doubt Jesus' huge compassion, his ability to forgive and the immensity of his spirituality. He was the saviour of the meek and the mild, the Good Shepherd who laid down his life for his flock. But was his spirituality inclusive of all living things, or did he just extend the covenant between man and God, leaving it separate from the rest of the natural world? There is little evidence in the New Testament that Jesus included the animal kingdom in his circle of compassion. Despite his concern for the 'meek and mild', there is little to suggest that this went beyond the human meek and mild or extended to all sentient beings, including not killing and eating them. Although Jesus extended the interpretation of the Old Testament's 'You shall not kill' to include not harming, he does not appear to take it beyond humans to include all living beings. But can compassion be complete if it is limited only to humans?

In his book *Animal Gospel*, leading animal rights theologian, Revd Professor Andrew Linzey says,

> *'When it comes to the ethical treatment of animals, we need to recognise frankly that some other religions have traditions of compassion that equal, even surpass, that of Christianity'*[5].

He compares Christianity unfavourably with Hinduism and Jainism in this respect and says of animal rights,

> *'Arguably, within the Christian tradition at least, animal rights insights are correctives to a tradition which has failed to reflect sufficiently creatively on some of its own most cherished ideas'*[6].

In his book *Animal Rights* Linzey says,

'It has, I think, to be sadly recognised that Christians, Catholic or otherwise, have failed to construct a satisfactory moral theology of animal treatment.'

Aldous Huxley points out in *The Perennial Philosophy*,

'Compared with that of the Taoists and the Far Eastern Buddhists, the Christian attitude toward Nature has been curiously insensitive and often downright domineering and violent. Taking their cue from an unfortunate remark in Genesis, Catholic moralists have regarded animals as mere things which men do right to exploit for their own ends.'

Gandhi too made the point when he wrote in *The Moral Basis of Vegetarianism*,

'It ill becomes us to invoke in our daily prayers the blessings of God, the Compassionate, if we in turn will not practice elementary compassion towards our fellow creatures.'

The Lost Teachings of Jesus

But did Jesus exclude animals from his moral circle? How well do the scriptures reflect the true nature of Jesus? According to Heidi Stephenson in her forthcoming book, *The Book of Life: The Lost Teachings of Jesus on the Animal Kingdom*, Jesus was a non-meat eater, although this was excluded from the edited testaments to suit those in religious power at the time. He was also an animal liberator. Certainly the early Christians, before the time of Saint Aquinas, reflected this and showed considerable compassion towards animals.

According to Stephenson, referring to the gospel of the Ebionites, Jesus was not a Pharisee or a Sadducee but a Nazarene, who were a peaceful, non-meat-eating group. Jesus of Nazareth was an incorrect interpretation of Jesus the Nazarene. She explains that when Jesus cleansed the temple, angrily turning over the tables of priests who were selling animals for slaughter to people who wanted to atone for their sins (Mark 11: 15-19), he was angry, not just because the house of his father had become a den of thieves, but because of the cruel treatment of the animals. The priests were not just stealing money, but stealing the lives of the animals, which included lambs, kids, calves, doves and pigeons. This was an act of animal liberation. In the gospel of The Ebionites, Jesus says,

> *'I have come to abolish sacrifice and if you do not cease from sacrificing, the wrath of God will not cease from you!'*
> *(Epiphin, Haeres, XXX,16).*

Jesus had come to replace the murderous fire of sacrifice with baptism in water. In Matthew 12:7 he says,

> *'If you had known what these words meant, "I desire mercy, not sacrifice" you would not have condemned the innocent'.*

The words he refers to were those of Hosea 6:6,

> *'I desire mercy, not sacrifice, acknowledgement of God, not burnt offerings'.*

The Gospel of the Ebionites, as quoted by Epiphanius, portray both John the Baptist and Jesus as vegetarians. The Ebionites, meaning 'the poor ones', were an early Jewish Christian movement that existed during the early centuries of the Christian era. They valued voluntary poverty and vegetarianism and sought to separate themselves from what they saw as the corruption of the temples.

The only time that Jesus is reported to eat flesh in the New Testament is when he feeds the five thousand with bread and fish. But, according to Stephenson, this was not literal, it referred to him feeding them on his words and wisdom. His words were the bread and the fish were his wisdom, as the Greek word for fish was ICHTHUS which is also the acronym for Jesus Christ, Son of God, Saviour (Iota Chi Theta Upsilon Sigma). After Jesus' death, whenever Christians met clandestinely to avoid persecution, they used the sign of the fish to mark their meeting places. Christians still use the sign of the fish today.

Paul's Letter on the Creation

When Paul writes in his epistle to the church in Rome, he writes, not about man waiting to be set free from bondage, but of the whole of creation waiting to be set free. He writes in Romans 8:19-22,

> *'For the creation waits with eager longing for the revealing of the children of God; for the creation was subjected to futility, not of its own will but by the will of the one who subjected it, in hope that the creation itself will be set free from its bondage to decay and will obtain the freedom of the glory of the children of God. We know that the whole creation has been groaning in labour pains until now.'*

Christian Attitudes towards Animals Today

Although today most Christians do not include animals in their moral circle, there are many modern day sections of the Christian Church that do include all sentient beings in their moral circle and make a positive difference to the lives of these animals. Many of the original founders of the animal welfare charity, the RSPCA (*www.rspca.org.uk*) were Christians, most notably the Rev. Arthur Broome who, as the Society's first secretary, spent time in prison for its debts. Others were notable vegetarians, such as Broome's successor as secretary, the Jew, Lewis Gompertz. Since then other Christian animal welfare charities have developed, including:

Anglican Society for the Welfare of Animals (*www.aswa.org.uk*);
Catholic Concern for Animals (*www.catholic-animals.org*);
Quaker Concern for Animals (*www.quaker-animals.co.uk*); and
Christian Vegetarians (*www.christianvegetarian.co.uk*).

Animals in the Catechism of the Catholic Church (CCC)

In October 1985 an extraordinary synod of Catholic bishops proposed that a commission of cardinals should prepare a draft of a Catechism to provide an authoritative and universal summary of the Catholic Church's faith which would synthesise all the previous teachings and doctrines. After many reviews and revisions a final document was drawn up in September 1997 which became the *Catechism of the Catholic Church.*

In her book *The School of Compassion*, former General Secretary of Catholic Concern for Animals and editor of their journal *The Ark*, Dr Deborah Jones, identifies four paragraphs in the Catechism that refer to animals, paragraphs 2415 to 2418. They are as follows:

Paragraph 2415:
1. The seventh commandment enjoins respect for the integrity of creation. 2. Animals, like plants and inanimate beings, are by nature destined for the common good of past, present and future humanity (Gen 1:28-31). 3. Use of the mineral, vegetable and animal resources of the universe cannot be divorced from respect from moral imperatives. 4. Man's dominion over inanimate and other living beings granted by the Creator is not absolute; it is limited by concern for the quality of life of his neighbour, including generations to come; it requires a religious respect for the integrity of creation (CA 37-38).

Paragraph 2416:
1. Animals are God's creatures. 2. He surrounds them with his providential care. 3. By their mere existence they bless him and give him glory (Mt 6:26; Dan 3:79-81). 4. Thus men owe them kindness. 5. We should recall the gentleness with which saints like St Francis of Assisi and St Philip Neri treated animals.

Paragraph 2417:
1. God entrusted animals to the stewardship of those whom he created in his own image (Gen 2:19-20; Gen 9:1-4). 2. Hence it is legitimate to use animals for food and clothing. 3. They may be domesticated to help man in his work and leisure. 4. Medical and scientific experimentation on animals is a morally acceptable practice if it remains within reasonable limits and contributes to caring for or saving human lives.

Paragraph 2418:
1. It is contrary to human dignity to cause animals to suffer or die needlessly. 2. It is likewise unworthy to spend money on them that should as a priority go to the relief of human misery. 3. One can love animals; one should not direct to them the affection due only to persons.

Highlighting the fact that the attitude towards animals by the Catholic Church has come a long way forward since the writings of its early theologians, such as Thomas Aquinas, Dr Jones suggests that it is still very anthropocentric. Although the catechism requires man to exercise his stewardship over animals wisely and not inflict unnecessary suffering on them, it still allows man to exploit them and states that animals should not be treated as equals with humans. However, Dr Jones points out that the Catechism may be subject to amendment and revision, and that work could still be done on the Catholic authorities to improve the Church's attitude towards animals.[7]

Islam

Six hundred years after Christ, the prophet Muhammad, believing that he was divinely inspired by the archangel Gabriel, wrote *the Qur'an* and Islam was born. *Islam* means 'submission to the will of God'. Muslims believe in the same God as the Jews and the Christians, but call him Allah. They believe that Muhammad is the last in a series of prophets, which includes Adam, Abraham, Moses and Jesus. Muhammad did not claim to have received a new revelation, but rather was getting back to the teachings of the prophets from a time before the Torah and the gospels, which he believed had drifted away from the core teachings of Adam and Abraham. He was going back to basics.

There are five pillars of Islam – declaration of faith, praying five times a day, giving money to charity, fasting and pilgrimage to Mecca. Muslims believe in *Jihad* or 'Holy War', which has been the cause of much controversy due to its misinterpretation. *Jihad* literally means 'struggle' or 'effort' and refers to three types of struggle. The first is the believer's internal struggle to live out the Muslim faith well, the second is the struggle to build a good Muslim community and the third is the struggle to defend Islam, with force if necessary. It is, however, the first type, the internal spiritual struggle, that is most important. This includes overcoming negative emotions such as anger, greed, hatred, pride and malice. Here the Muslim notion of Jihad is similar to the Jain notion of the spiritual Conqueror or *Jina*, who overcomes similar barriers to spiritual development.

Muslims undertake to help the poor and the weak, to do charitable works for humans and also to show love and kindness to animals. They believe that all creatures were made by Allah, who loves them all and they must, therefore, be treated with kindness and compassion. The Qur'an says,

> *'All the beasts that roam the earth and all the birds that soar on high are communities like your own. We have left nothing out in the Book. Before their Lord they shall be gathered all' (Qur'an 6.38).*

Muslims are instructed to avoid treating animals cruelly, over-working or over-loading them, neglecting them, hunting or fighting them for sport, cutting the mane or tail of a horse, or factory farming. In one story the Prophet was travelling with a man who took some eggs from a nest, causing the mother bird much distress. The Prophet told the man to return the eggs. When asked if Allah rewards acts of kindness to animals, the Prophet replied,

> 'Yes, there is a reward for acts of charity to every beast alive.' *(Bukkari Hadith 3:646)*

He also said,

> 'Whoever kills a sparrow or anything bigger without a just cause, Allah will hold him accountable on the day of judgement.'

In another story, an adulteress passed by a dog who was dieing from thirst. The woman drew water from a well and gave it to the dog to drink. For this she was forgiven *(Mishkat-el-Masabih).*

But, according to the Qur'an, although animals must be treated well, they can be used for human benefit, including for food and transport. The Qur'an also says,

> 'It is God who provided for you all manner of livestock that you may ride on some of them and from some you may derive your food. And other uses in them for you to satisfy your heart's desires. It is on them, as on your ships, that you make your journeys' *(Qur'an 40:79-80).*

Muhammad explained that killing for food would be a just cause, but only if it is necessary and the killing is undertaken mercifully. At that time, people were living in a desert environment, where a vegetarian diet would have been limited. The instructions for the method of the slaughter of animals, by a clean cut to the throat with a sharp knife, were given because this was the most humane method of slaughter available at the time, not because it was a strict rule which had to be obeyed whatever the circumstances. The fundamental principle was to do the most humane thing, not to obey a rule.

Muslim Attitudes towards Animals Today
Although most Muslims do not extend their moral circle to include animals, some Muslims do and there are a number of Islamic animal welfare organisations that promote non-meat-eating, such as:

Islamic Concern (*www.islamveg.com*);
Vegetarian Muslims group on Facebook; and
Green Prophet (*www.greenprophet.com*).

Zoroastrianism

Another monotheistic religion, which developed independently from the Abrahamic tradition, is Zoroastrianism. According to Karen Armstrong, Zoroaster was a priest who lived around 1,200 BCE as an Aryan on the Russian Steppes during the time when tribes were feuding amongst themselves and there was much violence. The chief deity at that time was Indra, the god of war. Zoroaster was sickened by the violence. The story goes that one day, at the age of thirty, whilst bathing in a river, Zoroaster was visited by the shining being, Vohu Manah (which means 'Good Mind'), who led him to the god Ahura Mazda, the Lord of wisdom and justice, and to the five other 'shining beings'. These represent truth and righteousness; holy devotion, serenity and loving kindness; power and just rule; wholeness and health; and long life and immortality. The god Ahura Mazda told Zoroaster to gather his people around him to fight a holy war against evil. Zoroaster became convinced that Mazda was not just another deity but the supreme God and so he set about writing the holy book of the Zoroastrians, *The Avesta*, from the revelations given to him at this time by Mazda. Eventually the Zoroastrians migrated south into Persia and the religion continues today in Iran.

Zoroastrianism is based on dualism, both cosmic and moral. There is believed to be an ongoing battle between good and evil in the Universe (cosmic dualism) and an ongoing battle between good and evil in humans (moral dualism). In the cosmic dualism, Ahura Mazda represents good and Angra Mainyu represents evil. Angra Mainyu is not conceived of as a god but as the destructive energy in the Universe. Mazda created a pure world through his creative energy, Spenta Mainyu, which Angra Mainyu continues to attack. Angra Mainyu manifests itself in old age, sickness, famine, natural disasters and death. Life is a mixture of opposing forces, life and death, night and day, good and evil. Moral dualism refers to the good and evil in the mind of man. God gave man the gift of free will so that he could choose between good and evil, honesty and deception, happiness and sadness. Ahura Mazda lived in Heaven and Angra Mainyu lived in Hell. It was believed that when a person died he would go to either Heaven or Hell depending on his behaviour in life. It is thought that the current concept of Heaven and Hell may have come from the Zoroastrian ideas [8].

The Zoroastrian God is believed to be all knowing, all powerful, everywhere and unchanging. He is the creator of life, the source of all goodness and happiness and impossible for humans to comprehend. Zoroastrians believe that, as everything God has created is pure, it must be treated with respect and love. They have traditionally protected the natural environment, not polluting the rivers, the land or the atmosphere and are widely regarded as the first ecological religion. All people are seen as equal, whatever their race or sex. Although animals are respected as part of God's creation, Zoroastrians traditionally did not abstain from eating meat. However, some later Zoroastrians have extended their compassion for the natural world to include non-meat-eating, although this is largely a personal choice, rather than a religious requirement.

Sikhism

A very recent monotheistic religion, which has developed separately from the Abrahamic tradition, is the Sikh religion, which emerged in the Punjab in India during the sixteenth century AD. It was founded by the Guru Nanak and is based on his teachings and those of the nine gurus who followed him, ending in the tenth and last guru, Guru Gobind Singh. The Sikh scriptures are recorded in *The Guru Granth Sahib*, which is itself considered to be a living guru.

Sikhism emphasises the importance of doing good works rather than just following rituals. It states that there are five ways to live a good life – to keep God in heart and mind at all times, to live honestly and work hard, to treat everyone equally, to be generous to the less fortunate and to serve others. Like other eastern religions, Sikhs believe in the cycle of birth, death and rebirth, and in karma. The only way to be liberated from the suffering of this karmic cycle is to experience and achieve union with God. This state of liberation is known as *Mukti* and cannot be achieved through learning but by the experience of contemplation, worship and compassion. God can be found both inside a person and around them in the natural world. To find him a person must look both inside himself and outside at the natural world. Self-centred pride and concern for material things blind people from the true reality of God. But no matter how wicked a person is, God exists in him and so he has the capacity for change. God's message has been written in the whole of creation and if a person opens their eyes and looks around them, they will see God's message. The Universe does not exist on its own. It exists because God wills it to exist and it is the manifestation of God's nature. Sikhism does not require renunciation of the world, but encourages its followers to work within the world to do good. By serving others, Sikhs serve God and eliminate their own ego and pride. Carrying out chores in the community and caring for the poor are important actions. The five vices of lust, greed, attachment to worldly things, anger and pride are avoided.

Sikhism is unique in that it combines the concept of monotheism with the eastern concepts of karma, suffering, the cycles of life and liberation and also with compassion and living in the world to do good things. However, it has not traditionally extended its respect for the natural world to sharing compassion with other sentient beings. The Sikh religion initially expressed concern for humans only, but later traditions within Sikhism have extended the moral circle to include animals and some practice non-meat-eating. But such concern for animals is a personal belief for the individual and does not form part of the religious requirement.

8

CONCLUSIONS
ON THE TRADITIONS OF COMPASSION

'It ill becomes us to invoke in our daily prayers
the blessings of God, the Compassionate,
if we in turn will not practice elementary compassion
towards our fellow creatures.'

Gandhi – The Moral Basis of Vegetarianism

Today the world's spiritual traditions and philosophies demonstrate varying degrees of compassion. Some spiritual traditions currently include only humans in their circle of compassion, whilst others extend it to include all sentient beings. Sadly, many of today's faiths condone or actively promote the exploitation of beings outside of their circle of compassion. In the past, those exploited often included people of other races, but today, those exploited are mainly other species. The variations over time have been enormous and we find ourselves living in a world today that has been shaped by history and the traditions adopted by our ancestors. But is it time to look again at what the various philosophies have to offer and ask ourselves if we have fully understood and taken on board what our traditions have actually taught, and also to ask whether we can learn from other spiritual philosophies and how they could benefit us?

Summary of Compassion in the Spiritual Traditions
Two of the earliest philosophies were the Hindu philosophy of India and the Taoist philosophy of China. Hindus believe in *Brahman*, the universal spirit that pervades everything in nature whilst, at the same time, transcending it. Similarly, the Taoist

philosophy of China sees the *Tao*, the Way of Heaven, as inhabiting everything in nature and existing in both the material and heavenly worlds. Both the Tao and Brahman are believed to have existed before the Universe and now live both in it and beyond it. The *Upanishads* and the *Tao Te Ching* describe how this universal spirit lives within all of us and within the whole of nature and how we can find union with this spirit through the practice of meditation and by living a simple and compassionate life. These philosophies show no prejudice between races, sexes or species. Hinduism, through the Upanishads, focuses on the inward study of the mind, in order to transcend the material world of suffering. Taoism advocates a life of Wu Wei, or going with the flow of nature and showing reverence for the natural world. Both are inclusive philosophies that place great emphasis on an appreciation of the natural world, environmental awareness and on compassion for all beings.

Philosophies of compassion are even stronger, however, in the Buddhist and Jain traditions. Both Buddha and Mahavira had been princes who realised that material comfort was the not the way to enlightenment. They also both tried the Hindu practices of meditation and austerity and still found that these were unsatisfactory. Whilst they could achieve enlightened states during the meditation practices, they soon lost these states once they came out of the meditation and continued to experience all their negative afflictions in everyday life. They both discovered that meditating on *compassion* was the way to experience enlightenment and maintain a peaceful state of equanimity afterwards. Buddha had attained his first enlightenment whilst reconstructing the feelings of empathy and compassion he had experienced as a child when he saw insects being killed by a plough. Mahavira's predecessor, Neminath, the twenty-second Tirthankar, received his enlightenment when he saw animals being held for slaughter for his wedding ceremony and felt empathy and compassion for them. But, for Buddha and Mahavira, it was not sufficient just to meditate on compassion, they believed that you had to go out and practice compassion, by helping fellow sufferers.

In ancient Greece, the Pythagoreans, the Orphic Sect and Socrates also based their spiritual practices on compassion and empathy for all living beings. Like the Jains and the original

Buddhists, they believed in extending compassion to all living things and refraining from harming any sentient being through the principle of ahimsa (non-violence) and this included non-meat-eating.

In the Abrahamic faiths, God placed man (Adam and his wife, Eve) in the Garden of Eden, a paradise where they lived in innocence, at peace with the wild animals and were instructed to eat a vegetarian diet. Man fell from grace by eating the fruit of the tree of knowledge of good and evil, which angered God who banished them from the garden, still instructing them to eat a vegetarian diet. However, mankind became corrupt and, amongst other sins, started to eat flesh. So, frustrated by this, God caused a mighty flood, after which He concedes that man, having fallen, can eat meat. But the prophets, particularly Isaiah and Hosea, prophesised about the return to a Peaceable Kingdom, a new Garden of Eden, where man and beast live in harmony with each other. They prophesised about a Messiah that will show mankind the way to the Peaceable Kingdom. When the Messiah, Jesus, came, he spent forty days in the wilderness, attended by angels and at peace with the wild animals.

Islam introduced some limitations on the extent to which non-human creatures could be harmed, but did not prevent their exploitation for human benefit, provided it was necessary and undertaken mercifully. This is also true of the other major monotheistic traditions.

A Personal View

If asked to rank the major spiritual traditions in order of their emphasis on compassion, I personally would rank Jainism at the top, as it demonstrates the widest circle of compassion. This extends beyond the human race to all sentient beings. Jains are also renowned for their pluralism and tolerance of other traditions and beliefs and there are very few reports of wars fought in the name of Jainism. The same cannot be said for some of the other major religions, which in many circumstances have been the main causes of wars. This is very sad. The tolerance of this eastern tradition stems from the belief that all spiritual traditions are partly true, but that they are not the whole truth. They see other religions as different paths leading to the same goal, which is the union of the individual soul with the universal spirit.

One of the major regrets I have in my life is that a full range of spiritual philosophies was not available to me when I was young. Instead, I was fed one particular view, both at school and in church. Whilst I respected this Christian tradition and learned much from it, it left me feeling incomplete. Other views were withheld from me that could have filled the gaps. Sadly, most societies still do not give their children a full range of views when it comes to spiritual traditions and that, I believe, is a serious miscarriage of justice.

My major concern about the faith that I was brought up in was the limitation it placed on its circle of compassion, which only includes the human species. I do, however, believe that this is mainly due to its misinterpretation, largely due to theologians such as Augustine and Thomas Aquinas, who, basing their rationalist theology on the teachings of Aristotle and saying that only man has 'reason', excluded the animals from our moral circle of concern. This totally ignored the teachings of the prophets, such as Isaiah and Hosea, who taught that man's purpose, having fallen from grace in the Garden of Eden, was to seek out the Peaceable Kingdom, a place where man and the animals lived together in peace and harmony. In the Peaceable Kingdom, as in the Garden of Eden, man and the animals did not eat each other.

As a result we live in a society which subjects other sentient beings to terrible suffering and institutional cruelty in factory farms, long distance transport, laboratories, circuses and many other commercial and sporting activities. Most of the current western religious traditions ignore or even condone this cruelty and that, I believe, is a major spiritual failing. My response has been to look to other spiritual teachings, particularly those that extend their circle of compassion to all sentient beings, and I have found much satisfaction in the Jain and Buddhist philosophies. This does not mean that I have turned away from Christian values, which still have much to offer. Many Christians experience personal mystical relationships with God or Christ that are rich, powerful and sustaining. Yet for me, the western interpretation of God is limited by its under-emphasis on compassion for all living beings and the rest of nature. For man is not the only species made in God's image. Surely the whole of nature, the whole of the Cosmos and all things in it are made in his image? They are, after all, his Creation. Everything is Brahman and everything follows the Tao. To limit God's image to the human form is not only conceited but, I believe, is a serious underestimation of the power of the universal spirit and compassion. I suspect the true Jesus knew this and for this he was crucified. Sadly, the New Testament and the Christian Church may never have given Jesus full credit for the extent of his circle of compassion.

I have not been able to cover all spiritual traditions and philosophies in this book, nor have I been able to explore all the details of the traditions that I have covered. But I hope that I have been able to give the reader a flavour of the major spiritual traditions and philosophies, with respect to their approach to empathy, altruism and compassion. I also hope that I have been able to assist the reader to look at each tradition with an open mind and to feel inspired to enquire further into the nature of other societies' values. In particular, I hope the reader will ask whether our individual attitudes and actions, and those of our societies, are adequate in terms of how we extend our compassion to the other sentient beings with whom we share a Universe.

.

PART 2

LIVES
OF
COMPASSION

9

THE PERENNIAL PHILOSOPHY
OF
SAINTS AND MYSTICS

'Not to hurt our humble brethren is our first duty to them,
but to stop there is not enough.
We have a higher mission –
to be of service to them wherever they require it.'

St Francis of Assisi
Quoted in the 'Life' by St Bonaventura

The Perennial Philosophy was a term coined by Leibniz and written about by Aldous Huxley in his book *The Perennial Philosophy*. It is so named because it is a philosophy that appears, time and time again, in all spiritualities. F.C. Happold thoroughly describes it in his book *Mysticism: A Study and an Anthology*, saying that it has four key principles. These are:

1. The world of matter and consciousness is only part of a greater reality of a more subtle nature, known as *The Divine Ground*, and is, indeed, a manifestation of that greater reality.

2. Conscious beings can access that reality through direct intuition and experience, through prayer and meditation. During that experience, the knower is united with the known.

3. Conscious beings have two selves:

i)   the 'ego', which identifies itself with the mind and body and fights for itself in the world. It is where the negative emotions reside, such as pride, anger, jealousy, hatred and greed; and

ii)   the 'eternal spirit' or 'higher Self', where positive emotions reside, such as humility, unconditional love and compassion.

4. It is, indeed, the goal of evolution for conscious beings to overcome their egoic self and to discover their true eternal Self and be united with the Divine Ground. This can be achieved if the individual makes the effort required.[1]

Mysticism

Happold suggests that it is the eternal quest of mankind to find the one ultimate truth, the final synthesis in which all partial truths are resolved. Mystics actually glimpse this truth.[2] The range of our normal perceptions is limited and so, in our normal lives, we only glimpse a fraction of what is really there and it is easy to be deceived. Also, what we see is filtered through our minds which hold prejudices based on our past experience. Professor W.H. Auden in his lecture at Oxford University in 1916 *Making, Knowing and Judging*, identified two levels of the mind, which he called the 'Primary Imagination' and the 'Secondary Imagination'. The primary imagination has contact with the sacred, the Divine Ground, and is observed without judgement and is just seen for what it is. The function of the secondary imagination is to give form to this undifferentiated awareness, to allow it to become incarnate. This is done by processing it through the mind to interpret and assess it, to translate it into words, concepts and images. Most minds, Happold argues, are conditioned to see the world through the secondary imagination and only the mystical experience allows one to clear the mind sufficiently of all its baggage to make the leap to the level of awareness of the primary imagination.[3]

Happold argues that the development of the primary imagination is part of the evolutionary process and says,

> *'What line may evolution be expected to follow? May it not be the growth of an ever higher level of consciousness... an expanding interiorisation and spiritualisation of man, which will result in an ability to see aspects of the Universe as yet only faintly glimpsed? And, if so, may we not see in the mystics the forerunners of a type of consciousness, which will become more and more common as man ascends higher and higher up the ladder of evolution?'* [4]

He describes it as a 'rare state of consciousness that is only found in the contemplative saints' and says that to attain that level of contemplation men and women withdrew from the world and followed a way of life entirely different from that led by those who remained in the world. Medieval theologians described it as 'mystical theology', 'experimental wisdom', and 'a stretching out of the soul into God through the urge of love'.[5] Aldous Huxley said that only those who were 'loving, pure in heart and poor in spirit' could achieve this level of enlightenment, reflecting what Jesus had said in the Sermon on the Mount when he blesses the poor, the meek, the hungry, the merciful, the pure in heart and the peacemakers, saying that they will inherit the Kingdom of Heaven.

Happold suggests that man has two conflicting urges in life, one towards the ego, to individualisation and separation and the other towards an escape from the loneliness of the ego, into something bigger and better than the self. These two urges are constantly at war within him. Clinging to selfhood and self-love, he struggles to let go of them and yet is longing for reunion with something which he feels he has been separated from, to return to that from which he has come.

In the mystical state, according to Happold, there is no time as we experience it in this life. It is both eternal and timeless. He says that man is 'a pilgrim of eternity, a creature in time but a citizen of a timeless world'. Neither are there any parts or any separation of those parts, just wholeness. There is no logic, so there can be no conflicts or inconsistencies. There are no impossible situations as we experience them in our world of time and space and the secondary imagination. For example, the statement 'A thing cannot at the same time be and not be' is true to our common sense perception in the current reality, but in the mystical world, where there is no time and space, such concepts are not applicable. The Zen Buddhists use 'koans', meaningless statements, which could not be grasped by logic and which forced the person to jump out of the 'here and now' mind-set into a higher level of conscious awareness.

Happold describes two types of mysticism, the *mysticism of love and union* and the *mysticism of knowledge and understanding*, which are not exclusive and often go hand in hand.[6] In the mysticism of love and union, the mystic joins with God, or the Atman joins with the Brahman, through feelings of great joy, devotion and adoration. In the mysticism of knowledge and understanding, the mystic seeks a comprehension of God by a direct experience of Him, where he sees reality as it truly is, in its wholeness, through integrated thought, rather than in parts, through analytical thought that tends to break down what it perceives into comprehensible units. Happold says that 'mysticism of knowledge and understanding springs from the urge, inherent in man, to find the secret of the universe, to grasp it not in parts but in its wholeness'.

He also breaks down mysticism into *nature mysticism, soul mysticism* and *God mysticism*. In nature mysticism the mystic experiences a sense of oneness with nature (typical of Taoism and Jainism). In soul mysticism the mystic finds his spirituality deep within himself (typical of meditation in Hinduism and Buddhism). In God mysticism, the mystic makes his relationship with God through prayer (typical of Judaism, Christianity and Islam).

So who were the mystics? Not only were they the founders of the major spiritual traditions, as we have seen in the previous chapters, but they were also the prophets of the Old Testament, the saints of Christianity and the Sufis of Islam and other individuals from the Jewish, Hindu and Buddhist traditions. One of the things they had in common was their affinity with and love of animals. Despite the popular view that the current Christian Church lacks any concern for animals, the Christian saints and mystics of the first twelve hundred years of the Christian Church were exceedingly concerned about animals and did many charitable acts towards them.

The Early Christian Saints

Until the thirteenth century AD, many Christians had been very compassionate people, particularly in their attitudes towards animals. The early Christian saints had rescued animals from hunters, talked with animals, shared their food with them and cared for them when they were sick and injured. Kindness to animals was recognised by the early Christians as a virtue. Many lived in the wild as hermits, modelling their quest for the Divine on prophetic figures who withdrew from society into the desert, like Abraham, Moses, Elijah, John the Baptist, Jesus and the Desert Fathers and Mothers of Egypt. They lived among wild animals who were their friends and protectors, returning in spirit to the Garden of Eden to live life as it was before the Fall and to live life as Jesus had done when he had lived in the wilderness for forty days:

> *'And Jesus was in the wilderness forty days, tempted by Satan; and he was with the wild beasts; and the angels ministered to him.' Mark 1 v.13.*

St Basil (330 AD – 379 AD) greatly influenced the Eastern Church and said in this prayer in the 'Liturgy of St Basil':

> *'The Earth is the Lord's and the fullness thereof. O God, enlarge within us the sense of fellowship with all living things, our brothers the animals to whom thou has given the earth as their home in common with us. We remember with shame that in the past we have exercised the high dominion of man with ruthless cruelty, so that the voice of the earth, which should have gone up to Thee in song, has been a groan of travail. May we realise that they live, not for us alone, but for themselves and for Thee, and that they love the sweetness of life.'*[7]

St John of Chrysostom (347 AD – 407 AD) who had been a powerful influence in the Byzantine Church, said,

> *'The Saints are exceedingly loving and gentle to mankind and even to brute beasts... Surely we ought to show them*

> *great kindness and gentleness for many reasons, but above all, because they are the same origin as ourselves.*[7]

St Benedict (480 AD – 550 AD) who founded the greatest international order of monks, the Benedictines, stated that monks should not eat meat, except when sick. As a result the original Benedictine monks were non-meat eaters. [7]

St Ciaran of Ireland (516 AD – 544AD) was converted to the Christian faith by St Patrick and began to preach to the Irish people, who were then mostly pagans. One day, feeling the need for a period of quiet, Ciaran went to a lonely woodland district and started to build himself a cell. Sitting down by a tree, he noticed a fierce looking boar. Ciaran spoke gently to the boar calling him 'Brother Boar', as he treated all animals as his brother and sister. The boar realised that Ciaran was a friend and not a foe and so he helped Ciaran to build his cell, tearing down strong branches with his teeth and bringing them to Ciaran. When the cell was finished the boar stayed with Ciaran and soon many other animals joined them, including a wolf, a fox, a badger, a deer and many birds. Ciaran called them all the first brother monks of his little monastery. Later, as people joined them and Ciaran started a larger monastery, he never forgot his animal friends who continued to live with him.[8]

St Melangell is the Welsh patron saint of animals. In 604 AD the Prince of Powys, Brochwel Ysgithrog, went hare hunting at Pennant in the Derwyn Hills. His hounds pursued their prey into a bramble thicket and, following them, he found a young woman praying and given up to divine contemplation, with the hare lying under the fold of her garments. The baying hounds also came under her calming influence and the exasperated prince gave up the chase and sat to listen to her story of escape and exile from Ireland. Impressed by her piety and courage, he made a vow to present her with his lands for the service of God, that they might be a perpetual asylum, refuge and defence. Melangell lived there as a solitary for 37 years, after which a church with a shrine was built over her cell. Her church remained a place of sanctuary throughout the Middle Ages and the hares continued to be protected in the parish. The conservation society, Cymdeithas Melangell, now promotes animal welfare.[9]

St Isaac the Syrian, who lived in Syria in the 7th century AD, answers the question 'What is a charitable heart?' as follows:

> *'It is a heart which is burning with love for the whole of creation, for men, for the birds, for the beasts...for all creatures. He who has such a heart cannot see or call to mind a creature without his eyes being filled with tears by reason of the immense compassion which seizes his heart; a heart which is softened and can no longer bear to see or learn from others of any suffering, even the smallest pain being inflicted upon a creature. That is why such a man never ceases to pray for the animals... [He is] moved by the infinite pity which reigns in the hearts of those who are becoming unified with God.'*[7]

St Cuthbert (7th century AD) was a Scottish shepherd boy until he was fifteen, when he became a monk in Melrose Abbey. Later, he became a hermit, living on Farne Island in a small cell. There he made friends with the birds, giving them his protection from hunters and sharing meals with them.[7]

St Anslem (1033 AD - 1109 AD) was born in Italy and became Archbishop of Canterbury. He openly condemned cruelty to animals and once rescued a hare from huntsmen.[7]

The Hermit of Eskdale rescued a wild boar from a hunt in 1159 AD. Outraged at the disruption of their bloodsport by this early hunt saboteur, the huntsmen attacked him and mortally wounded him. The Abbot rallied to the support of the hermit who, before he died, forgave his murderers but ordered them, as a penance, to build a breakwater on the beach at Whitby to prevent the erosion of the land. Until the twentieth century this penance was remembered by the driving in of stakes into the sand on each Ascension Day.[7]

St Francis of Assisi (1181 AD - 1226 AD) is known as the *Patron Saint of Animals* and is commonly thought to be the main saint who showed concern for animals. But, as we have seen, he was not alone. A great many of the saints before him, particularly those who lived a solitary and ascetic life, bestowed compassion on animals, returning to the spiritual state man had been in when he resided in the Garden of Eden, communicating with animals and living in harmony with nature.

St Francis was famously known to preach to the animals and he is reputed to have persuaded a wolf to stop attacking the town's people of Agobio if those people promised to feed the wolf for the rest of his life. Francis was a radical who broke away from traditional monastic life and founded a group of itinerant preachers which, in 1209, was given papal approval. For Francis, the divine was in everything in nature, such as the sun, the moon, mountains, wind and water and, of course, in animals. He called everything his 'brother' or 'sister', such as 'Brother Sun' and 'Sister Moon'.[10] This great sense of the interconnectedness and interrelatedness of things was expressed in his famous *The Canticle of Brother Sun* or *Praise of the Creatures:*

> *Most high, omnipotent, good Lord,*
> *Praise, glory, and benediction, all are Thine,*
> *To Thee alone do they belong, Most High,*
> *And there is no man fit to mention Thee.*
> *Praise be to Thee, my Lord, with all Thy creatures,*
> *Especially to my worshipful brother sun,*
> *The which lights up the day, and through him dost Thou brightness give;*
> *And beautiful is he and radiant with splendour great;*
> *Of Thee, Most High, signification gives.*
> *Praised be my Lord, for sister moon and for the stars,*
> *In Heaven Thou hast formed them clear and precious and fair.*
> *Praised be my Lord for brother wind,*
> *And for the air and clouds and fair and every kind of weather,*
> *By the which Thou givest to Thy creatures nourishment.*
> *Praised be my Lord for sister water,*
> *The which is greatly helpful and humble and precious and pure.*

Praised be my Lord for brother fire,
By the which Thou lightest up the dark,
And fair is he and gay and mighty and strong.
Praised be my Lord for our sister, mother earth,
The which sustains us and keeps us
And brings forth diverse fruit with grasses and flowers
bright.
Praised be my Lord for those who for Thy love forgive,
And weakness bear and tribulation.
Blessed those who shall in peace endure,
For by Thee, Most High, shall they be crowned.
Praised be my Lord for our sister, the bodily death,
From the which no living man can flee.
Woe to them who die in mortal sin,
Blessed those who shall find themselves in Thy most holy
will,
For the second death shall do them no ill.
Praise ye and bless ye my Lord and give Him thanks,
And be subject unto Him with great humility.

St Francis said,

'Not to hurt our humble brethren is our first duty to them,
but to stop there is not enough. We have a higher mission
to be of service to them wherever they require it.'[11]

'If you have men who will exclude any of God's creatures
from the shelter of compassion and pity, you will have men
who will deal likewise with their fellow men.'[11]

Meister Eckhart (1260 AD – 1329 AD) was a German Dominican priest and mystic who espoused a form of pantheistic mysticism and saw God in all creation. He said of animals,

'All creatures are the utterances of God.'

'Apprehend God in all things, for God is in all things.
Every single creature is full of God and is a book about
God.

Every creature is a word of God.
If I spent enough time with the tiniest creature, even a
caterpillar
I would never have to prepare a sermon.
So full of God is every creature'.

'We ought to understand God equally in all things,
For God is equally in all things.
All beings love one another.
All creatures are interdependent.'

St Philip Neri (1515 AD – 1595 AD) was an unusually late saint to be concerned with animals. Although he is best known as the founder of the Oratory Movement, he embraced vegetarianism on the grounds of animal welfare, not just on the grounds of abstinence. Once, passing a butcher's shop he said, 'If everyone was like me, they wouldn't kill animals'. He also set captive birds free which, by their own choice, would not leave him. Animals were attracted to him. At one time, someone found a young bird in the chapel and brought it to him. Philip told them not to squeeze the bird or hurt it, but to open the window and let it fly away. But afterwards he worried whether he had done the right thing, as it was so small that it wouldn't know where to go. On another occasion he was given a brace of live partridges for a meal, but he set them free. He would also insist on flies being let out of the window instead of being swatted. He released captured mice into places of safety and expressed pity for animals on their way to slaughter. He cared for humans as well as for animals and saved an ex-Dominican heretic from execution.[12]

St John of the Cross (1542 AD – 1591 AD) was a Spanish mystic and a Carmelite friar who became a Roman Catholic saint. He wrote a poem called *The Dark Night of the Soul* which describes the dark journey of the soul from its bodily residence to its divine union with the love of God. But he said of his relationship with animals,

'I was sad one day and went for a walk. I sat in a field. A rabbit noticed my condition and came near. It often does

not take more than that to help at times - to just be close to creatures who are so full of knowing, so full of love that they don't chat, they just gaze with their marvellous understanding'.

Other Saints of note include St Jerome (373 AD – 420 AD) who, like the Roman slave Androcles, took a thorn from the paw of a lion who repaid him by giving up eating other animals and serving at the monastery until he joined St Jerome in death. St Columba ordered his monks to care for an injured crane, and his follower, St Waleric, used to caress the woodland birds. Other saints became hunt saboteurs. St Neot saved hares and stags from huntsmen and St Godric of Finchdale rescued birds from snares. St Aventine rescued a stag from hunters and St Carileff protected a bull that was being hunted by King Childebert. Both St Hubert and the Roman general, St Eustace, saw visions of the crucifixion between the antlers of stags they were hunting, leading St Hubert to renounce hunting. St Isidore in Spain protected a hare from huntsmen. [7]

10

THE RISE OF SPECIESISM

'The speciesist shows a sentimental tendency
to put his own species upon a pedestal,
but he or she does so on totally inadequate grounds.
There is no scientific justification for the speciesist prejudice.
There is no logic in it.'

Dr Richard D. Ryder – The Political Animal

St Francis was one of the last of the plethora of early Christian saints who included animals in their moral circle. With a few notable exceptions, nearly the whole of the Catholic Church excluded animals from its moral circle after St Francis. So what caused this dramatic paradigm shift?

St Augustine (354 AD – 430 AD)
Despite the love of Creation shown by so many of the Catholic saints up until the time of St Francis, there were a few, even in those times, who were highly anthropocentric. One of the most outstanding of these was St Augustine who was Bishop of Hippo Regius in the Roman province of Africa and is often known as St Augustine of Hippo. He was a writer and a theologian and was very influential in the development of western Christianity and philosophy. In his book *City of God* the question arises as to who the commandment 'Thou shall not kill' applies to. Augustine states that this can only apply to man because,

> *'The irrational animals that fly, swim, walk, or creep ... are*
> *dissociated from us by their want of reason, and are*

> *therefore by the just appointment of the Creator subjected to us to kill or keep alive for our own uses'.*[1]

He acknowledges that animals feel pain but argues that this is of no importance,

> *'For we see and appreciate from their cries that animals die with pain. But man disregards this in a beast, with which, as having no rational soul, he is linked by no community of law.'*[2]

His writings formed the foundation for much of thinking in the later Catholic Church.

St Thomas Aquinas (1225 AD – 1274 AD)

A year before St Francis died in 1226 AD, another saint was born, Thomas Aquinas. He founded his teachings more on Augustine and Aristotle than on Jesus Christ, and almost single-handedly introduced speciesism into the Catholic Church. The writings of Aristotle had recently been rediscovered. Aristotle was the pupil of Plato, who had, in turn, been the pupil of Socrates. Plato had been greatly influenced by Pythagoras, who had taught and practised compassion to all living beings and had been a non-meat eater, as had the Pythagoreans who followed him. But Aristotle had turned away from their principles and had taught that man was related to the gods and was superior to women, slaves, foreigners and animals. These members of society had no rights and were to be exploited. Aristotle demonstrated the very prejudices that Socrates would have challenged with his dialectic debates.

Thomas Aquinas was raised as a Benedictine monk, but left the Benedictines to join the Dominicans and became the Church's leading theologian. He distorted Christianity to accommodate the newly rediscovered teachings of Aristotle. He taught that charity did not extend to animals and, like Aristotle, argued that animals lacked reason and had no fellowship with humans. He considered it to be the natural order that animals existed for the benefit of man and said that there was 'no sin in using a thing for the purpose for which it is'. Animals were put on earth to be exploited, killed and eaten by man. There was no room for compassion for animals. He said,

> *'If in Holy Scripture there are found some injunctions forbidding the infliction of some cruelty towards brute animals... this is either for removing a man's mind from exercising cruelty towards other men, lest anyone, from exercising cruelty upon brutes, should go on hence to human beings; or because the injury inflicted on animals turns to a temporal loss for some man.'* [3]

From then on society would be different. The whole of the Catholic Church based its theology on the teachings of Aquinas. The lives of compassion lived by the great early Christian saints ended there and western society became increasingly sexist, racist and speciesist.

The speciesism encouraged by Thomas Aquinas grew to nightmarish proportions during the Middle Ages with animals being horribly brutalised and slaughtered. There was dog fighting, bear baiting, bull baiting, cock fighting, cock stoning, cat persecution, the abuse of cattle being driven to market and, of course, the terrible treatment of horses, who provided the main means of transport for centuries. There was also the horrible vivisection of living, conscious animals for scientific purposes.

Acquinas' Straw

In December 1273, a year before he died, Aquinas had a significant religious experience after which he stopped writing. He said,

> *'I can't continue writing. Everything I have written seems to me like so much straw compared to what I have seen and what has been revealed to me.'* [4]

Aquinas may have had a direct and mystical *experience* of God and realised that his experience far transcended any of the *reasoning* he had used in his theology in the past - the same reasoning which he had used when he had separated man from the other animals. Unfortunately, he did not go on to share this new experience and he left the Catholic Church with his former writings, from which they developed their speciesist theology.

Descartes and Dualism

The callous arrogance of Aquinas was extended by René Descartes (1596 AD to 1650 AD) who announced that animals had no souls and could experience no pain. He came to epitomise the dualistic thinking of his time and encouraged the live vivisection of animals. When he and others experimented on them, their screams, he said, were no more significant than the creaking of a door. Dogs and horses were pinned down and, fully conscious, were slowly dissected.[5]

The Early Animal Rights Movement

But there were many others who reacted strongly against this. In 1683 *Thomas Tyron* wrote of birds complaining,

> *'What law have we broken, or what cause given you, whereby you can pretend a right to invade and violate our part, and natural rights, and to assault and destroy us?'*

This was probably the first written mention of animal 'rights'. Others also complained of the terrible cruelty suffered by animals at the hand of man, including the poets, *Blake, Burns, Wordsworth, Coleridge* and *Shelley*. The vivisectors, with their inability to think beyond the limitations of rationalism, clashed head on with the poets, who were more disposed to empathetic and compassionate thinking. In 1789 the philosopher *Jeremy Bentham* said,

> *'The day may come when the rest of the animal creation may acquire those rights which never could have been withheld from them but by the hand of tyranny.'*

The speciesists argued that man was superior to the animals, as man could talk and reason. Animals could not. Bentham replied,

> *'The question is not, can they reason? Nor, can they talk? But can they suffer?'*

He argued that it didn't matter that animals couldn't talk or reason. Man should show compassion to them because they could *suffer*. But it has been demonstrated that not only do non-human animals suffer, but that they *do* talk and they *do* reason. The French philosopher *Montaigne* remarked,

> *'The defect that hinders communication betwixt them and us, why may it not be on our part as well as theirs?'*

He was suggesting that communication was not necessarily only achieved through the medium that humans were most familiar with, i.e. speech. There could be many methods of communicating, of which vocalising was only one. If we wanted to communicate with other species we had to look at the alternative methods of communication. Demonstrations that animals can talk and reason are discussed in more detail in chapter 15 'The Minds of Animals'.[5]

The animal rights movement continues to the present day. Animal rights author Henry Salt (1851-1939) wrote the books *Animal Rights* and *The Creed of Kinship*. In the later he wrote:

> *'The religion of the future will be a belief in a Creed of Kinship, a charter of human and sub-human relationships'.*

Speciesism

Speciesism is a word coined by the ethicist, psychologist and animal welfare campaigner *Dr Richard D. Ryder* in 1970 and adopted by many other animal welfare campaigners of the twentieth century who came after him, including Peter Singer. It refers to the widespread discrimination that is practised by man against the other species[6]. Speciesism and racism are both forms of prejudice that are based upon appearances. Ryder has written extensively on the subject of speciesism in various books, which include *Victims of Science,* 1975, *Animal Revolution,* 1989, *The Political Animal,* 1998 and most recently, *Speciesism, Painism and Happiness,* 2011. Peter Singer also wrote about it in *Animal Liberation,* 1975, as have many others.

Ryder responds to the common criticism of the speciesist that the non-speciesist is anthropomorphic and sentimental by saying,

> *'It is the exploiter of animals, not the animal protectionist who is being irrational or emotional when attempting self-*

justification. The speciesist shows a sentimental tendency to put his own species upon a pedestal, but he or she does so on totally inadequate grounds. There is no scientific justification for the speciesist prejudice. There is no logic in it. But thank goodness we can all feel a natural spark of sympathy for the sufferings of others. I believe we need to catch that spark and fan it into a fire of rational and universal compassion.[7]

Despite the writings of the great philosophers and poets of the seventeenth, eighteenth and nineteenth centuries, such as Jeremy Bentham, the speciesist view continued to remain the norm. Even *Charles Darwin* feared popular opinion and it took him twenty years to summon up the courage to publish his evidence for evolution through natural selection. He finally took the leap when he heard that his rival, Alfred Russel Wallace, was catching up with him in discovering evolution and could publish his findings first. And despite the discoveries of great scientists, such as Darwin, and the writing of very eminent contemporary philosophers, such as Richard Ryder and Peter Singer, people still cling to speciesist views today.

I have always found the prejudice of speciesism to be logically challenging. Not only is the prejudice that separates the human animal from all other sentient beings illogical, but so too is the prejudice that results in the different treatment of different species and even members of the same species. For example, in the West we find the eating of cats and dogs shocking, but we happily eat sheep and pigs. This is despite the scientific evidence that suggests that pigs are more intelligent that dogs. We are shocked at the idea of eating horses, but take the eating of cows for granted. We find the idea of keeping song-birds cooped up in cages distasteful, but happily support the confinement of hens in battery cages through our thoughtless buying habits. We prosecute those who abuse domestic dogs, while there are some in our Society who want to bring back fox hunting, when a fox is a species of dog. The determining factor of whether an animal is a companion or a pest is determined by our level of familiarity with it and on competition for resources, not on any inherent attributes of the species. A domestic bunny can be a pet, whilst a wild rabbit can be classified as a pest. This sort of speciesist logic is deeply flawed and is perpetuated by either a lack of intelligent thinking or by a mental resistance that keeps us in denial about the inconsistency of our morality. We are the victims of conditioning and habit, puppets that favour prejudice over clear and rational thinking. This state is surely unworthy of an intelligent species. Indeed, it is not the behaviour of an intelligent species.

Painism

After coining the term *Speciesism* Richard Ryder went on to formulate his theory of *Painism*. He said,

> *'Morality is essentially about how we treat others, and by others I mean all those who can suffer pain or distress, that is to say, all those who are painient.'*

He goes on to explain that pain is pain, regardless of who or what experiences it. If alien visitors from outer space turn out to be painient, or if we manufacture machines that are painient, then we would have to widen the moral circle to include them. Carl Sagan also questions what our moral position would be if we were to meet aliens from another planet, who would certainly be of a different species to us, and would probably be more intelligent. Both he and Ryder ask whether they would have the right to exploit us, simply because they were more intelligent than us.

In his book *Speciesism, Painism and Happiness*, Ryder suggests that there are moral principles such as justice, freedom, equality and brotherhood. But these are not the roots of morality, but branches that stem from it. The root of morality is pain. Just as we seek to avoid pain in ourselves so, for morality's sake, we should seek to prevent causing pain to others. Ryder's notion of pain is similar to the Buddhist notion of suffering. Pain is not only physical, such as toothache, but also mental, such as fear, stress or boredom. The notion of morality being based on avoiding causing pain to others is similar to the Jain notion of ahimsa or avoiding causing harm.

Ryder also notes that you cannot take a Utilitarian view towards pain. You cannot say that pain is acceptable because the sum of the pleasures that it creates in many individuals outweighs the pain caused to the sufferer. This argument is frequently used to support vivisection (as well as the argument that humans are superior to animals), to state that the suffering of a small number of animals is justified in order to prevent a disease in many humans. Ryder argues that such a Utilitarian view would justify gang rape, if the sum of the pleasures of the many rapists outweighed the suffering of the one victim. Clearly, Ryder says, this is nonsense. You cannot sum the pains of many individuals, as everyone experiences their pain separately and individually.[8]

You Are, Therefore I Am

The title of Satish Kumar's book, *You Are, Therefore I Am* stands up for non-dualistic relationships, in sharp contrast to Descartes' *I think, therefore I am.* It comes from the Sanskrit dictum *So Hum.* Descartes' dictum sowed the seeds of dualistic thought and individualism, which formed the basis of our selfish, greedy and ultimately destructive western societies. In *You Are, Therefore I Am* Satish Kumar, speaking from a Jain perspective, tries to counter this and says,

> 'The culture of non-violence goes beyond the more rational and more humanist tradition of the West. In the consciousness of progressive groups there is a move away from the violence of nationalism, racism, sexism, and religious intolerance. Yet, groups still practise what I'd call speciesism, in which the human species is considered superior to all other species. The violence to non-human species often remains unnoticed. This causes grave harm to animals, forests and wildlife of all kinds. This attitude of human superiority is the foundation of the culture of violence...We have to recognise the fundamental unity of all life and develop a reverence for it'.[9]

> 'Human beings...have no more rights than any other species. All living beings, human and other-than-human, have an equal right to life. Not only do humans have no absolute rights...but they also have extra obligations to practise non-violence.'

In *Resurgence* magazine, Satish comments that,

> '*One important dimension is missing from our environmental agenda and that is the plight of the pigs, cows, cats, dogs, horses, monkeys and other animals that humans use for food, medicine and entertainment...I call upon all environmental activists and organisations to remedy this and embrace the cause of animal rights as an integral and important part of the environmental movement.*'[10]

Ryder says that 'the ethical arguments against speciesism are formidable and expose the irrationality and sentiment of the anthropocentric position'. In the closing paragraph of his book *The Political Animal – The Conquest of Speciesism* he says,

> '*All people are born with the potential for compassion. How far that compassion is extended and nurtured is dependent on culture and experience. We no longer perceive an unbridgeable gulf between ourselves and those of other species, who share with us this short interlude of consciousness and pain that we call life. Instead, we all feel part of the same community of pain; we view non-humans now as fellow sufferers in the cosmic game. With even greater clarity we can see that pain, in the broadest sense, is the common enemy and the best focus for a new morality. The concern for the welfare of non-humans is a truly moral quest in what is often seen as an increasingly amoral world.*'[11]

11

PHILANTHROPY
AND THE HUMANE MOVEMENT

'If the enormous volume of philanthropy of the present day were wisely directed it would, I believe, in the course of a few years, change the face of England.'
Joseph Rowntree

'Am I not a Man and a Brother?'
Josiah Wedgwood

During the Axial age, 2,500 years ago, the Greek playwright Aeschylus wrote the play *Prometheus Bound* in which he told the myth of how primitive creatures were made to become human. In the play these creatures lived in caves, in darkness and in fear. They had no knowledge or skills or culture. The king of the gods, Zeus wanted to destroy them, but one of the Titans, Prometheus decided to save them out of his *Philanthropos Tropos* or 'humanity-loving character'. He gave the creatures two life-enhancing gifts. One was fire, which symbolised knowledge and skills, and the other was optimism. With optimism and skills they could improve their condition which would enable the creation of humankind as civilised beings.[1] Thus the concept of philanthropy was formed and developed in Ancient Greece. *Philanthropia* was defined in the Platonic Academy's philosophical dictionary as 'a state of well-educated habits stemming from the love of humanity. A state of being productive for the benefit of humans'.

The Romans developed their own form of Philanthropia from this, which they called *Humanitas*, although this existed in a society that was extremely ruthless. Both the Greeks and the Romans kept slaves and the Romans were particularly cruel in their sports in the arena and in their actions at conquering and ruling other nations. After the fall of the Greek and Roman empires both Philanthropia and Humanitas fell into a long Dark Age.[2]

The Protestant Movement

The concept of philanthropy was revived in the sixteenth century when Sir Francis Bacon used the word *Philanthropia* in his essays. This started the rebirth of the philanthropic spirit. Philanthropy was seen as a form of enlightenment and as an essential key to human happiness that involved living in harmony with nature and with one's own circumstances. This coincided with various reform movements in the Christian Church. The Protestant church had split away from the Catholic Church in the sixteenth century following the reformation movement started in Germany by Martin Luther.

The Protestants felt that religion did not require the intermediary of the Catholic priests or their hierarchy in Rome and they wanted to get back to spiritual basics. In England this movement was supported by King Henry VIII, whose desire to break away from the Catholic Church in Rome was largely motivated by his wish to divorce his first wife, Catherine of Aragon. But many individuals in the Protestant movement did not feel that the movement had gone far enough and sub-divisions developed such as the Puritans and the Presbyterians.

The Quakers

One of these groups was the Quakers, also known as the Religious Society of Friends, which was set up by George Fox in 1640. Fox believed that everyone could have a direct experience of Christ without the mediation of the clergy. The Quakers believed that they were restoring the true Christian Church after centuries of separation of the Church from its original spiritual values. They believed in working hard which led them to accumulate considerable wealth. However they also held the view that it was wrong to hold on to material wealth, as the Bible said that it was easier for a camel to pass through the eye of a needle than for a rich person to enter the Kingdom of Heaven. So the Quakers, practising philanthropy, set about redistributing their wealth to the needy. Many of the Quaker business people invested in improving the lives of their employees, building them accommodation and amenities. Such philanthropical Quakers included the families that founded the firms Rowntrees, Cadburys, Frys and Clarks. Other wealthy Quaker families, such as the bank-owners Barclays and Lloyds, and the owners of friendly societies such as Friends Provident, redistributed their wealth to the poor and to worthy causes. Others were great social reformers such as Elizabeth Fry who led the prison reform movement, giving prisoners a purpose in life.

Quaker mysticism, as it came to be called, focused on 'the outwardly directed witness'. Rather than withdrawing from the world, the Quakers sought to translate their mysticism into action through social and political activities. They believed that such action leads to greater spiritual understanding.[3]

The Abolition of Slavery

The major reform issue of the eighteenth century was the abolition of slavery. In 1696 the Quakers in America declared their opposition to slavery and in 1774 they formed an anti-slavery society. Two years later they excluded slave-owners from their membership. In 1783 the first British abolitionist organisation was founded by a group of Quakers who presented a petition to Parliament through Sir Cecil Wray, the MP for Westminster. They then set up the non-denominational 'Committee for the Abolition of the Slave Trade' to lobby parliament which was led by the Anglican, Thomas Clarkson. Josiah Wedgwood, grandfather of Charles Darwin and founder of the famous Wedgwood pottery business and a great philanthropist, also joined them. In 1787 he designed a pottery medallion, which read '*Am I not a Man and a Brother?*'

The Quakers themselves were dissenters and they were unable to become members of Parliament, so they approached William Wilberforce, an Anglican Evangelist, to become the leader of their parliamentary campaign. Wilberforce championed the *Slave Trade Act* which was passed in 1807, but slavery itself was not finally abolished in the British Empire until 1833 with *The Slavery Abolition Act*. It was later abolished in the French colonies in 1848 and in the United States in 1865.

Martin's Act, the RSPCA and the NSPCC

Following the successful abolition of the slave trade with the *Slave Trade Act* in 1807, many of its pioneers went on to fight for the legal protection of animals. A bill brought by Sir William Putney and supported by the MP Richard Martin and others in 1800 to outlaw bull baiting had failed. With his considerable experience of re-introducing unsuccessful bills to parliament and not giving up, William Wilberforce supported its reintroduction, but it again failed.

In 1809 Thomas, Lord Erskine brought a wider bill against 'Wanton Cruelty' which succeeded in the Lords but failed in the Commons. They continued to fight for legal protection for animals and in 1822 Erskine and Richard Martin were finally successful in securing *Martin's Act* in the Commons. This made it an offence to 'wantonly beat, abuse or ill-treat any horse, donkey, sheep, cow or other cattle', provided it was not the property of the offender. This was a landmark in that it was the first piece of parliamentary legislation against animal cruelty. However it was very limited in scope, as it failed to prevent many forms of cruelty to animals, including bull-baiting and it did not stop a person from being cruel to an animal they were deemed to own. Other Acts however were introduced and these were later consolidated into *The Protection of Animals Act 1911*. Martin's Act also set a precedent for other countries that followed its lead and set up their own animal protection legislation.[4]

In 1824, two years after Martin's Act was passed, a group of men met in a coffee house in London, ironically named 'Old Slaughter's' after its first Landlord, and founded a Society for the Prevention of Cruelty to Animals, the SPCA. Anti-slavery MPs William Wilberforce and Thomas Foxwell Buxton were joined by MPs Richard Martin, A. Warre and Sir James Mackintosh. There were also three churchmen, one of whom was the Rev. Arthur Broome who became the Society's first secretary. The SPCA was the world's first successful animal welfare society. Its objects stated,

> *'The object of the Society is the mitigation of animal suffering and the promotion and expansion of the practice of humanity towards the inferior classes of animated beings*

> *– a practical duty equally deducible from reason, from the natural feelings of man, and from the benevolent spirit and precepts of the Christian Religion.'*

They set up two committees, one to publish literature and influence public opinion and the other to adopt measures for inspecting the markets and streets, the slaughterhouses and the conduct of coachmen. They also defined morality as 'the desire, rationally directed, to promote general happiness', thus bringing the Society within the Utilitarian canon as defined by Jeremy Bentham.

The Society had a difficult start. It employed Mr. Wheeler and some others intermittently as inspectors and in its first year the Society brought 150 prosecutions for cruelty, campaigned against bull-baiting, dog-fighting, the abuse of horses and cattle, the cruelty of the meat markets and painful experiments on animals. The Society immediately fell into debt and its first secretary, the Rev Arthur Broome, was thrown into prison but was later bailed out by Richard Martin. The second secretary, Lewis Gompertz, turned the Society's finances around, enabling it to continue. However he was persecuted by his enemies for being a Jew and a vegetarian and was forced to resign. But the Society's fortunes changed when the young Princess Victoria showed an interest in the Society's work and accepted its invitation to become Lady Patroness. In 1840, when she was queen, she gave the Society her royal patronage and it became the Royal Society for the Prevention of Cruelty to Animals, the RSPCA.

Money was raised from philanthropists, including the wealthiest woman in Britain, Angela Burdett-Coutts of the Coutts banking dynasty, and the Society took off. Soon, similar societies started appearing across Europe and America following the example of the RSPCA. These were followed by societies springing up for the protection of children. In 1874 a prosecution was taken by Henry Bergh of the American Society for the Prevention of Cruelty to Animals to protect an abused child in New York. As there was no mechanism for prosecuting to protect children, the system for protecting animals was employed instead. Shortly afterwards, in 1875, the New York Society for the Prevention of Cruelty to Children was established, which was the first children's society. Shortly after this, members of the RSPCA helped to establish the NSPCC in the UK and they shared offices during the early years of their establishment.

RSPCA founders James Mackintosh and Richard Martin also went on to oppose the death penalty for minor offences and Martin campaigned for the establishment of a system of legal aid and fought for the poor and starving people on his estates in Ireland, which earned him the nickname 'Humanity Dick'. These pioneers were part of a general compassionate movement that encompassed both humans and animals. What is remarkable is the considerable opposition they faced from those with a vested interest in maintaining both slavery and animal abuse. The cruelties they fought against at that time were inconceivable in both their intensity and their ubiquity. The fact that such people did take a stand against abuses, and established protective legislation and humane societies, is something for which we should all be grateful. What would society be like today if these reforms had not been made? We are indeed indebted to these reformers.[5]

Anti-Vivisection Societies

In America Caroline Earle White, who had been very active in the anti-slavery movement, also founded the American National Anti-Vivisection Society, the 'NAVS' in 1883 to campaign against the cruelty of experimentation on animals. In 1898 the social reformer and suffragist, Frances Power Cobbe, set up the British Union for the Abolition of Vivisection, the 'BUAV'. Campaigns against vivisection had started in 1824 when the French experimenter François Magendie provoked an outcry in London with his physiological demonstrations on cats and dogs. Reports of similar atrocities in France, such as the slow, live dissection of tied down, unanaesthetised horses at a veterinary college in Alfort inflamed the campaign, which was often supported by British scientists and veterinary surgeons. Richard Martin denounced the practice in parliament and the RSPCA brought a prosecution against a French scientist, Eugene Magnan, for publicly experimenting on dogs at a medical conference in Norwich. A petition was organised by the campaigner Frances Cobbe, which was signed by many notable Victorian philanthropists, including Lord Shaftesbury.[6] Queen Victoria wrote strong letters on the subject to her prime ministers William Gladstone and Benjamin Disraeli and to the president of the RSPCA, Lord Harrowby. Extracts from her letters read as follows:

> *'The Queen hears and reads with horror of the sufferings which the brute creation often undergo from the thoughtlessness of the ignorant, and she fears also sometimes from experiments in pursuit of science.'*
> **Letter from Queen Victoria to Lord Harrowby, President RSPCA, 1874.**

> Later she wrote, *'The Queen has done all she could on the dreadful subject of vivisection, and hopes that Mr. Gladstone will speak strongly against a practice which is a disgrace to humanity and Christianity.'*
> **Letter from Queen Victoria to Mr. Gladstone, 1881.**

> *'There is, however, another subject on which the Queen feels most strongly, and that is this horrible, brutalising, <u>unchristian-like vivisection</u>. That poor dumb animals should be kept alive as described in this trial <u>is revolting and horrible</u>. This <u>must</u> be stopped. Monkeys and dogs – two of the most intelligent amongst those poor animals who cannot complain... Dogs, "man's best friend", possessed of more than instinct, to be treated in this fearful way is <u>awful</u>. She directs Sir William Harcourt's attention <u>most strongly to it.</u> It really must not be permitted. It is a disgrace to a civilised country.'*
> **Letter from Queen Victoria to Sir William Harcourt, Home Secretary.**[7]

In 1875, due to the monarch's intervention, the government set up a Royal Commission of Inquiry that recommended that such research should be licensed. In 1876 an advisory committee was established for the regulation of pain.

Today, throughout the world, vivisection on animals is still seen as a necessity for the advancement of human knowledge for both medical and non-medical research. It has grown to industrial proportions globally, with billions of sentient creatures suffering in the name of research every year. Often its only justification is that it can be used by organisations as a defence in litigation to claim that their products were legally tested and compliant. Pain is still 'regulated' in some parts of the world. In the UK *The Animal Scientific Procedures Act 1986* was set up to oversee the regulation of pain and in 2011 Europe issued a directive for animal testing to regulate the treatment of animals in experimentation.

Disappointingly, in 1947 the courts in the UK ruled that the National Anti-Vivisection Society and other organisations that campaign to end animal experimentation cannot be charities because a charity must be set up for the public benefit. Medical research, they argue, is for the public benefit and an organisation that seeks to abolish one of the tools of medical research cannot therefore be a charity.

Non-Violent Resistance Movements

The efforts of the philanthropists and others in the humane movement had done much to resolve human suffering, by abolishing slavery and alleviating poverty, but their fight for the protection of other sentient beings still has a long way to go. Animals suffer as slaves in many human industries, not just in laboratories. They suffer slavery conditions in factory farms, sport and zoos where they are routinely denied the 'rights' of freedom and respect that are given to the human species, as established in the United Nation's Declaration of Human Rights. Today, those who seek to exploit animals for their own greed have given the phrase '*Animal Rights*' negative connotations. It has been associated with the violent actions of a minority who have become frustrated by their inability to relieve animals of the suffering inflicted on them by other human beings. But the humane movement should not be about violence, but about non-violence and ahimsa. It must continue to fight non-violently for the freedom and dignity of all sentient beings.

Gandhi fought two resistance campaigns against injustice during his lifetime. The first was in South Africa against the Europeans' abuse of Indians under their apartheid regime, particularly after their introduction of *The Black Act*. The second was in India where he fought for Indian independence against British rule and particularly against the unfair salt taxes. In both cases he applied *satyagraha* or 'non-violent resistance', based on the principle of ahimsa. Martin Luther King also applied peaceful protest during the civil rights movement in America in the 1950s and 1960s and Nelson Mandela largely applied it during his struggles against apartheid in South Africa. For Gandhi, satyagraha went beyond passive resistance and became a force in practising non-violent actions. He said,

> *'Truth (satya) implies love, and firmness (agraha) engenders and therefore serves as a synonym for force. I thus began to call the Indian movement Satyagraha, that is to say, the Force which is born of Truth and Love or non-violence and gave up the use of the phrase 'passive resistance' in connection with it...* [8]

Gandhi calls satyagraha a *love force* or a *soul force*. He says,

> *'In the application of satyagraha, I discovered in the earliest stages that pursuit of truth did not admit of violence being inflicted on one's opponent, but that he must be weaned from error by patience and compassion.'*

These are wise words that should continue to be practised by the humane movement today. We must not fight violence with violence, but equally we must not sit back and allow violence to be enacted on other sentient beings and do nothing to prevent it. The humane movement must continue in the footsteps of Gandhi and exert the compassionate force of satyagraha in standing up and resisting the many current practices of violence against sentient beings.

12

COMPASSIONATE GENIUSES

'A great soul, the noblest part of creation,
is ever compassionate'.

Francis Bacon - Advancement of Learning

The evolution and anatomy of the brain identifies common sites within the brain's structure for both creative ability and compassion (see chapter 14). Is it any wonder therefore that some of history's greatest geniuses from the fields of mathematics, astronomy, poetry, art and music also have a great propensity for compassion? Many of these are famous for their views on compassion to all sentient beings and were strong advocates of non-harming and non-meat-eating. Some examples are discussed below in date of birth order. The quotations attributed to them have been painstakingly collected over many years by Jon Wynne-Tyson who published them in his book *The Extended Circle – A Dictionary of Humane Thought*. I am most grateful to him for allowing them to be re-quoted here.

Pythagoras (570 BCE – 495 BCE) was the famous Greek mathematician and philosopher, who is best known for the mathematical theory that was named after him. Pythagoras was also the founder of esoteric teachings and founded the sect known as the Pythagoreans, which discussed and developed theories on mathematics, science and music and undertook spiritual practices, which included the ethics of non-violence to all living things. The Pythagoreans were non-meat-eaters and refused to take part in the sacrifice of animals. They also practised a form of yoga and were peaceful and tolerant people. They saw the divine in nature through the beauty of mathematics, geometry, science, astronomy and music. Pythagoras is reported in *The Metamorphoses*, written by the Roman poet Ovid, as saying,

> *'Animals share with us the privilege of having a soul.'*

Ovid also attributes to Pythagoras the quotation,

> *'As long as man continues to be the ruthless destroyer of lower living beings, he will never know health or peace. For as long as men massacre animals, they will kill each other. Indeed, he who sows the seed of murder and pain cannot reap joy and love.'*[1]

Ovid (Publius Ovidius Naso) (43 BCE – 17 AD), who is best known for his erotic poetry says in his epic poem *Metamorphoses*:

> *'Take not away the life you cannot give;*
> *For all things have an equal right to live.*
> *Kill noxious creatures where 'tis sin to save;*
> *This only just prerogative we have;*
> *But nourish life with vegetable food,*
> *And shun the sacrilegious taste of blood.'*[2]

Plutarch (46 AD – 120 AD), was a Greek historian, mathematician, philosopher and author. His works included *Parallel Lives* and *Moralia*. Plutarch shared a Platonic view of the divine realm and believed in the importance of ethics. He says in *Moralia*,

> *'The obligations of law and equity reach only to mankind, but kindness and benevolence should be extended to the creatures of every species, and these will flow from the breast of a true man, as streams that issue from the living fountain.'*[3]

Leonardo Da Vinci (1452 – 1519) was the genius Italian Renaissance polymath, who was a painter, sculptor, architect, musician, scientist, mathematician, engineer, inventor, anatomist, geologist, cartographer, botanist and writer. He famously purchased caged birds in the marketplace in order to set them free. In his notes he has written,

> *'I have from an early age abjured the use of meat, and the time will come when men such as I will look upon the murder of animals as they now look upon the murder of men.'*

He also wrote,

> *'Truly man is the king of the beasts, for his brutality exceeds theirs. We live by the death of others: We are burial places!'*[4]

Thomas More (1478 – 1535) was Lord Chancellor to Henry VIII from October 1529 to May 1532 and author of the book *Utopia* about an ideal, imaginary island nation. In Utopia he says,

> *'The Utopians feel slaughtering our fellow creatures gradually destroys the sense of compassion, which is the finest sentiment of which our human nature is capable.'*[5]

Francis Bacon (1561 – 1626) has been called the father of empiricism, having popularised inductive methodologies for scientific inquiry, often called the Baconian method or the scientific method. In *Advancement of Learning* he writes,

> *'Nature had endowed man with a noble and excellent principle of compassion, which extends itself also to the dumb animals – whence this compassion has some resemblance to that of a prince towards his subjects. And it is certain that the noblest souls are the most extensively compassionate, for narrow and degenerate minds think that compassion belongs not to them; but a great soul, the noblest part of creation, is ever compassionate'*[6]

John Locke (1632 – 1704), an empiricist like Francis Bacon, a philosopher and physician and regarded as one of the most influential of enlightenment thinkers says,

'And they, who delight in the suffering and destruction of inferior creatures, will not be apt to be very compassionate or benign to those of their own kind. Children should from the beginning be brought up in an abhorrence of killing and tormenting any living creature.'[7]

Sir Isaac Newton (1642 – 1727), the English physicist, mathematician, astronomer, natural philosopher, alchemist and theologian, has been considered by many to be the greatest and most influential scientist who ever lived. He is famous for his books *Philosophiae Naturalis* and *Principia Mathematica* and for laying the foundations of classical mechanics, which included universal gravitation and the three laws of motion. However his appreciation of science did not diminish his appreciation of religious matters. He says,

'Gravity explains the motions of the planets, but it cannot explain who set the planets in motion. God governs all things and knows all that is or can be done.'

Isaac Newton was known for his love of animals and his concern for his cat's needs to get in and out of the house led to his invention of the cat flap. Voltaire said of him in *Elemens de la Philosophie de Newton*,

'There is in man a disposition to compassion as generally diffused as his other instincts. Newton had cultivated this sentiment of humanity, and he extended it to the lower animals. With Locke he was strongly convinced that God has given to them a proportion of ideas, and the same feelings, which he has to us.'[8]

Alexander Pope (1688 – 1744) the famous English poet, best known for his satirical verse and his translation of Homer says in his *Essay on Man*,

'All are but parts of one stupendous whole, whose body Nature is, and God the soul.'[9]

131

Charles Darwin (1809 – 1882) was the English naturalist famous for the discovery of evolution through natural selection, his five-year voyage on the HMS Beagle and as author of *The Origin of Species* and *The Descent of Man*. In *The Descent of Man* he writes,

> *'The love for all living creatures is the most noble attribute of man.'* He also writes, *'There is no fundamental difference between man and the higher mammals in their mental faculties...The difference in mind between man and the higher animals, great as it is, certainly is one of degree and not of kind.'*

Again in the Descent of Man, he writes,

> *'We have seen that the senses and intuitions, the various emotions and faculties, such as love, memory, attention and curiosity, imitation, reason, etc., of which man boasts, may be found in an incipient, or even sometimes in a well-developed condition, in the lower animals.'*[10]

Henry D. Thoreau (1817 – 1862) was an American author, poet, philosopher, naturalist and abolitionist. He wrote books on natural history, the environment and ecology and is best known for his book *Walden* a reflection on simple living. In Walden he says,

> *'I have no doubt that it is part of the destiny of the human race, in its gradual improvement, to leave off eating animals, as surely as the savage tribes have left off eating each other when they came in contact with the more civilised.'*

He also says,

> *'I believe that every man who has ever been earnest to preserve his higher or poetic faculties in the best condition has been particularly inclined to abstain from animal food, and from much food of any kind.'*[11]

Leo Nikolayevich Tolstoy (1828 – 1910) was a Russian writer of novels, short stories, plays and essays. His two most famous novels were *War and Peace* and *Anna Karenina*. Tolstoy was brought up as the son of a wealthy Russian nobleman and he enjoyed gambling and womanising, but he later gave up his wealth and extravagant lifestyle in an act of renunciation inspired by Christ, Buddha and St. Francis. He was inspired by Christ's Sermon on the Mount and his ideas on non-violent resistance, expressed in such works as *The Kingdom of God is Within You* had a profound impact on Mohandas Gandhi and Martin Luther King. In *The First Step* he writes,

> *'If man aspires towards a righteous life, his first act of abstinence is from injury to animals.'*

He also writes,

> *'This is dreadful! Not the suffering and death of the animals, but that man suppresses in himself, unnecessarily, the highest spiritual capacity – that of sympathy and pity toward the living creatures like himself – and by violating his own feelings becomes cruel. And how deeply seated in the human heart is the injunction not to take life! But by the assertion that God ordained the slaughter of animals, and above all as a result of habit, people entirely lose their natural feelings'.*

In *On Civil Disobedience* he says,

> *'A man can live and be healthy without killing animals for food; if he eats meat, he participates in taking animal life merely for the sake of his appetite. And to act so is immoral.'*

In a letter to Mrs. C.P. Farrell in July 1909 he writes,

> *'What I think about vivisection is that if people admit that they have the right to take or endanger the life of living*

*beings for the benefit of the many, there will be no limit for
their cruelty.'*[12]

Mark Twain (1835 – 1910) was the American author of *Tom
Sawyer* and *The Adventures of Huckleberry Finn*. He wrote in
What is Man?,

> *'The fact that man knows right from wrong proves his
> intellectual superiority to the other creatures; but the fact
> that he can do wrong proves his moral inferiority to any
> creature that cannot.'*[13]

Thomas Edison (1847 – 1931) was the American inventor and
businessman who invented many devices including the light bulb,
the phonograph and the motion picture camera. He was the fourth
most prolific inventor in history holding 1,093 US patents as well
as patents in the United Kingdom, France and Germany. He writes
in *Harpers Magazine* in 1890,

> *'Non-violence leads to the highest ethics, which is the goal
> of all evolution. Until we stop harming all other living
> beings, we are still savages.'*[14]

Albert Einstein (1879 – 1955) was the famous theoretical
physicist and developer of the theory of relativity who won the
Nobel Prize for Physics in 1921. Realising that Newtonian
mechanics were insufficient he developed the 'special' theory of
relativity. But later he discovered that this did not cover
gravitational fields, so he went on to develop his 'general' theory
of relativity. Einstein wrote in *The New York Post*,

> *'A human being is part of the whole, called by us the
> 'Universe', a part limited in time and space. He
> experiences himself, his thoughts and feelings, as something
> separate from the rest – a kind of optical delusion of his
> consciousness. This delusion is a kind of prison for us,
> restricting us to our personal desires and to affection for a
> few persons nearest to us. Our task must be to free
> ourselves from this prison by widening our circle of*

> *compassion to embrace all living creatures and the whole of nature in its beauty. Nobody is able to achieve this completely, but the striving for such achievement is in itself a part of the liberation and a foundation for inner security.'*

In a letter to *The Vegetarian Watch-Tower* on 27 December 1930 he wrote,

> *'It is my view that the vegetarian manner of living by its purely physical effect on the human temperament would most beneficially influence the lot of mankind.'*[15]

Thomas Hardy, OM (1840 – 1928), was the famous Dorset author of classic novels such as *Far From The Madding Crowd, Tess of the d'Urbervilles* and *The Mayor of Casterbridge* which commented on the way people struggled and got caught up in life's difficulties. Although Hardy was brought up in the Anglican faith, such suffering caused him to question the idea of an omnipotent God who cared for the world, although he maintained his faith by his belief in a universal consciousness. He says,

> *'The Christian God – the external personality – has been replaced by the intelligence of the First Cause...the replacement of the old concept of God as all-powerful by a new concept of universal consciousness. The 'tribal god, man-shaped, fiery-faced and tyrannous' is replaced by the 'unconscious will of the universe' which progressively grows aware of itself and 'ultimately, it is hoped to be sympathetic.'*

He wrote in a letter to *The Humanitarian* in 1910,

> *'The establishment of the common origin of all species logically involves a readjustment of altruistic morals, by enlarging the application of what has been called the Golden Rule from the area of mere mankind to that of the whole animal kingdom'.*

He also wrote in the same letter,

'The discovery of the law of evolution, which revealed that all organic creatures are of one family, shifted the centre of altruism from humanity to the whole conscious world collectively. Therefore, the practice of vivisection has been left by that discovery without any logical argument in its favour.'[16]

George Bernard Shaw (1856 – 1950) was a prolific writer of more than 60 plays which included *Arms and the Man*, *Pygmalion* and *The Chocolate Soldier*. His plays were mostly satirical comedy that examined religion, government and class privilege. He was a socialist and humanitarian, he founded the London School of Economics and also wrote speeches for the Fabian Society. He held strong views on vivisection and meat-eating. He says in the preface to his play *Back to Methuselah*,

'Now the general conception of Evolution provides the humanitarian with a scientific basis, because it establishes the fundamental equality of all living things. It makes killing an animal murder in exactly the same sense as the killing of a man is murder.'

He also says,

'This sense of the kinship of all forms of life is all that is needed to make evolution not only a conceivable theory, but an inspiring one.' He continues, *'Our vanity, and our snobbish conception of Godhead as being, like earthly kinship, a supreme class distinction instead of the rock on which Equality is built, has led us to insist on God offering us special terms by placing us apart from and above all the rest of his creatures. Evolution took that conceit out of us; and now, though we may kill a flea without the smallest remorse, we at all events know that we are killing our cousin.'*

Of vivisection he says in the preface to the play *The Doctor's Dilemma*,

'Vivisection is a social evil because if it advances human knowledge, it does so at the expense of human character.'[17]

Mohandas Gandhi (1869 – 1948) was the pre-eminent political and ideological leader of India, who led the Indian independence movement through satyagraha or resistance to tyranny through mass civil disobedience, based on the principle of ahimsa. He is also known as *Mahatma*, 'great soul' Gandhi or *Bapu*, 'father' as he is honoured as the father of the nation in India, which celebrates his birthday on 2 October with a national holiday as the international day of non-violence, 'Gandhi Jayanti'. He undertook satyagrahas first in South Africa in the struggle for civil rights for Indians and later in India against British Imperialism. Gandhi wrote in *The Moral Basis of Vegetarianism*,

'The greatness of a nation and its moral progress can be judged by the way its animals are treated.'

He also writes,

'It ill becomes us to invoke in our daily prayers the blessings of God, the Compassionate, if we in turn will not practice elementary compassion towards our fellow creatures.'

In *The Words of Gandhi* he says,

'I want to realise brotherhood or identity not merely with the beings called human, but I want to realise identity with all life, even with such things as crawl upon the earth.'[18]

Dr Albert Schweitzer, OM (1875 – 1965) won the Nobel Peace Prize in 1952 for his philosophy of *Reverence for Life*. His address *The Problem of Peace* which he delivered on receiving the prize was considered to be one of the best speeches ever given. Schweitzer had been brought up as a Christian in Germany and studied music and theology. He then worked as a church deacon and wrote books about theology. He later studied medicine and worked as a missionary doctor in Africa. However he based his life on the Jain principle of ahimsa and was a non-meat-eater. His passionate quest was to discover a universal ethical philosophy, anchored in a universal reality, and make it directly available to all of humanity. After receiving the Nobel Peace Prize he spent the remainder of his life working for nuclear disarmament alongside Albert Einstein. He writes in his book *Civilisation and Ethics*,

> *'The disastrous feature of our civilisation is that it is far more developed materially than spiritually. Its balance is disturbed... A civilisation which develops only on its material side, and not in the sphere of the spirit... heads for disaster.'*

He explains,

> *'Ethics in our Western world has hitherto been largely limited to the relations of man to man. But that is a limited ethics. We need a boundless ethics, which will include the animals too.'*

He continues,

> *'A man is really ethical only when he obeys the constraint laid on him to aid all life which he is able to help, and when he goes out of his way to avoid injuring anything living. He does not ask how far this or that life deserves sympathy as valuable in itself, nor how far it is capable of feeling. To him life as such is sacred.'*

He explains that

> *'Ethics is in its unqualified form extended responsibility to everything that has life.'*

In his Nobel Peace Prize address *The Problem of Peace in the World Today* he says,

> *'The human spirit is not dead. It lives on in secret...It has come to believe that compassion, in which all ethics must*

take root, can only attain its full breadth and depth if it embraces all living creatures and does not limit itself to mankind.'

In a letter to Aida Flemming in 1959 he writes

'Our civilisation lacks humane feeling. We are humans who are insufficiently humane! We must realise that and seek to find a new spirit. We have lost sight of this ideal because we are solely occupied with thoughts of men instead of remembering that our goodness and compassion should extend to all creatures. Religion and philosophy have not insisted as much as they should on the fact that our kindness should include all living creatures.'

Albert Schweitzer's most famous quote, from *The Philosophy of Civilisation* is,

'Until he extends the circle of compassion to all living things, man will not himself find peace.'[19]

Aldous Huxley (1894 – 1963) was a humanist, pacifist, satirist and the author of *Brave New World* which was about the dehumanising aspects of scientific progress, mass production and Pavlovian conditioning. Although he was born in Surrey and educated at Eton and Oxford, Huxley later became a Vedantist and practised ahimsa through meditation and non-meat-eating and wrote widely on spiritual values. In his book 'The Perennial Philosophy' he says,

'Compared with that of the Taoists and the Far Eastern Buddhists, the Christian attitude toward Nature has been curiously insensitive and often downright domineering and violent. Taking their cue from an unfortunate remark in Genesis, Catholic moralists have regarded animals as mere things which men do right to exploit for their own ends.'

He adds,

'Modern man no longer regards Nature as being in any sense divine and feels perfectly free to behave toward her as an overweening conqueror and tyrant.'[20]

Ernst Friedrich Schumacher (1911 – 1977) was the influential economic thinker, ecologist and writer who wrote the book *Small is Beautiful: A Study of Economics as if People Mattered*. He says in the book,

'There have been no sages or holy men in our or anybody else's history who were cruel to animals or who looked upon them as nothing but utilities, and innumerable are the legends and stories which link sanctity as well as happiness with a loving kindness towards lower creation.'

Schumacher was born and brought up in Bonn in Germany, but unwilling to live under the Nazi regime, he moved to England where he was interned on an isolated farm. During his internment he wrote a paper titled *Multilateral Clearing* which captured the attention of the economist Maynard Keynes. Keynes was so impressed by Schumacher's abilities he had him released from internment and found him a position at Oxford University. Schumacher became an influential economic thinker and statistician and became Chief Economic Advisor to the Coal Board for two decades. He is best known for his critique of western economies and his proposals for small-scale, decentralised and humane technologies. His *Buddhist Economics* recommended production from local resources for local needs. He was heavily influenced by Mahatma Gandhi who he described as 'the greatest people's economist', as his economic thinking was compatible with spirituality rather than materiality. After his death the Soil Association, the Schumacher College in Dartington in Devon, England and the New Economics Foundation were founded in his memory.[21]

Yehudi Menuhin, OM (1916 – 1999) the famous violinist, conductor, child prodigy and musical genius says in his book 'Just for Animals',

'Why is compassion not part of our established curriculum, an inherent part of our education? Compassion, awe, wonder, curiosity, exaltation, humility – these are the very foundation of any real civilisation, no longer the prerogatives, the preserves of any one church, but belonging to everyone, every child, in every home, in every school.'

Yehudi means 'Jew' in Hebrew, and Yehudi Menuhin's Russian Jewish parents named him 'Jew' after an incident which made them determined that there should be no misunderstanding that they were Jewish and to demonstrate that they were proud of it. They had sought an apartment when living in the United States and the landlady had unwittingly said, after offering it to them, 'And you'll be glad to hear I don't take Jews.' He studied yoga under B.K.S. Iyengar and became a committed yogi, environmentalist and non-meat-eater. He also founded the famous Yehudi Menuhin school in Stoke D'Abernon, Surrey.[22]

Carl Sagan (1934 – 1996) was an American cosmologist of Ukrainian Jewish descent and author of many science fact and science fiction books. He presented the famous television series *Cosmos* and wrote the novel *Contact* that led to the film of the same name. He was a professor at Cornell University and a Director of the Laboratory for Planetary Studies. He worked at NASA on the space probes programme and designed the message on the plaques attached to Pioneer 10, Pioneer 11 and Voyager space probes. These were designed so that they could be understood by any extraterrestrial intelligence that might find them. He was instrumental in setting up SETI, the search for extraterrestrial intelligence. In his book *The Dragons of Eden* he writes,

'The cognitive abilities of chimpanzees force us, I think, to raise searching questions about the boundaries of the community of beings to which special ethical considerations are due, and can, I hope, help to extend our ethical perspectives downward through the taxa on earth and upwards to extraterrestrial organisms, if they exist.'[23]

He also writes,

> *'If chimpanzees have consciousness, if they are capable of abstractions, do they not have what until now has been described as "human rights"?   How smart does a chimpanzee have to be, before killing him constitutes murder?* '[24]

PART 3

THE EVOLUTION OF COMPASSION

13

THE EVOLUTION
OF THE UNIVERSE, CONSCIOUSNESS AND
COMPASSION

'For we are the local embodiment of the Cosmos
grown to self-awareness.
We have begun to contemplate our origins:
starstuff pondering the stars;
organised assemblages of ten billion billion billion atoms
considering the evolution of atoms;
tracing the long journey by which, here at least,
consciousness arose.

Carl Sagan – Cosmos

To understand the evolution of compassionate conscious life on Earth we must go right back to the origin of the Universe, because without its origin life would not have been possible. It will also enable us to consider the relatively short and recent time that conscious life has existed on Earth compared to the life-span of the Universe.

The Cosmic Calendar
Scientists believe that the Universe was created 13.7 billion years ago in an event known as the Big Bang. Some scientists have described the history of the Universe since that event by using the analogy of a calendar of one year, with the Big Bang event occurring at the first moment of 1st January. Every billion years corresponds to twenty-six days on the calendar.

On this calendar the Milky Way galaxy was formed on 1st May. Our solar system originated on 9th September, with the sun forming as a second or third generation star, coalescing from the remnants of a nearby supernova explosion. The Earth was formed on 14th September and the earliest life on Earth emerged on 25th September. But it was not until 1st December that there was sufficient oxygen in the Earth's atmosphere for organic life to evolve and it was not until the 18th December that the first plankton and trilobites flourished. Then, on 19th December, the first fish, which were the first vertebrates, appeared. This was probably when conscious life on Earth first emerged, in the latter half of the last month of the year! Plants colonised the land on 20th December and the first insects appeared on 21st December. On the 22nd December the first amphibians emerged and on 23rd December the first trees and reptiles evolved. Dinosaurs arose on 24th December, but the first mammals did not evolve until the 26th December. These were followed by the first birds on 27th December. Then on 28th December the dinosaurs became extinct. The first cetaceans and primates appeared on 29th December and the first hominids arose on 30th December.

The first humans did not appear until 31st December at 10.30pm and they did not draw their first cave paintings until 11.59pm. Buddha, Mahavira, Socrates and Laotse were born at 11.59.55pm, Christ was born at 11.59.56pm and Muhammad was born at 11.59.57pm.[1] Now it is the first second of New Year's day. What will happen next? Whatever humans do to themselves or the planet, we can be fairly sure that the rest of the Universe will carry on regardless.

A Universe Teeming with Life
Conscious life, we observe, probably did not appear on Earth until around 19th December on the Cosmic Calendar and compassionate conscious life would have appeared sometime after this. The Universe waited a lifetime to realise itself. But can we assume that the Earth is the only place in the Universe to develop compassionate conscious life? There are over 100 billion stars in our Milky Way Galaxy and beyond that there are over 100 billion galaxies, each with hundreds of billions of stars, in the known Universe. Surely compassionate conscious life cannot be unique to the Earth? Even if the smallest percentage of stars have planets orbiting them that are capable of supporting life, that could still add

up to a very large number of places where life has evolved and some of those places could conceivably have developed conscious, compassionate life.

The building blocks of life are everywhere. Throughout the Universe stars have been forging the atoms that form those building blocks through the process of nuclear fusion. During the Big Bang, 13.7 billion years ago, quarks combined to form electrically neutral neutrons, positively charged protons and negatively charged electrons. The strong nuclear force combined the neutrons and protons together to form the nuclei of hydrogen atoms and the opposing electrical forces of the protons and electrons attracted each other, causing electrons to orbit the nuclei to form whole atoms. The simplest atoms were hydrogen which were made up of one proton and one electron and these were created in abundance. The second simplest atom was helium, which was made up of two neutrons, two protons and two electrons, formed from the fusion of four hydrogen atoms. Ninety nine percent of the Universe is made up of hydrogen and helium.

Gravity then attracted the matter so that it condensed into huge masses. As the masses increased, the pressures increased and the temperatures rose. When the pressures and temperatures became high enough nuclear fusion began, with the hydrogen atoms fusing to form helium atoms and giving off energy in the form of photons. Stars were switched on and there was light. At the higher pressures and temperatures found in stars in their late red giant phase, helium fused to form carbon, which has six protons. As the temperature rose further in these stars helium fused with carbon to form oxygen, which has eight protons. For stars the size of our sun, this is where the fusion ended, with the dying star forming a beautiful nebula. But in massive stars, much bigger than the sun, this fusion continued with increasing temperatures by the addition of two extra protons from the helium atom to form neon with ten protons, then magnesium with twelve protons, then silicon with fourteen protons and then sulphur with sixteen protons. This continued all the way up to iron with twenty-six protons. At the much higher temperatures reached in supernova explosions, atoms with more protons than iron, such as gold and uranium, were formed[2][3].

All these atoms are found in life on Earth. Iron is found in blood, calcium is used in teeth and bones, nitrogen is used in DNA, oxygen is essential for respiration and we are made of carbon. These atoms combine to form organic molecules that are the beginnings of life and give life its diversity. Atoms of carbon, hydrogen, oxygen and nitrogen, form the molecules called amino-acids which combine to form proteins from which DNA is made, which forms the building blocks of life. Cosmic rays from distant supernova explosions cause hereditary changes called mutations that enable evolution to take place. We are made of star-stuff and this star-stuff is abundant everywhere in the Universe and the processes that lead to the creation of organic life are commonplace, if not inevitable, where the conditions are right[4]. In fact, organic molecules have been found on meteors that have fallen to Earth, demonstrating that organic molecules can form extra-terrestrially in space[5]. The probability of life on Earth being unique, even compassionate, conscious life being unique, is extremely low. Even if the probability of a single star having an orbiting planet with attributes suitable for life is extremely low, the possibility that the Universe is teeming with life remains high, given the billions and billions of stars in the Universe.

Sadly, because of the vast interstellar distances in space and the limitation of the speed of light being the maximum speed at which anything with a mass can travel, we are unlikely ever to communicate with or meet up with other conscious life forms. The nearest star to us is Proxima Centauri which is 4.3 light years away, which means that, even if we could travel at the speed of light, it would take 4.3 years to reach it. The Voyager interstellar spacecraft is travelling at one thousandth of the speed of light and will take 40,000 years to reach Proxima Centauri[6]. Scientists are trying to listen for communications from intelligent life in space with radio telescopes as part of the SETI project, the 'Search for Extra-Terrestrial Intelligence'. At the time of writing no communications have yet been received. Scientists have speculated about the possibility of travelling through wormholes, which provide short distant links to distant parts of the Universe through warps in the fabric of space, but so far such ideas have remained a fantasy in the realms of science fiction. So the possibility of communicating with or meeting up with other forms of life that have evolved in the Universe is highly remote.

But supposing such an encounter were to occur, how would we react to our fellow sentient beings with whom we share the Universe, our fellow travellers on the journey of life? Would we treat them with compassion and respect, or would we capture them and keep them as exhibits in zoos or even experiment on them in laboratories? How intelligent or powerful would they have to be before we accorded them the same rights as we accord ourselves? How would we define intelligence? Would not the fact that they were, like us, conscious life forms, be enough for us to apply the golden rule to them, and to treat them as we would want them to treat us? Should SETI ever become successful in their quest, we would have to address these serious ethical questions. Are we ready for such an eventuality?

We can assume that the evolution of organic life throughout the Universe is highly probable, if not inevitable. But what about the evolution of consciousness and compassionate, conscious life? How likely are these to occur? In order to answer this question we need to look at how consciousness in life on Earth evolved.

The Evolution of Consciousness
Consciousness in living beings on the planet Earth can be seen to be abundant with mammals, birds, reptiles and fish having a brain and displaying behaviour typical of consciousness. Indeed they would be unlikely to be able to get around and do their business without consciousness. Even insects probably have some form of consciousness to direct them about their business. Their actions are far more complex than the actions that result from sensory responses to external stimuli that we see occurring in species which do not have a brain, such as plants. It could be inferred that consciousness is necessary for animal life to exist. The boundary at which the sensory responses to external stimuli, exhibited by primitive life forms, become a conscious experience may be very hard to define or pinpoint. But, at some stage, evolution must have ensured that the process of natural selection selected in favour of conscious beings, thus accounting for the proliferation of conscious life on Earth. These beings presumably could make decisions that were a little more complicated than 'move slowly towards the

light' to decisions like 'move quickly away from a predator' or 'go and search for food'.

The flexibility that conscious thought provides for animals to search for food and avoid predators makes conscious thought a likely winner in the natural selection stakes. The more complex the decisions that the organism is able to make, the more flexibility it will have for survival. So the development of consciousness into intelligence, and then the increasing development of intelligence, was more likely to improve the chances of survival. Natural selection would select against the less intelligent conscious beings in favour of the more intelligent conscious beings, particularly in an environment that depended on organisms competing for food and sex, or predating on each other. Intelligence could develop in different ways and the type of intelligence suitable for one form of conscious being may not be the most appropriate type of intelligence for another form of conscious being. For example, the ability to make swift decisions to pounce on prey may be the strategy adopted by one type of organism, whilst the ability to make a tool may be the strategy adopted by another type of organism. This is why cats do not make bows and arrows and why humans cannot chase and catch things at the speed that cheetahs do.

The Evolution of Compassion

So we can see how the processes of evolution and survival of the fittest can explain the natural selection of conscious creatures and then more intelligent conscious creatures. But does this explain the evolution of compassion? Logically it could be argued that compassion has developed through our parental natures. The offspring of parents who cared for them were more likely to survive than the offspring of parents who did not care for them. The surviving offspring of the parents who cared for them were then more likely to carry the caring genes of their parents and hand them on. Hence, by the principle of natural selection, those creatures, which carried the caring gene, were more likely to survive and to evolve into animals that cared themselves. Furthermore, many animals had to work together and co-operate in order to survive. This increased the chances of success in hunting for food or defending territory from attack. So those who cared for their family or for their neighbours and friends and co-operated with them, were more likely to survive than those who did not co-operate.

But caring for other members of your family or community and co-operating with them is not the same as altruism and compassion. This requires following the golden rule and caring for those who are not part of your in-group and even caring for your enemies. It is difficult to imagine how natural selection would select in favour of those who showed compassion for others outside of the in-group. Compassion is something that goes over and above the call of duty of caring for your family and community and co-operating with them. In fact, such co-operative behaviour with the in-group could also lead to tribalism, which would result in non-altruistic behaviour. Perhaps this is why we see so many examples of humans behaving in uncompassionate ways and exhibiting selfish behaviour and prejudices such as racism, sexism, ageism, speciesism and general hostility to members of other groups. In fact, natural selection should select in favour of selfishness and greed, where loyalty only extends as far as the personal in-group and where co-operation benefits the survival of that in-group, including the individual who is part of it.

Perhaps compassion is not a natural evolutionary behaviour at all, but an aberration that actually conflicts with the conditions for personal survival. We see around us a world full of greed and selfishness, where there are endless wars and where half the world die of hunger, while the other half consumes far more natural resources than it needs. But we also see great acts of compassion that defy the norm. Why is this?

The Selfish Gene
In his book *The Selfish Gene,* Richard Dawkins suggests that the basic unit of natural selection is not the individual or the community of individuals or even the species, but it is *the gene.* The gene is basically selfish because it is competing for survival with all other genes to continue its potentially immortal life. Unlike the life forms the gene inhabits, which are born, live and die, the gene continues its life indefinitely, being passed on from one generation to another in the chromosomes of the bodies it inhabits. Dawkins describes the life forms that the genes inhabit,

(which include elephants, viruses and you and me) as '*survival machines*' for those genes, as they reproduce and pass the genes on through the generations in their chromosomes.[7] Dawkins agrees that,

> '*Universal love and the welfare of the species as a whole are concepts that simply do not make evolutionary sense.*'

He suggests that biological nature will provide little help in building a society in which individuals co-operate generously and unselfishly towards a common good. However, he points out that animals have brains and cultures (memes) that are capable of over-riding the instructions of their genes. The biggest rebellion that humans use against their genes is the use of contraception, as this defies the genes' objective of continuing life in the future generations of its survival machines. He says,

> '*Let us try to teach generosity and altruism, because we are born selfish. Let us understand what our own selfish genes are up to, because we may then at least have the chance to upset their designs.*'

He points out that genes, whether selfish or not, are virtually irrelevant to the understanding of human nature. This leads on to the 'nature versus nurture' debate.

There is a theory called '*group selection theory*'. This argues that a species, or population within a species, whose individual members are prepared to sacrifice themselves for the welfare of the group, may be less likely to become extinct than a rival group whose individual members place their own selfish interest first. Thus, the world becomes populated mainly by groups that consist of self-sacrificing individuals. But Dawkins argues that this will not work because, if there is just one selfish individual (and there will probably be more than one selfish individual), who is prepared to exploit the altruism of the rest, then he is more likely to survive and pass on his genes. His children will inherit his selfish trait and after several generations of natural selection, the altruistic group will be overrun with selfish individuals. Even if the altruistic group never had selfish individuals of its own, there would be nothing to stop selfish individuals from other groups migrating into the altruistic group.[8]

The Unselfish Consciousness

In terms of natural selection, therefore, we are doomed to be selfish if we follow the instructions of our genes. In order to break the cycle we have to use our brains, our consciousness, our culture and our memes to create an altruistic society. Dawkins says,

> *'Whatever the philosophical problems raised by consciousness, for the purposes of this story it can be thought of as the culmination of an evolutionary trend towards the emancipation of the survival machine as executive decision-takers from their ultimate masters, the genes'.*[9]

Why would any species evolve something surplus to or even in conflict with personal survival? Some scientists have commented on the ability of human beings to demonstrate mental abilities in other fields, such as mathematics, which also go far beyond anything that evolution would have selected in favour of for personal survival. There have been no survival benefits during the evolution of man that required him to have the ability to calculate the theory of relativity or Newton's laws or do any of the higher abstract thinking of which he is capable. So how has the human brain reached this level of intellectual ability without the pressures of natural selection to drive it? Indeed, what thoughts go through the minds of other animals with large brains, such as cetaceans, elephants and great apes?

Altruistic compassion, like high level intellectual capabilities, seems to be either a by-product of a large brain that evolved for other survival reasons, or something that evolved through some mechanism not fully explained by natural selection. In terms of survival value, why should anyone show compassion for other sentient beings? Could the explanation for the feelings of empathy and compassion for others, outside of one's own personal in-group, be the result of a need for the individual consciousness to return to a collective consciousness?

The Vegetarian Gene

Another interesting subject for evolutionary theory is the question of vegetarianism. Human beings have evolved to be omnivorous, but some choose to be non-meat-eaters. There have been a number of surveys in different countries which have sought to identify what proportion of the country's population was vegetarian. Unfortunately, there do not seem to be any global surveys that would indicate what proportion of the world's population as a whole was vegetarian. The findings from the various surveys were collated by the *Raw Food Health Journal*[10], which suggests that the percentages of vegetarians by country are 3.2 per cent for the United States[11], 6 per cent for England[12], between 2 per cent and 4 per cent for most other European countries[13] and 40 per cent for India. Is this due to nature or nurture?

Millions of years ago in our evolutionary history, before our omnivorous ancestors lived as hunter/gatherers on the African plains after descending from the forest canopies, their arboreal ancestors ate only fruits. Is it possible that the fruit eating genes of these fruitarian ancestors have continued down through the generations to emerge in a small proportion of the human population, such that these people are natural vegetarians? Most non-meat-eaters, however, choose to give up meat due to lifestyle changes brought about by compassionate concern for other animals. This is either because they believe that the animals have as much right not to be eaten as humans do or because they are concerned about the way animals are treated in modern day farming systems, or both. But there are individuals who do not like eating meat, regardless of their ethical views and other individuals who have chosen to stop eating meat for ethical reasons, but who still crave meat. Could the practice of non-meat-eating be both nature and nurture? Could it be both genetically driven and the result of compassionate decision-making? This is an interesting area where more research would be helpful.

We can therefore conclude that we are innately selfish, driven by our selfish genes, seeking our own survival. Natural selection has selected those individuals who selfishly sought to survive, did survive and passed their selfish genes on to future generations. Where parental care and co-operation with the in-group assisted personal survival, such attributes were also positively selected for. But we have the choice to use our brains and our consciousness not to behave selfishly. Whilst our past survival may have depended on selfish behaviour, maybe the human population is now so large and so powerful that selfishness can only ultimately lead to its own destruction. Maybe now is the time to use our brains to override our selfish genes with compassion. In later chapters we will look at why this might be necessary for our survival, but first we should look in a little more detail at the evolution and structure of the brain to determine how we could use it to be more compassionate.

How can anyone fail to be struck with awe, when one considers that we are here, now, 13.7 billion years after the birth of our Cosmos, able to contemplate our place in it? And we can contemplate this:- having evolved a body, a brain and consciousness through a process of natural selection, driven by our selfish genes, we now have the opportunity to use that consciousness to over-ride those selfish genes and develop our compassion and altruism to create a better world in which to live.

14

BRAIN
EVOLUTION & STRUCTURE

*'The discovery of the law of evolution,
which revealed that all organic creatures
are of one family,
shifted the centre of altruism from humanity
to the whole conscious world collectively.'*

Thomas Hardy - a letter to The Humanitarian, 1910

In the previous chapter we concluded that evolution and natural selection were driven by genes, rather than by the activities of their survival machines, and that these genes were basically selfish. Therefore any compassionate or altruistic behaviour in the individual survival machine required the genes to be over-ruled by the brains of those survival machines. So how does the brain function, how did it evolve and how can compassion emerge from it? Did the brains of different species follow the same or different evolutionary paths and are some species more conscious or more intelligent than others? Do some species feel more pain and suffer more than others? Are the brains of humans so different from those of other species that this justifies us in treating those other species differently from us? And within our own species, why do some people behave with compassion when others do not? Why do some people think rationally while others think creatively? In order to understand these questions a little better we need to look at the evolution of the brain and its anatomy.

The Evolution of the Animal Brain

No two individuals are alike, either in physical appearance or in mental behaviour. All organisms on Earth are made up of DNA and share the same genetic language, which has evolved from a single ancestor at a single instance in the origin of life on Earth, around four and a half billion years ago. A typical DNA molecule or chromosome of a human-being is made up of around five billion pairs of nucleotides, each containing four bits of information, which make up this genetic language. Therefore, an average human chromosome is made up of some twenty billion bits of information, which means that the likelihood of two human beings appearing exactly the same is highly improbable.

The likelihood of two minds being alike is even more improbable. The human brain contains about ten billion neurons, each containing between 1,000 and 10,000 synapses, or connections with other neurons, which define the different states that the brain can be in. The average human brain has more different possible states than the number of electrons or protons in the entire Universe. Thus the mental state of two individuals can never be alike and the behaviour of a single individual may itself have many internal inconsistencies.[1] So how did such a complex organ as the brain evolve?

Neural Chassis: The earliest recorded brains were in primitive fish, which had a spinal chord with a small swelling on the front, which has been called a hindbrain. By around five million years ago fish also developed a midbrain and a tiny forebrain, which still exist in fish today, and is called the neural chassis. Throughout evolution the brain developed new layers, while never eliminating the earlier layers, which still exist in all modern animals today.

Reptilian Complex: Several hundred million years ago the brain developed a new layer around the neural chassis called the reptilian complex, which was a feature of the reptiles that evolved from fish. Control of our basic behaviours, such as fight and flight, is still based in the reptilian complex. These faculties include dominance behaviour, aggression and sex drive. Regulation of bodily functions such as the heart, the circulation and respiration also reside here.

Limbic System: About a hundred and fifty million years ago another layer evolved around the reptilian complex in mammals called the limbic system. This area is related to strong and vivid emotions and it is the area that is affected if psychedelic and hallucinogenic drugs are used. It controls emotions that we tend to think of as uniquely human, but as this part of the brain is shared with other mammals, it is fair to conclude that these other animals experience them too. The limbic system includes the *hypothalamus* which is associated with drives, the *amygdala*, which is associated with emotions and the *hippocampus*, which is associated with memory. The master gland, the *pituitary gland*, which influences other glands and controls the *endocrine system*, also resides in the limbic system. Different states of mind are rooted in changes within the endocrine system, which affects the moods experienced by mammals.

The limbic system is also the home of the *olfactory cortex*, which controls the sense of smell. Memories stimulated by smells can evoke strong emotional feelings. Love and altruistic behaviour are also affected by the limbic system.[2] During the 1950s, Paul MacLean, physician and neuroscientist at the US National Institute of Mental Health, suggested that the positive emotions of compassion, joy, serenity and maternal affection emanated from the limbic system.[3] If this is the case, we share these positive emotions with other animals.

Although modern-day fish have not evolved a limbic system around their brains, similar structures to those contained in the limbic system of other animals have evolved in their forebrains, making modern day fish more highly evolved than their primitive ancestors. Modern-day fish have a hippocampus and an amygdala in their forebrains, which reside in the limbic system in mammals. Thus modern-day fish should be capable of feeling pain and of experiencing emotions and are therefore capable of suffering.[4]

Neocortex: The most recent evolutionary layer is *the neocortex,* which sits around the limbic system and is present in most mammals. It developed several tens of millions of years ago. This has further evolved to an even more advanced size in primates, whales, dolphins and elephants. The neocortex is the site of the cognitive functions. It is divided into four major lobes including the frontal lobes, the parietal lobes, the temporal lobes and the occipital lobes. The *frontal lobes* are associated with deliberation and regulation of action, the *parietal lobes* are associated with spatial perception and communication between the brain and the rest of the body, the *temporal lobes* are associated with memory and a variety of complex perceptual tasks and the *occipital lobes* control vision.

Embryonic Brain Development: All animals go through the evolutionary process as they develop as embryos before birth. A human embryo's brain, for example, will go through the brain forms of their evolutionary ancestors during gestation. The brain development starts with the neural chassis, which resembles the brain of a primitive fish. As the embryo develops the brain grows by building up different layers in the same way as brains evolved. The reptilian complex develops around the neural chassis, the limbic system then develops around the reptilian complex and the neocortex finally develops around the limbic system.[5]

Anatomy of the Animal Brain

The Frontal Lobes and the Sense of Self: The frontal lobes of the neocortex are particularly developed in humans and are, perhaps arrogantly, seen as the area that makes us different from other animals. They are associated with anticipation of the future and are the sites related to anxiety and guilt. They have also enabled the human upright posture, which freed the front feet, allowing them to develop into hands and achieve the skills of tool-making and writing. The frontal lobes are also the region that creates the sense of self. We infer this because patients who have had prefrontal lobotomies have been described as losing a continuing sense of self and the feeling that they are a particular individual who has control over their life. It could be assumed that, the more developed the frontal lobes, the stronger the sense of self and therefore the greater the ego. Another human characteristic is language, which includes reading, writing and arithmetic, but this appears to require the co-operative activities of all four lobes, especially the dominant temporal-parietal areas.[6]

Mirror Neurons and Empathy: Also in the frontal lobe region of the brain lies the system of mirror neurons. Mirror neurons are brain cells which are activated when a person does something, feels an emotion or thinks a thought. But they are also activated when that person observes someone else doing something, feeling an emotion or thinking a thought. This provides the person with the ability to understand what the other person is doing, feeling or thinking and enables the sense of empathy with that other person. It is the basis for intuition and emotional intelligence. It enables us to empathise with another's suffering and may also be the basis for morality.

Mirror cells were first discovered by accident in monkeys in 1995 by Giacomo Rizzolatti at the University of Parma, whilst he was experimenting on them. Rizzolatti had implanted electrodes in their pre-motor cortices, which were being used to measure their nerve cell activity when they picked up food. During a lull in the experiments one of the experimenters picked up some of the monkey's food and ate it himself with the monkey watching, but not eating. The equipment registered activity in the same cortical cells of the monkey as it did when the monkey was picking up the food himself. Further experiments were conducted and mirror cells were discovered in monkeys.[7] This not only was the discovery of the root of empathy but it also demonstrated that monkeys can empathise! I wonder how the equipment would have registered if the experimenters had plugged the electrodes into their own brains?

Neurotransmitters and Moods: Moods are created in the brain by different neurotransmitters or brain chemicals. The main ones include serotonin, which creates moods of serenity and optimism; enkaphalins and endorphins, which reduce stress and create a feeling of calm; oxytocin, which creates a sense of oneness with others and feelings of warmth and trust and is produced during sex and childbirth; dopamine, which generates feelings of desire, anticipation and excitement to motivate us into action and which creates the feeling of meaning in our lives; and noradrenaline, which creates heightened moods.[8] Changes in the balances of these neurotransmitters affect our moods and drives and determine whether we are happy, depressed or manic. Depression or mania can, to some extent, be treated with drugs that alter the balances of these chemicals in the brain.

Left and Right Hemispheres: The most striking thing about the neocortex is that it is divided into two separate hemispheres, which are connected by an organ called the *corpus callosum,* through which each hemisphere communicates with the other. Each hemisphere has separate functions, but they work together, one acting as a checker and balancer of the other. Research conducted during the 1960s by Roger Sperry of the California Institute of Technology suggests that the two hemispheres behave differently to each other.[9] The left hemisphere processes information sequentially and the right hemisphere processes information simultaneously.

Scientists believe that, in right-handed people, the *left hemisphere* is largely responsible for rational thought and critical thinking, whilst the *right hemisphere* is largely responsible for creativity and intuition. The left hemisphere generally controls such things as logic, language and writing, whilst the right hemisphere generally controls such things as music, poetry and art. The right hemisphere is good at grasping wholes, while the left hemisphere likes detail. This could be explained by the different physical structure of the two hemispheres. The left hemisphere is made up of more grey matter than the right hemisphere, which is made up of more white matter than the left hemisphere. The axons in the right brain are longer than those in the left brain, which means that they connect neurons that are, on average, further away from each other. The right brain is better equipped to draw on several different brain modules at the same time, which is why it is better at lateral thinking.[10] However, it has been discovered that, in the case of left handed individuals, some of these functions may be reversed. Also, parts of the brain are capable of taking over the functions of other parts of the brain if they become damaged, so there is flexibility in the system.

Great insights, it is suggested, originate from the intuitive right hemisphere. This can give people their Eureka moments. It has been suggested that when one is analysing a problem, the left hemisphere is working by processing the information in sequence. When you stop analysing the problem and go away and do something else, the right hemisphere sometimes takes over and, because it is capable of processing information simultaneously, can come up with the answer. The experience of the thinker when this happens may be one of surprise and exhilaration.

Such resolutions of problems sometimes occur in dreams. The human brain has three common states; awake, the dream-state and dreamless sleep. Scientists have suggested that in the dream-state, while the conscious mind is suppressed, the unconscious mind continues to function, which sometimes results in the solution to a problem or the awareness of new insights.

In a balanced personality, both hemispheres are operating and co-operating with each other. The scientist Dr. Carl Sagan said in his book *The Dragons of Eden,*

> *'There is no way to tell whether the patterns extracted by the right hemisphere are real or imagined without subjecting them to left-hemisphere scrutiny. On the other hand, mere critical thinking, without creative and intuitive insights, without the search for new patterns, is sterile and doomed. To solve complex problems in changing circumstances requires the activity of both cerebral hemispheres: the path to the future lies through the corpus callosum'.*[11]

The balanced personality may be the result of millions of years of natural selection. Both creativity, in responding to a changing environment, and the rational analysis of a problem are required in order to survive. Therefore natural selection should favour a balanced personality. But as we mentioned above, the trillions of different possible states of the mind, arising from the multitude of synapses, ensures that no two individuals are the same. Everyone will have a different balance between the two hemispheres, some may lean more to the left and others may lean more to the right. Some people are more rational and less sensitive than others and very often the rational people and the sensitive people disagree with each other. Sometimes this disagreement can be quite strong as they find it difficult to see the other's point of view. Perhaps a little pluralism is required here. And perhaps we need a little more self-awareness of any left or right hemisphere bias in our personalities and should make positive efforts to counter that bias. As well as there being differences between individuals, animals are often internally inconsistent within themselves, swinging between a left bias and a right bias depending on their mood. Socrates described our minds as being like a chariot with two horses, one black and one white, pulling in different directions with a weak charioteer in control.

Brain Redundancy: It could be argued that if we were to design an animal brain from scratch we would not come up with anything like the animal brain that we see today, which was the product of millions of years of evolution. Such a designed brain would have logically coherent parts and no redundancy. Evolution gave us a brain that was developed by the gradual addition of many separate new parts. At the same time the older parts were never discarded but continued to be used alongside the new parts and were never considered obsolete. Thus we flit between the very old fish and reptilian areas of the brain and the newer areas of the frontal lobes of the neocortex. The result is a very complicated and often unpredictable and emotional animal.

Brain Centres of Compassion: But if we need to use our complex brains, with all their hereditary baggage, to override our selfish genes in order to develop compassion, how are we to achieve this? Compassion is a complex, positive emotion. It is not part of the wild emotions that reside deep in our limbic systems that cause us to lose control of our rationality. Rather, it is an emotion that we can rationally control. To develop compassion we should aim to balance the left and the right hemispheres of the neocortex. Our positive emotions of unconditional love should be encouraged to rise up in our right hemispheres, checked by the rationality of our left hemisphere to ensure that such love does not turn into jealous, possessive love or lose its position to negative emotions such as hate or envy.

Differences between the Human Brain and the Brains of Other Animals

It is clear that the human brain shared the same evolutionary path as the brains of other animals and shares the same structures as they do, but many humans still perceive their brains to be superior to those of other animals. What differences could have developed in the human brain in recent evolutionary history that could justify such a prejudice? In *Dragons of Eden* Sagan examines the evolution of the brain and tries to determine where the rubicon exists between the mental state that we call *animal* and the mental state that we call *humanity*. He examines the evolution of the human brain by making comparisons with our evolutionary ancestors and cousins, relating to both the overall size of the brain and the ratio of brain weight to body weight. He compares these to modern man, *Homo Sapiens*, who has a brain volume of 1,100cc – 2,200cc and a body to brain ratio of 45.

Australopithecus Africanus: one of our earliest ancestors was Australopithecus Africanus or the 'Gracile Australopithecine'. The earliest known specimen lived around six million years ago and was an imperfect biped with a slight forehead, who used stone and bone tools. He stood between 1 metre to 1.25 metres tall, weighed between 20kgs – 30kgs and had a brain volume of between 430cc – 600cc, giving him a body to brain weight ratio of 50.

Australopithecus Robustus: related to him, but evolving much later at around 3.5 million years ago, was the stronger and heavier Australopithecus Robustus, who was also an imperfect biped but who had a low forehead and was not known to have used tools. He was 1.5 metres tall, weighed around 40kg - 60kg and had a brain volume of 500cc – 550cc, giving him a body to brain ratio of 90.

Homo Habilis: around 3.7 million years ago the first Homo Habilis emerged. He was completely bipedal, had a high forehead and used stone tools and possibly constructed buildings. He stood between 1.2 metres – 1.4 metres tall and weighed around 30kgs – 50kgs. He had a brain volume of 500cc – 800cc, giving him a body to brain ratio of 60. It is possible that both Australopithecus Robustus and Homo Habilis both evolved from the earlier Autralopithecus Africanus. Both were different and only Homo Habilis has been identified by us as being 'Human' by being given the name 'Homo'.

Homo Erectus: around 1.5 million years ago Homo Erectus emerged. Like Homo Habilis he was completely bipedal, had a high forehead and used stone tools. He is also credited with the discovery of fire. He stood 1.4 metres – 1.8 metres tall, weighed around 40kgs – 80kgs and had a brain capacity of 750cc – 1,250cc, giving him a body to brain ratio of 65.

Great Ape Body to Brain Ratios

Species	Height	Weight	Brain capacity	Ratio – Body to Brain Weight
Australopithecus Africanus	1.0m – 1.25m	20kgs– 30kgs	430cc – 600cc	50
Australopithecus Robustus	1.5m	40kgs – 50kgs	500cc – 550cc	90
Homo Habilis	1.2m – 1.4m	30kgs – 60kgs	500cc – 800cc	60
Homo Erectus	1.4m – 1.8m	40kgs – 80kgs	750cc–1,250cc	65
Homo Sapiens	1.4m – 2.0m	40kgs – 100kgs	1,100cc-2,200cc	45

It is clear from the body to brain ratios that there was little difference between the Gracile Australopithecines (50), Homo Habilis (60), Homo Erectus (65) and modern man, Homo Sapiens (45). They are all bipedal tool users. It is assumed that the growth in brain size is directly related to tool using and walking upright. Charles Darwin suggested that tool making was both the cause and effect of walking upright. One could not be said to have caused the other and both were dependent on the other. Walking upright freed the hands for tool making and the use of tools encouraged walking upright. We saw earlier, when discussing the anatomy of the brain, that the frontal lobes of the neocortex played a part in enabling man to stand upright. So too did the shape of his spine, which unlike any other animal, has four curves, enabling the vertebrae to stack up on top of one another, while the body is in the vertical position.

Homo Sapiens has demonstrated abilities and achievements that exceed those of the other species, but if the ratio of body weight to brain weight are similar, the difference must be in the size of the brain. The Homo Sapiens' brain of 1,100cc – 2,200cc is almost twice the size of the brain of Homo Erectus, which was 750cc – 1,250cc. Humans are the only animals known to experience pain in childbirth, due to the size of the baby's head. In the story of The Garden of Eden in Genesis, the punishment for man for eating the fruit from the tree of knowledge of good and evil was to suffer pain in childbirth. Understanding of the difference between good and evil is an abstract concept that resides in the frontal lobes of the neocortex and enables man to make moral judgements.

The Scottish anatomist and anthropologist, Sir Arthur Keith (1866 – 1955), proposed a rubicon in the evolution of the human brain, suggesting that uniquely human qualities begin to emerge in a brain of around 750cc, which would include Homo Erectus. Chimpanzees have an average brain volume of 400cc and a gorilla has an average brain volume of 500cc, which is not far behind this rubicon.

How then do we account for the much larger sizes of the brains of whales, dolphins or elephants when we measure 'human' qualities? But size alone might not be the only relevant factor. Specific developments in the frontal, temporal and parietal lobes may also have a bearing on 'human' qualities. So too may the large number of neural connections or synapses in the brain. Clearly we have to examine all of the four factors of the brain discussed above when we attempt to determine 'humanness', i.e. the overall size of the brain, the ratio of body weight to brain weight, the structure of the lobes in the neocortex and the quantity of synapses.[12]   In the end, any differences were summed up perfectly by Charles Darwin, when he said in *The Descent of Man*,

> *'The difference in mind between man and the higher animals, great as it is, certainly is one of degree and not of kind'.*[13]

Therefore our brief overview of the evolution and structure of the brain in this chapter raises two key issues in our quest to understand compassion. The first is that we need to use our brains to develop compassion. This is because our genes are basically selfish and we have been naturally selected as selfish beings in order to survive, although such survival included parental care and co-operation within our social in-groups. But compassion and altruism requires more than this. It requires us to assist individuals outside of our in-group, possibly at some cost to ourselves. Richard Dawkins showed us that such behaviour is not determined biologically, but that our brains can override our selfish genes and we can learn to be compassionate. Compassion is a positive emotion that can be nurtured, but this requires the control by the frontal lobes of the neocortex over the emotions that arise in the hypothalamus and the balanced development of the left and right hemispheres of the neocortex.

The second key issue raised by our review of the evolution and structure of the brain is the comparison between the human brain and the brains of other animals. Human brains shared most of their evolutionary history with those of other animals. Whilst human brains may be bigger than most, but not all, other animal species' brains and whilst humans generally have a larger brain to body mass ratio, human brains are different *only in degree and not in kind* to most other animal brains. Thus there is little justification for the prejudice shown by man against other animals.

15

THE MINDS OF ANIMALS

'We have seen that the senses and intuitions,
the various emotions and faculties,
such as love, memory, attention and curiosity,
imitation, reason, etc., of which man boasts,
may be found in an incipient,
or even sometimes in a well-developed condition,
in the lower animals.'

Charles Darwin – The Descent of Man

If we have shared our evolutionary path with other animals and have evolved similar physiologies and brain structures to them, as demonstrated in the previous two chapters, surely it follows that we must share both our intelligence and our emotional lives with them also? In chapter 10 we showed that, although Jeremy Bentham had said in 1789, *'The question is not, can they reason? Nor, can they talk? But can they <u>suffer</u>?'* some animals, such as chimpanzees, *can* reason and talk. By using sign language chimpanzees can develop quite complex vocabularies. Many animals, such as primates and corvids, can use tools and demonstrate complex problem solving abilities and one chimpanzee was observed to experience a Eureka moment on solving a problem. Other experiments have demonstrated quite complex problem-solving abilities in other species, such as rats who find their way around mazes and remember it.

Animals *Can* Reason and Talk
The question of whether primates can communicate has been demonstrated by a series of studies. The first serious research was conducted by *Alfred Russel Wallace*, the co-discoverer of evolution

by natural selection, whilst working with orang-utans in Indonesia. He concluded that orang utans behaved exactly like a human child in similar circumstances and displayed similar facial expressions.

At the University of Nevada, *Beattrice and Robert Gardner*, realised that the pharynx and larynx of a chimpanzee were not suitable for speech and looked for a form of symbolic language that could employ the strengths rather than the weaknesses of the chimpanzee anatomy. They recognised the immense dexterity of their chimpanzees and decided to teach them sign language, known as Ameslan. In a short space of time Washoe, Lucy, Lana and other chimpanzees were signing and using a vocabulary of between 100 and 200 words. By comparison, the human vocabulary comprises some 1,000 commonly used words. They also started to invent new words and phrases. For example, when Lana was introduced to an orange for the first time she signed for the colour orange and for apple, i.e. orange apple. A New York Times reporter was very moved by his experience of meeting the chimpanzees. Born to deaf and dumb parents, the first language he was taught was sign language. When he met the chimpanzees he was deeply moved and said, 'suddenly I realised that I was conversing with a member of another species in my native tongue.' – or in his native hand![1]

Chimpanzees have also proved their abilities at solving problems. At a research station on Tenerife, a chimpanzee named Sultan was observed by Wolfgang Kohler connecting rods together to reach an otherwise inaccessible banana. We have already mentioned the chimpanzee, reported by *Konrad Lorenz*, who appeared to experience a Eureka moment when he worked out that he could reach a banana that was hanging up just beyond his reach if he brought a box over to where the banana was hanging and stood on it.[2]

Primatologist *Jane Goodall* reported chimps using tools in the form of twigs to extract termites from their nest to eat. In addition mother chimps were teaching their babies how to do this. Cultural differences have emerged in the way groups of primates behave. For example one group of monkeys may know how to eat birds eggs and the neighbouring group may not. In another observation macaques were observed trying to pick grains out of the sand to eat, which was a very laborious process. One macaque learned to throw a handful of grains and sand in the water and exploited the fact that the sand sank whilst the grain floated, thus separating the grain and making it easier to eat. Other young macaques worked out how to copy this behaviour, although the older ones were less willing to learn. After a few generations all the macaques in the group were separating the grain from the sand in this way.

In his book 'The Dragons of Eden' *Carl Sagan* examines the evolution of intelligence and includes a review of the various studies on the intelligence of our nearest relative the chimpanzee. He concludes,

> *'The cognitive abilities of chimpanzees force us, I think, to raise searching questions about the boundaries of the community of beings to which special ethical considerations are due, and can, I hope, help to extend our ethical perspectives downward through the taxa on earth and upwards to extraterrestrial organisms, if they exist.'*[3]

Having demonstrated that chimpanzees can both talk and reason, Sagan writes,

> *'If chimpanzees have consciousness, if they are capable of abstractions, do they not have what until now has been described as "human rights"? How smart does a chimpanzee have to be, before killing him constitutes murder? What further properties must he show before religious missionaries must consider him worthy of attempts at conversion?'*[4]

Cognitive Ethology
In addition to intelligence, what about *emotions* that have developed during the earlier stages of the evolution of the brain and can be found in the deeper limbic system? If humans have emotions, surely some other animals must have them too? If evolution required cooperation, in order to survive, then surely all animals who evolved in a cooperative environment will demonstrate the behavioural outcomes of such cooperation? If humans can be loving, such other animals should be too. If

humans can have morals and show compassion, then is it not possible that other species do so?

Cognitive ethology is the scientific study of the mental and emotional lives of animals. These studies demonstrate that many species have complex thoughts and rich emotional lives. In his book *The Age of Empathy: Nature's Lessons for a Kinder Society,* Frans De Waal explains that empathetic behaviour is not a recent, easily shed virtue, but an ancient part of our biology, whose beginnings can be traced far further back in evolutionary time than to just our primitive cousins. In fact empathy, like a Russian doll, is multi-layered. Cognitive ethologist, Marc Bekoff says,

> *'Arguments that ignore evolutionary relationships and continuity are bad biology and result in the establishment of false boundaries that have dire consequences for species deemed lower than others.'*[5]

Animal Cooperation

In the original Darwinian approach to evolution, where the most successful species were those who followed the rules of survival of the fittest, the concept of *competition* was dominant, i.e. competition for food, for space and for sex. However, the cognitive ethologists recognise that, equally important, if not more important, to successful survival was the concept of *cooperation*. Animals who lived in social groups were better able to defend themselves from attackers and could share responsibilities for hunting and gathering and for child care.

Ethologists have developed two widely accepted explanations for the cooperative and selfless behaviour shown by animals, including humans. The first is *kin selection*, which was proposed by evolutionary biologist William Hamilton in 1964. This suggests that by helping one's own kin relatives, one is indirectly investing in one's own genes. Many studies have shown that individuals will sacrifice immediate self-interests to benefit close relatives. But there are also many examples of animals acting compassionately to others who are not their own kin. This is the second theory of selfless behaviour, known as *reciprocal altruism*, which was developed by the evolutionary biologist Robert Trivers in 1971.[6]

There are many examples of reciprocal altruism where animals share food with others. Jane Goodall reported it in chimpanzees in the 1970s and after that researchers reported food sharing in baboons, naked mole rats, jackdaws, capuchin monkeys and vampire bats. Another example of reciprocal altruism is where animals, such as meerkats and Canada geese, stand on sentry duty to protect the group. The raising of another animals' young is another example, as researches on elephants, dolphins, wild dogs, fruit bats and marmosets have shown, where animals take on responsibility for orphans. Also many females act as midwives while another female gives birth.[7]

Animal Morality

In order to live successfully in a society you have to adhere to certain rules of behaviour and these constitute *morals*. Such morals are not necessarily the same as our morals and, indeed, different species may require different sets of morals, relevant to their own circumstances. In their book *Wild Justice: The Moral Lives of Animals* Marc Bekoff and Jessica Pierce demonstrate that animals, like humans, have morals. They define morality as 'an evolutionary adaptation to social living'.

Not all animals may abide by the rules of their morality. As with humans, there are bad guys as well as good guys and there may even be a criminal element. Animal societies often have rules for dealing with those members of their societies who contravene what is viewed as acceptable behaviour. Commonly, such members are ostracised from the group.

Animal Emotions

In addition to having morals, animals have emotions and these are beautifully described by Jonathan Balcombe in his book *Second Nature: The Inner Lives of Animals.*

Animals display negative emotions such as fear, anxiety, depression and grief. We are all familiar with monkeys who rock from side to side when held captive without sufficient mental stimulation, due to boredom and frustration. But in one experiment, described in Balcombe's book, starlings, who are social and inquisitive by nature, were also shown to demonstrate repetitive behaviour patterns and higher levels of the stress hormone corticosterone, when confined alone in small cages.[8]

Emotional fever has been demonstrated during research in rats, lizards and turtles, where the body temperature rises as a result of stressful situations. This is much the same as when humans blush and show an increase in body temperature when under stress. It was demonstrated when the animals were being handled by strangers. Once the animal had got used to the handler and knew them to be friendly, the temperature rise stopped occurring, but when a new unfamiliar handler came along, they experienced the rise in temperature again.[9]

Animals show grief and experience bereavement. Studies of baboon behaviour in Botswana have shown that mothers grieve the loss of a child and that their levels of glucocorticoid hormones rise for several weeks, as they do in human mothers who lose a child. Close family members and friends show similar hormonal changes in proportion to their social connection to her. Like humans, baboons have coping methods, such as expanding their social networks and engaging in more grooming activity.[10]

Elephants are very emotional animals and have been observed to cradle their dead relative's bones in their trunks and shed tears. In Zimbabwe a group of three elephants lived near the Imire Safari Ranch owned by the Travers family, where three adult Rhinos were kept for protection against poaching. The elephants lived just outside the ranch because they felt safe there and often accompanied the rhinos. One tragic night, four members of the army attacked the ranch, tied up the guards and shot the three rhinos, leaving a baby rhino orphaned. They then hacked off what was left of their horns, the rhinos having previously been dehorned in order to protect them. After the rhinos had been buried, the elephants visited the burial site and wept, and one of the screaming elephants tried to dig out a buried rhino who had been her friend.[11]

In other stories told by Jonathan Balcombe in *Second Nature: The Inner Lives of Animals*, Bison mourned the death of one of their number who was shot in Yellowstone Park and a Zebra mourned the death of his son, returning four times to his dead body and repeatedly trying to rouse him. Observers have noted that dairy cows remain distressed for days when their new-born calves are taken away from them prematurely. This is done on a massive scale to billions of cows and their calves in order for the cow to produce milk for humans rather than for her calf, as nature intended.

Owners of domestic animals, not only cats and dogs, are only too aware of the emotional capacities of their pets, showing love and loyalty, distress in stressful situations, such as visits to the vets or the boarding kennels, and also separation anxiety. They show excitement at positive things such as the prospect of a walk and guilt when they know they have wrong, such as damaging the furniture.

Animal Compassion and Altruism

There have been many studies which demonstrate that animals not only show the emotions of friendship and cooperation, of stress and grief, but also of compassion to others. For example, research has shown that monkeys will go for days without food rather than give a painful shock to another monkey.

Elephants often come to the assistance of others. In Kenya's Samburu reserve one female elephant, Grace went to the aid of another female elephant, Eleanor who had fallen down, even though she was from another group of elephants. Grace tried to help Eleanor up by using her tusks and foot. Unfortunately, Eleanor fell again and soon died. During the following weeks, elephants from five different family units visited the body. A team, led by the Douglas-Hamiltons to study them, concluded that elephants show compassion towards one another and have an awareness of death.[12]

Elephants also feel regret. After a tragic incident at the Elephant Sanctuary in Tenesee, an elephant called Winkie, accidentally knocked one of his human carers over and trod on her, killing her. Winkie was depressed for weeks.[13]

Dolphins have been reported to protect humans against shark attack by surrounding them until the danger has passed, even though the human is a complete stranger. Such a dramatic experience is described by Leah Lemieux in her moving book *Rekindling the Waters: The Truth About Swimming with Dolphins.* Dolphins show not only tremendous parental instincts and in-group co-operation, they not only demonstrate considerable social skills, but they also, in such examples, show highly advanced levels of altruism.

There have been many stories of unusual animal cross-species friendships. Examples include the 130 year-old tortoise who lived at Haller park sanctuary in Mombasa who became the surrogate mother to Owen, a two year-old hippopotamus who was brought to the sanctuary after he was orphaned in the 2004 Indian Ocean tsunami. At the Kenya Wildlife Service Orphanage in Nairobi a seven month old baboon named Gakii was reported to have adopted a three month-old bush baby. There are many stories of inter-species surrogate mothers, where a mother who has lost her infant and is strongly driven hormonally to behave as a mother takes on and often milk-nurses orphans from another species. Examples have included a German Shepherd who adopted some Bengal tiger cubs, a Chihuahua who adopted a baby marmoset, and a cat in Japan, named Hiroko, who, after losing her kittens and being left in a room with a pair of suck eggs, hatched the eggs and mothered the ducklings.[14] For further beautiful examples of such relationships, see the *Unlikely Friendships* series of books.

Animal Creativity and Art

The ability to be creative and artistic is something that we think of as a purely human attribute. It demonstrates the highest capacity for consciousness and cognitive abilities. But what if other animals demonstrated an artistic ability? Wouldn't we have to acknowledge their higher cognitive abilities too? At the *Asian Elephant Art and Conservation Project (AEACP)* in Thailand, elephants have been taught to paint and they have an ability to paint beautifully.

Traditionally the elephants had been used in the logging industry but, with most of the forests destroyed, the elephants were left redundant and had no home to return to. The charity AEACP rescued the elephants and, without the space to keep them fully stimulated and occupied, taught them to paint. The elephants held the paint brush with their trunk. Some elephants eagerly took to painting and were encouraged, while others preferred not to paint and were left to do their own things. The elephants who wanted to paint were taught through positive reinforcement techniques and were praised and encouraged. Such elephants continued to hone their skills and develop their own personal style. Two types of art emerged, abstract expressionism and figural works, such as flowers and self-portraits. The paintings then began to sell and raise funds for the charity. Here is a clear example of animals being creative and artistic.[15]

A Sixth Sense

Many animals demonstrate abilities that are beyond the experience of the human being, some we can explain and others we cannot. These include, for example, the homing abilities of pigeons, the ability of salmon to swim across an ocean and return to the place where they originally spawned and the migration of birds who, having flown thousands of miles, return to the same place every year, knowing both when and where to migrate to. There are stories of cats and dogs, too, who travel long journeys to return home. Some are even known to go and find their owner who has left home. One remarkable story is that of Prince, an Irish terrier in World War 1. In August 1914 Prince's owner, Private Brown, left his home in Hammersmith to go to Flanders with his battalion, leaving Prince at home with his wife. In late September 1914 Prince went missing. A few weeks later he turned up in the trenches in Flanders and found Private Brown. The only possible explanation was that Prince must have got in with some troops and crossed over the Channel with them, but how he knew where to go or how to find his master is currently a mystery.[16]

Another wonder of nature is the spectacle of a flock of starlings flying in formation. In the same instant they all change direction and they don't all bump into each other. How do they know when and in what direction to turn? Some shoals of fish do the same thing. There are guide dogs that are trained to tell their owners when the owner is about to have an epileptic fit and, in some parts of the world, people look at the behaviour of snakes, to predict an earthquake.

Wildebeests in Kenya have a mysterious ability to detect rainfall thirty miles away and use this ability to move to greener pastures. Many trees have produced a swamp-or-starve strategy to deter seed predators, where they produce very few seeds most years and then, one year, produce many. Squirrels have developed a sense to detect when trees are going to do this and they interrupt the weaning of their first litter of pups and produce another litter ahead of the impending food surplus. It is not known how squirrels know when to do this. Howler monkeys know when there is about to be a storm and howl and mangabey monkeys rely on their memory of recent patterns of temperature and solar radiation to decide whether or not to travel to a particular patch of fruit. Estaurine crocodiles have an amazing long-distance homing ability. In one study of them, a crocodile was shipped 250 miles from his home and he managed to return there within three weeks.[17]

In his book *Dogs That Know When Their Owners Are Coming Home: The Unexplained Powers of Animals* Rupert Sheldrake investigates the unexplained abilities of animals. These include psychic connections with those close to them, such as pets and their owners (telepathy), premonitions about events (precognition) and long-distance homing abilities (sense of direction). He gives examples from his extensive research.

In one case a midwife and social worker in Norway, who worked odd hours and would return home at irregular times, was always greeted by her husband with a cup of tea. Her husband always knew when she was coming home because their dog, Tiki, would rush to the window and stand on the windowsill, with sufficient time between when Tiki first sensed his mistress' return and her actual return, for the husband to get the kettle on and make the tea.

In another example a woman would always know when it was her husband ringing her on the telephone rather than anyone else as, whenever it was her husband that rang, their cat Whiskins would rush to the telephone and paw at the receiver. Often he would knock the receiver off the hook and meow at the husband. Whenever anyone else phoned, Whiskins showed no interest.

A woman in England moved house and took her horses, Badger and Tango with her. A few weeks after the move, the gate was blown open in a storm and the two horses left their field and returned to their old home over nine miles away on a route they had never taken before.

On 17 October 1989 a woman in Santa Cruz was amazed when her cat ran up into the attic to hide, which she had never done before. She was terrified and would not come down. Three hours later the Loma Prieta earthquake struck, devastating the centre of Santa Cruz.

My own father tells the tale of how he returned home at the end of the Second World War, after four years away in Burma. As he turned into the road in which he lived, his dog Bruno, a black Labrador, came running down the street to greet him, excited and wagging his tail. Not only had Bruno remembered my father after four years separation, but he somehow knew when he was returning home.

Sheldrake tested these reports, during his research, with computers and video cameras, recording the behaviour of the animals reported to him by their owners. He has collected a significant amount of data on the subject. He concludes that, as yet, there is no scientific explanation for this, but proposes the hypothesis of *morphic fields* and suggests that further scientific studies should be undertaken into them. Morphic fields, Sheldrake proposes, are fields, like gravity and electromagnetic fields that exert influence over long distances and are particularly strong between animals (including humans) where strong bonds have been formed. Morphic fields are examined in more detail in chapter 18. Sheldrake suggests that humans may have been able to sense these, but have lost their ability to tune into them during their evolutionary development, as humans developed language and reasoning instead.[18]

Such insights into the minds of animals, who have shared their evolutionary development with us, leads us on to examine that deepest of all mysteries – consciousness.

PART 4

CONSCIOUSNESS

16

STUDIES IN CONSCIOUSNESS

'The establishment of the common origin of all species
logically involves a readjustment of altruistic morals,
by enlarging the application of what has been called
the <u>Golden Rule</u>
from the area of mere mankind to that of
the whole animal kingdom'.

Thomas Hardy - letter to The Humanitarian in 1910

One cannot stop at considering the evolution and functioning of the brain and the nervous system without going on to consider the most remarkable brain function of all – consciousness. What is it and how does it work? What purpose does it serve that evolution should select in favour of it? Who do we share the phenomenon of consciousness with, both on this planet and within the entire Cosmos? Was consciousness a prerequisite of the Universe, destined to be from the beginning of time?

Consciousness Studies
Despite considerable research on consciousness, science has not yet found a conclusive theory or explanation for it. There have been considerable discoveries concerning the functioning of the brain, in terms of which parts of the brain are responsible for which activities and there have been many theories on consciousness, but there have been no real scientific conclusions on what consciousness is or how it works. As the physicist and mathematician Roger Penrose says in his book, *The Emperor's New Mind,*

'The phenomenon of consciousness cannot be accommodated within the framework of present-day physical theory'.

Science has made some amazing discoveries about the working of sub-atomic particles and the creation of the Universe, but it hasn't even touched on the subject of consciousness. Scientists have formulated detailed theories about the first three minutes of the creation of the Universe after the big bang, but have no explanation of what came before the big bang. They do not even know if the concept of 'before the big bang' is a meaningful one. At that point they have reached the boundary of current scientific endeavour. In the same way, whilst detailed studies have been made of the brain, an understanding of consciousness seems to lie beyond the boundary of what current science can tell us. Surely understanding consciousness must therefore be the most exciting scientific endeavour of our time?

In her book *Conversations on Consciousness* Susan Blackmore interviewed twenty-one leading philosophers and scientists who were experts in consciousness, in order to find an answer to the question of what consciousness is. She asked questions such as,

'Why is consciousness such a special and difficult issue for twenty-first century science?' and

'How does the subjective experiences we call consciousness arise from the physical brain?' and

'Can zombies – people who behave outwardly just like others but have no inner mental life – exist?'

Her conclusions were that, even amongst the experts in the field, there was very little agreement, the whole field was utterly confusing and there was almost no unanimity in the answers she received.[1]

Socrates was one of the first philosophers to investigate consciousness in around 420 BCE. He saw consciousness as man's true self or 'Nous' which comes from the soul or 'Psyche'. It is the faculty of intuitive insight, which allows man to distinguish between good and evil and to choose good. For Socrates the aim of life was to nurture the psyche, by attaining knowledge of the self. This theory was known as '*dualism*' as it emphasised the dual existence of the body and the soul. The body resided in the physical world, while the consciousness resided separately in a non-physical world.

Later Socrates' student Plato expanded on this theory and emphasised the importance of the interaction between the body and the psyche. He argued that the body influences the soul through the senses, informing it of the nature of the outside world. The soul provides man with the method of making sense of the world and relating to it through the operation of reason. This theory became known as '*dualist interactionism*'. The body inhabits the material world and its sensations provide the soul with information about that world's ever-changing appearances. But these appearances are mere reflections of the unchanging patterns or universal forms that underlie the structure of the world. Both the forms and the soul live in a world of the underlying structures, known as the Platonic Realm. Just as Plato's mathematical truths lived in this realm of ideas, so too did the soul. And for Socrates and Plato consciousness was the soul.

The theory of *dualist-interactionism* was further developed by the seventeenth century French philosopher Réné Descartes, during a time when the intellectual climate was dominated by the opinion that the material Universe was nothing more than insensate corpuscles or atoms. Descartes believed that the bodies and brains of humans and animals could be nothing more than machines, whose operations were determined purely by mechanical principles. But whereas animals and machines had no soul, man, Descartes proposed, had two distinguishing faculties that made him superior to animals and machines. These faculties were language and reason, and because man had these abilities he had consciousness and therefore a soul.[2]

These philosophers saw the Universe as being split into two separate realms; the material Universe, which was filled with physical stuff, which had a location in space and time and the non-material Universe or spirit world, which was filled with thinking stuff, which had no location in space. Others took a more

183

rationalist view, known as '*monism*', and saw consciousness as just a part of the physical functioning of the brain, which existed only in the material world. They saw brain purely as a complex network of neurons and synapses, through which electrical and chemical stimuli pass, creating what we know as consciousness. The details of how consciousness comes to life from this physical system were and are still not understood. The nearest analogy for consciousness was proposed by neuropsychologist and author Richard Gregory. He likened it to the creation of electricity when a piece of copper wire is coiled around a moving magnet, (or conversely, the creation of magnetism when electricity is passed through a piece of coiled copper wire). The materialists propose that there is something in the layout of the brain structure that, although not understood, generates consciousness.[3]

A number of further questions arise. When does consciousness start? Does it suddenly switch on when the brain attains a certain level of development or does it stir gradually through various levels of sleep? At which point in the evolution of life did consciousness first appear? At which point in the development of a foetus does consciousness first appear? What is the lowest form of life today that exhibits signs of consciousness? These questions raise profound ethical implications on a range of issues including abortion and animal welfare. Any form of life that is conscious has the potential to suffer and therefore should deserve our protection. Where there is doubt about the level of consciousness experienced by a living being, surely that living being should always be given the benefit of the doubt? We should assume that the being is conscious, can suffer and therefore should be protected.

The Seat of Consciousness
Where in the brain is the seat of consciousness? Studies have demonstrated that the conscious waking state depends on quite a small and specific part of the brain in both humans and animals. Researches conducted by Moruzzi and Magoun in 1949 and Bogen in 1995 have demonstrated that the waking state can be abolished in all animals by a very small lesion in one of two places. The first involves a lesion of less than one cubic centimetre in the brainstem reticular formation, which is an area concerned with arousal. The

other involves an even smaller bilateral cut in an area known as the intralaminar nuclei of the thalami, which is the gateway for sensory inputs to the cortex and sits on the brainstem. Baars argues that the seat of consciousness lies in these primitive parts of the brain.[4]

Others, such as Bermond, however, argue that consciousness occurs in the cortex and that the reticular formation of the brainstem and intralaminar nuclei of the thalami act as switches to consciousness, so that if they are damaged consciousness is switched off in the cortex. Bermond argues that Baars is wrong to suggest that the primitive areas are where consciousness lies, as he fails to understand their role as switches to consciousness within the cortex. It should be noted, however, that Bermond also argues that animal suffering may only be expected in anthropoid apes![5]

Very large volumes of the cortex can, however, be lost without impairing waking consciousness. In fact an entire hemisphere of the cortex can be removed without loss of consciousness. These studies imply that the seat of consciousness lies in the most primitive part of the brain, the brainstem, a part of the brain shared by all mammals, birds, reptiles and fish. Any other brain material is purely additional to the purpose of consciousness, comprising the peripheral add-ons for doing other intellectual functions. Indeed a bigger and more developed brain may add more intelligence to an animal, but it may not change its level of consciousness.[4]

Some scientists suggest that only the human animal is conscious and it is anthropomorphic to assume that other animals could also be conscious. Indeed large numbers of scientists spend huge amounts of taxpayers money researching into whether or not animals are conscious! They argue that we should not infer that, simply because animals appear to behave in a way that appears to result from conscious thought, they actually experience conscious thought. But such an assumption would require a bizarre event in the recent history of evolution, whereby something happened to humans that had neither happened before in the whole of evolution, nor had happened to any other species, which caused humans to become conscious. Improbable as such a late evolutionary event would be, given that humans have shared the largest part of their evolutionary history with other animals, some scientists argue that this event was language and that language determines consciousness. As no animal other than humans have language, they argue, no other animal can be conscious. This of course requires the assumption that no other animal has language. Just because an animal does not have vocal chords does not mean that it cannot use a language of another sort that we humans have not yet fathomed. But if you need language in order to have consciousness, how do you learn the language? Do you not need to be conscious in order to learn the language in the first place? Are human babies not conscious until they have learned to speak a language? And where does this consciousness start? Is it when the baby has learned the words 'Mama' and 'Papa' or is it at some more developed stage of their linguistic abilities? Clearly the argument that language is necessary for consciousness is nonsense.

Rather than fearing anthropomorphism, is it not more logical to assume that natural selection selected in favour of consciousness at a much earlier stage in the evolutionary process? The flexibility that conscious thought provides for animals to search for food and avoid predators makes conscious thought a likely winner in the natural selection stakes. Consciousness allows for more complex decision making than the simple sensory responses to external stimuli demonstrated by some presumably unconscious beings, such as plants and simple animal life forms, which do not possess a brain and a nervous system. The more complex the decisions that the organism is able to make, the more flexibility it will have for survival. As studies have demonstrated that the seat of consciousness lies in ancient parts of the brain, the argument that mammals, birds, reptiles and fish are conscious would appear to be very strong.

Freewill

As regards conscious decision making, there has been much research and debate into whether there is such a thing as conscious free will at all. Experiments carried out by the neuroscientist Benjamin Libet in 1985 suggested that people do not have freewill, as the conscious decision to take an action comes after the action has been initiated. He tested volunteers, fitted with EEG sensors, who were asked to make voluntary hand movements. He noted that the brain processes required to make the act occurred about half a second before the act, as registered by a fluctuation in neural activity, called a readiness potential (RP). However the volunteers reported making the decision to move their hands about 350 – 400 milliseconds after the brain activity had been registered. Libet discovered that the unconscious brain initiates an action before the conscious brain is told about it. He concluded that the fact that the conscious brain thinks that it has taken the decision to act is an illusion. The result of this, he argues, is that we have no free will.

Many have criticised the experiment and doubted the ability to accurately time the events, although the experiments have been repeated since. I question whether we can compare a decision to make a hand movement, which, whilst not being the same as a reflex action, is a minor decision, with a major life changing decision, such as whether to accept a new job and leave your current position, which requires a significant amount of consideration. Doesn't thinking drift between conscious and unconscious thought all the time? For example, when driving a car one often also listens to some music and thinks about whatever is 'on your mind'. When the driving is simple, such as on an open road, your conscious thought may focus on your 'thinking subject' and the driving may be done unconsciously. When the driving gets tricky, such as the approach to a roundabout, you may take your conscious mind away from your thoughts and concentrate on your driving. When a good piece of music comes on the radio, your conscious thought may follow the music with the driving and the thinking drifting to 'the back of your mind' temporarily. As Freud said, the conscious mind is merely the tip of the iceberg. But whether conscious will is an illusion or not, there is no reason to assume, given the shared evolutionary history, that humans are different from animals in this respect.[6]

Artificial Intelligence
Another fundamental question is, if consciousness can be generated by the systems of the animal brain, can it be created by other systems? Can a silicon system produce consciousness, such as that used in computers? Can artificial intelligence (AI) lead to consciousness? Can robots be given the gift of conscious life? If they can, then this too would raise fundamental ethical questions about the way we treat those computers and robots. Computers

have become very smart. Not only do they perform mathematical problems at a level of complexity and a speed far beyond the abilities of the human brain, but they have also been programmed to solve problems. In 1955 the RAND Corporation in America developed the programming language IPL1 and later IPL2, which enabled computers to express strategies used by humans. From this they produced the 'General Problem Solver' (GPS), a programme for solving logic problems which required strategy. It could play chess and prove theorems. By the early 1980s chess programmes were beating the human chess masters. The programme Chess Champion Mark V not only beat the UK grand master, but also found three solutions to a chess problem that was believed to have only one solution. The chess problem had been printed in newspapers around the world and no human had found the other two solutions. Shortly afterwards, IBM's computer 'Deep Blue' defeated the reigning international chess champion.[7]

Programs have been designed which respond to questions asked by human subjects, who have failed to spot that the 'person' they were conversing with was not human. An early example of this was a psychotherapy program developed by Joseph Weizenbaum of the Massachusetts Institute of Technology (MIT), which fooled the subject into thinking that he was conversing with a human psychologist. Such logic and strategy solving problems are relatively easy to programme into serial, digital computers in a manner that enables the computer to considerably exceed the abilities of the human brain. But there are many functions that the human brain can perform which are not easily programmed into computers. For example, computers have difficulty translating languages because they do this literally and are not sensitive to the nuances. An early computer used for translation proved the point. It was asked to translate the sentence 'Out of sight, out of mind' into Chinese, which it did. When it was asked to translate it back again in to English it produced the phrase 'Invisible Idiot'. Computers also have difficulty in recognising complex patterns such as faces.[8]

But it has been suggested that computers' inabilities to deal with such problems have more to do with the programmers' inabilities to specify their requirements than it has to do with the nature of computers. In order to address these problems it was recognised that programmers would have to design a different architecture for their programmes that would more readily reflect the architecture of the animal brain. More recent systems have been developed to use multi-layered, artificial neural nets whose internal connections are either strengthened or weakened over a learning period, according to pre-set learning rules. This architecture more closely resembles the neural network of the brain than the previous serial systems did. Thus the computer is able to learn from its 'experiences' and as a result, pattern recognition by computers has come on in leaps and bounds. At MIT a robot called *Cog* was developed who was brought up to learn sensory and cognitive skills. He had a 'nervous system' of parallel architecture, which was designed to learn from and interact with the world. He was programmed to learn language rather than be given a databank with a language already programmed into it. He had ears that could differentiate between different human voices and speech synthesis software. He was equipped with a motivation structure, with internally programmed goals and preferences, similar to human desires. After twelve years of learning, Cog had made human-like eye movements and head and neck orientations, he could reach a visual target, detect faces and eyes and play the drums. But he had not learned a language. Sadly, the Cog program was shelved.[9]

But would any of this have meant that Cog would or could attain consciousness? Afterall, intelligence is not the same thing as consciousness. And if he could, how would we know that he was conscious? If he did achieve consciousness, would emotions also arise with it or are these a separate function that would require additional programming? Could such programming give Cog positive emotions whilst sparing him the negative ones? Would Cog have been capable of experiencing compassion? Could Cog have achieved enlightenment and Buddhahood?

Consciousness Studies by Experience

How can we explain consciousness? Some rationalists have argued that it is not scientific to examine it in the first person, i.e. by examining one's own experience of consciousness, but that consciousness must be examined in the third person, by observation of the behaviour of a subject. This has two fundamental flaws. Firstly when the third person examines the results of his experiments, perhaps say from electro-encephalograph (EEG) scans, he too is using his conscious experience of observing the outputs to interpret them. This not only has the same flaws as using first person experience, it is also one step removed from the first person experience and therefore is less likely to be as accurate. The second flaw is that you cannot prove that the third person is conscious except by extrapolation from your own experience of consciousness. It is possible that you are living alone in a world constructed in your own mind, in which the other beings that you think of as conscious, are figments of your imagination. You cannot prove otherwise, you can only assume that because they behave like you do, and you know from your own experience that you are conscious, that they too must be conscious. So the only real understanding of what it is like to be conscious must come from our own experiences.[10]

The Hard Problem

Consciousness expert David Chalmers, who has been Director of the Center of Consciousness Studies at the University of Arizona and Director of Consciousness Studies at the Australian National University in Canberra, split the problem of consciousness into two parts. These are the *easy problem* and the *hard problem*. The easy problem is to understand how the functioning of the brain produces behavioural activities, such as thinking, perceiving and remembering. The hard problem is to understand how the functioning of the brain produces the subjective experience of being conscious. This seems to imply a duality between the physical matter of the brain, its hardware of neurons, synapses and brain tissue, and the non-physical stuff called '*qualia*' or *experiences*.

Many experts believe that there is nothing more to being alive than complex, interrelated biological functions. Therefore once the functions of thinking, perceiving and remembering are understood, there will be nothing left to investigate. David Chalmers and others believe that this alone will not explain consciousness and that this will require further investigation. David Chalmers raises the concept of a zombie, who behaves like an intelligent conscious creature, but who actually has no consciousness. The easy problem would explain such a zombie because his brain functions would determine his behaviour, but the hard problem would not explain him, as he would not be conscious. In such a zombie, the lights would be on, but no-one would be home. Cog was such a zombie. Furthermore, David Chalmers suggests that although science is objective, consciousness is subjective, so consciousness must be explored from the first person perspective.[11]

David Chalmers also suggests that it is wrong to try to find a cause for consciousness and that it is irreducible and fundamental to physics in the same way that space, time, mass or charge are fundamental and irreducible. Stuart Hameroff, who has also been Director of the Center of Consciousness Studies at the University of Arizona, takes a similar view. He suggests that there are two types of explanation for conscious experience. One explanation is '*emergence*' where the brain does a lot of complex information processing which produces something completely different called conscious experience. The other explanation is that consciousness is a *fundamental property* of the Universe, like mass, charge or spin. Both he and Roger Penrose believe that consciousness exists at the lowest level of reality at the Planck scale, the level at which space-time geometry is no longer smooth but quantized or granular. They believe that qualia are embedded as patterns in this fundamental granularity of space-time geometry. Roger Penrose also suggests that Platonic values in mathematics and ethics are embedded there too. Stuart Hameroff suggests that quantum computing occurs in protein structures called 'microtubules' which make up the internal scaffolding of the neurons.[12]

The Self Conscious Universe

A recent theory on consciousness is '*Reflexive Monism*' which consciousness expert, Dr. Max Velmans has proposed in his book *Understanding Consciousness*. It is a *monistic* approach because he believes that the mind and the brain exist in one physical universe, as opposed to the dual universes of Socrates, Plato and Descartes, where the brain exists in the physical world while consciousness exists in the non-physical realm. It is *reflexive* because consciousness is the Universe's way of appreciating itself.

Velmans suggests that self-realisation is the ultimate achievement of the Universe. He says,

> *'Whatever the truth of this may be, who can doubt that our bodies and our experience are an integral part of the Universe? And who can doubt that each one of us has a unique, conscious perspective on the larger Universe of which we are a part? In this sense, we participate in a process whereby the Universe observes itself – and the Universe becomes both the subject and the object of experience. Consciousness and matter are intertwined in mind. Through the evolution of matter, consciousness is given <u>form</u>. And through consciousness, the material Universe is <u>real-ised</u>.'*[13]

The psychologist Carl Jung held a similar view. He realised this when he sat alone in a game reserve outside Nairobi and looked with awe at the dramatic scene before him. He wrote,

> *'We view life as a machine calculated down to the last detail, which along with the human psyche, runs on senselessly, obeying foreknown and predetermined rules. In such a cheerless, clockwork fantasy there is no drama of man, world or God: there is no 'new day' leading to 'new shores', but only the dreariness of calculated process.... Human consciousness created objective existence and meaning, and man found his indispensable place in the great process of being.'*

So Velmans and Jung suggest that the ultimate achievement of the Universe is self-realisation, the evolution of consciousness that is capable of looking back at the Universe and appreciating itself, much as we look inquisitively at ourselves in a mirror. But was this only the natural conclusion of the Universe's evolutionary process, or was consciousness already inherent in the Universe, as a fundamental property, like mass, charge or spin, as Penrose and Hameroff suggest? Is it like the Hindu Brahman? Are conscious beings the offspring of this universal consciousness, looking to be reunited with their parent?

17

THE MYSTERY
AT THE END OF THE UNIVERSE

'If we do discover a complete theory,
it should be in time understandable in broad
principle by everyone.
Then we shall all,
philosophers, scientists and just ordinary people
be able to take part in the discussion
of why the Universe exists.'

Stephen Hawking – A Brief History of Time

In order to understand compassion we need to understand consciousness, and in order to understand consciousness we need to understand the Universe because, as we will later discover, the two are deeply interconnected.

The Problem of Cause and Effect
In the first place, why does the Universe exist? It is most remarkable that the Universe should exist. Surely it would have been much easier for it not to have bothered to come into existence at all! But we know it exists because we are here, living in it and observing it. So where did it come from? Did it have a beginning or has always been here? How can it always have been here? It must have come from somewhere. But if it came from somewhere, if it had a beginning, what came before it and what caused it to come into being?

These questions are impossible to answer from our normal perspective of reasoning and our everyday lives, where we expect all effects to have causes or explanations. For some people the solution to this conundrum is that God created the Universe. But then we are left with the question of where did God come from? The answer provided by the proposers of the God theory is that God just is and that's that! God expects us to believe in him. It is therefore blasphemous to question his existence and that is the end of the story. Others believe that the Universe started with a big bang, but that just leaves us with the question of what caused the big bang and what came before it? Their answer is that there was nothing before the big bang, no space and no time, so it is meaningless to ask such questions. Like the God theory, the big bang just happened and that's that! In our world of cause and effect, neither theory is satisfactory.

Then there is the question of how big the Universe is. Does it have an edge? If it has an edge, what lies beyond the edge and how far does that go on for? If it doesn't have an edge, it must be infinite, but how can anything be infinite? In the opening of his book *A Brief History of Time*, Stephen Hawking likens these conundrums to a charming theory that the world is balanced on a turtle. When the question is asked as to what the turtle is balanced on, the answer is another turtle. Then one must ask what the other turtle is balanced on and one gets the answer that it is balanced on yet another turtle and so on. But then we hit the problem of there being an infinite number of turtles, each supporting the previous one. Or perhaps, like the God theory or the big bang theory, there is a super turtle at the bottom of the tower of turtles, which supports all the rest. In the end we are always hit with two conundrums, 'Does the Universe have an edge or is it infinite?' and 'Does the Universe have a beginning and an end or is it eternal?'.[1]

Classical Theories of the Universe
There have been many scientific theories to explain these conundrums. Originally it was believed that the Universe was infinite and eternal, but that lay beyond our comprehension. Then came the big bang theory, which suggested that the Universe exploded out of a highly dense and minutely small thing called a singularity in a strange quantum event 13.7 billion years ago. There was no need to explain what came before this event as nothing existed before it. Time and space were created as part of

the big bang event and had no prior existence, so it would be meaningless to talk about time and space before this event.

The theory has been supported by the discovery of a cosmic microwave background (CMB) all around us in space, which forms the remnants of the explosion that took place at the time of the big bang.[2] We also observe, from the red shifts in the spectrum of their light, that distant galaxies are rushing away from us, as a result of a huge explosion, consistent with the big bang theory.[3] We are then confronted with the question of whether the Universe will go on expanding indefinitely or whether it will stop expanding and will fall back in on itself. Whichever it is will depend on the amount of matter in the Universe and the gravity that matter exerts. Scientists do not believe that there is enough visible matter to prevent the Universe from expanding indefinitely, but there may be enough invisible 'dark' matter to make the difference. It is the current view that only four percent of the matter in the Universe is visible matter, the remaining 96 percent being both dark matter and dark energy. At the time of writing, the debate as to whether there is enough dark matter in the Universe to cause it to contract still continues and is not conclusive, although the most popular current view is that there is insufficient dark matter and that the Universe will expand indefinitely.[4] If the Universe expands indefinitely we will be faced with a cold, bleak future when the stars burn out and all the stuff in the Universe is so widely distributed that space becomes a very cold, dark and empty place.[5] If the expansion of the Universe slows down sufficiently to start contracting again, it will fall back in on itself until it eventually returns again to a singularity, where the fabric of space and time and all of the laws of physics break down and are no more.

Maybe that will be the end, or maybe the singularity will explode out again in another big bang event to create a new universe. If it does, will that universe be similar to the one we inhabit, or will it be remarkably different, with alternative dimensions of space and time and different laws of physics? This could all depend on the conditions existing in the first few fractions of a second following the big bang.

Some scientists have hypothesised that we live in an *oscillating universe*, which goes through great cycles of expansion and contraction. In this hypothesis the Universe explodes out of a singularity in a big bang event and then expands. When the expansion has slowed down sufficiently the Universe contracts under the force of gravity, until it returns once more to a singularity. Then it goes through the process all over again and keeps repeating it. The theory suggests that we are living in one of many cycles.[6]

Some scientists have suggested that we may live in one of many universes, which exist independently of each other in a *'multiverse'*, and that universes regularly and spontaneously pop out of singularities. Each may be different, due to having slightly different conditions during the first few micro-seconds after their big bangs, which lead to differences in the structures of those universes and their laws of physics. Some may be sterile and doomed, but others may thrive and go on to develop conscious life which observes and reflects on their home universe. Maybe most proto-universes fail in a system of natural selection and we are the product of a rare, maybe unique, universe whose conditions have randomly been just right for the development of conscious life. Among an infinite number of universes ours may be one in which all the conditions happen to be right for life and consciousness.[7]

The Hindus first created the concept of an oscillating universe, believing that the Universe underwent an infinite number of births, deaths and rebirths. Hinduism is also the only religion whose time scales correspond to those of modern cosmology. They estimated that each oscillation of the Universe is represented by a day and a night of Brahma, which extends for 8.64 billion years. This is not as much as that estimated by today's cosmologists, but it is certainly of the same order of magnitude. However there is no guarantee that the time scales used by today's cosmologists are more than ballpark figures. The estimate of the time between now and the big bang of 13.7 billion years has been revised a few times and we certainly have no time scale for the end of the life of the Universe. In Hinduism each day and night of Brahma, each oscillation, is part of a Brahma century, during which Brahma dreams the cosmic dream. At the end of this century Brahma falls into a dreamless sleep, when the Universe dissolves for another hundred Brahma years. Then Brahma stirs and begins to dream of the Universe again for another hundred Brahma years. And so it continues endlessly. The Hindus were also the first to develop the idea of many universes living alongside each other. They believed that there were an infinite number of Brahmas all dreaming their own cosmic dream.[8]

The Hindu creation god Shiva is depicted in a famous image as the Lord of the Dance, representing the creation of the Universe at the beginning of each cosmic cycle. In the upper right hand of Shiva is a drum, which symbolises the sound of creation. In the upper left hand is a tongue of fire, agni, which reminds us that the newly created Universe will one day be destroyed billions of years from now. Shiva stands on the prostrate form of Apasma-rupurusa, the symbol of human ignorance, above a lotus pedestal, the symbol of enlightenment, from which an aureole of fire emanates, representing the rhythm of the Universe.[9]

But even in an oscillating universe, there still remains the nagging question of when and how did all the oscillating start? What *caused* it to start? Was there a first universe that exploded in a big bang, expanded and contracted again into a singularity and started the whole oscillating universe process? If so, what caused this first universe to come into being? Or has there always been an oscillating universe for eternity? Like the turtles supported by other turtles, we still have the problem of where did it all start? Is there a super-turtle at the bottom of the tower of turtles or are there an infinite number of turtles?

Our current method of logic and understanding, which is based on cause and effect and an explanation for every event, breaks down here. But maybe there is a solution. Maybe it is possible for the Universe to be bounded in the past and yet not come into existence abruptly at a singularity. This could be made possible by the theory of quantum cosmology, which is based on the theory of quantum physics.

Quantum Cosmology
The problems of cause and effect resulting from classical theories of the Universe could be resolved by quantum cosmology which is based on quantum physics. Quantum physics applies to the very small micro-world of atoms and sub-atomic particles. It does not apply to the macro-world of things bigger than atoms. In the macro-world the normal laws of physics apply. For example, planets follow Newton's laws of motion. These laws are

deterministic, whereby every cause has an effect and vice versa. In the sub-atomic world of quantum physics things are not deterministic and are uncertain. The theory is based on *Heisenberg's Uncertainty Principle*, which states that all measurable quantities (e.g. position, motion and energy) are subject to unpredictable fluctuations and hence to uncertainty in their value. As a result quantum events are not determined by preceding causes. The outcome of a quantum event is neither known nor knowable, although the probability of an outcome of an event can be calculated.

If you want to predict the future state of a thing, you need to know its position and momentum. In the macro-world position and momentum can be measured and used to calculate the future state of that thing. For example, it is possible to predict the position of a planet at a given time in the future from a knowledge of its present position and momentum. In the quantum world, however, you cannot measure both position and momentum. So you cannot predict the future state of an electron, for example, because if you are certain about its position, you cannot be certain about its momentum and vice versa. In fact the more certainty you have about one condition, the less certainty you have about the other condition. As a result quantum particles can disappear and spontaneously reappear in other parts of the Universe.

Furthermore, at the quantum level things shift between behaving like particles and behaving like waves. There is a duality to their state. Light, for example, comes in waves but is also measured as particles called photons. Electrons behave in the same way. In the famous slit experiment an electron can be beamed at a flat surface on the other side of a card with two slits in it. The electron can be seen to pass through both slits as if it were a wave, but at the same time only one electron particle is seen to hit the flat surface beyond. However, even though you cannot calculate the future states of quantum things individually, you can calculate the *probabilities* of their future states. Thus the quantum world is a world of uncertainty to which the laws of probability apply.[10]

Some cosmologists propose that quantum physics provides a way of circumventing the problem of the origin of the Universe, because it weakens the link between cause and effect. This is the theory of *quantum cosmology*, which suggests that a universe could spontaneously appear as a result of a quantum fluctuation. Such fluctuations occur at the Planck scale, named after Max Planck, whose experiments led to the creation of quantum theory, later developed by Heisenberg and Bohr. At this scale the separate dimensions of space and time become indistinguishable. As the Universe expands, the familiar dimensions of three-dimensional space and the one dimension of time come into being. In addition, quantum cosmologists argue that the Universe is finite but unbounded. What does this mean?

A Finite but Unbounded Universe

First, let us consider the concept of space being finite but unbounded. Imagine you are travelling in a straight line around the world. Although you appear to be travelling in a straight line, you will eventually come back to where you started because you were passing over the curved surface of a globe. The surface that you thought was flat was actually curved but, because of the scale, this was not apparent to you. The flat surface was actually folding round on itself. The same is true of space.

Next, imagine space as being like a balloon being inflated. The balloon expands as time goes forward. An observer's position in space could be anywhere on the surface of that balloon. If you were to make a journey in a straight line through space you would eventually (if you could live long enough and hypothetically had a spaceship powerful enough) come back to where you started, because the fabric of space is curved, like the surface of the balloon. Another point about the balloon is that, as the balloon is inflating, everything around you on the surface of the balloon appears to be moving away from you at an equal speed, as the balloon is inflating evenly. This is exactly what we see when we observe galaxies in space, they all appear to be rushing away from us at an accelerating rate. This is measured by the red shift in the spectrum of the light they emit, using the Doppler effect. As light moves away from you, the light waves get extended and move towards the longer (red) end of the spectrum.[11]

Because all the distant objects in the Universe show a red shift in the light waves they emit, we can tell that they are moving away from us. Indeed, all the distant galaxies we observe in the Universe are moving away from us. Therefore, we are either in the highly unlikely position of being at the centre of the Universe, or the dimensions of space are curved, as in the balloon analogy, so that as space expands everything moves away from everything else[12]. Thus, space is finite but unbounded.

The Hartle and Hawking Model

But what about time, how is time finite but unbounded? James Hartle and Stephen Hawking describe an interesting hypothesis. Imagine you have a flat sheet of paper on which you draw two axes, a horizontal axis and a vertical axis. The horizontal axis represents the three dimensions of space and the vertical axis represents time. The bottom of the piece of paper, at the foot of the vertical 'time' axis, represents the moment of the big bang. As you move up the vertical time axis you move forwards through time. With the paper lying flat, the three dimensions of space have an edge at either side, represented by the edges of the piece of paper. Hence space is finite and bounded.

Next, roll the piece of paper into a cylinder and join each end of the horizontal axis together. Now space is finite but unbounded, as you can keep going round and round the surface of the cylinder on the horizontal space axis. This is similar to the analogy of the balloon. But this can now be extended to take time into account.

Hartle and Hawking then suggest to convert the cylinder into a cone, with the point of the cone at the bottom, representing the beginning of time. As time moves forward, space expands (up the cone). The increasing circumference of the cone represents expanding space as time moves from the bottom of the cone to the top of it. Time is bounded at the bottom of the cone.[12]

But the most profound proposal made by Hartle and Hawking in the cone analogy comes in the next stage. In the classical theory of the big bang, as predicted by classical physics, there is a point at the bottom of the cone, which reflects a single point in time and space when the Universe began. Time has a beginning in the classical theory of the creation of the Universe. However, in the theory of quantum cosmology, time and space merge together so that there is no distinct time and place of creation. The point at the bottom of the cone in their analogy gets rounded off and made into a bowl-shape. Hartle and Hawking propose that at this period of the creation of the Universe, time is just another dimension of space and so it does not exist as time. Although time is still finite in the past, there is no well-defined beginning. *There is no big bang singularity.* Geometrically all points on the bottom of the bowl are equivalent, so there is no point that is uniquely the beginning of time.

Hartle and Hawking propose that there is no origin of the Universe, but neither is it infinitely old. Time is limited in the past but has no boundary. Stephen Hawking says, *'The boundary condition of the Universe is that it has no boundary'.* [13] The Universe has no boundaries in either space or time. It therefore was not created. It simply is!

18

QUANTUM COSMOLOGY
AND CONSCIOUSNESS

*'Consciousness dances on the edge
between the quantum world and the classical world.
And the more we are influenced and in touch
with the quantum subconscious world of enlightenment,
the happier we can be.'*

Stuart Hameroff – Conversations on Consciousness

*'Even if there is only one possible unified theory,
it is just a set of rules and equations.
What is it that breathes fire into the equations and
makes a universe for them to describe?'*

Stephen Hawking – A Brief History of Time

In the previous chapter we saw how quantum theory helped to resolve the twin conundrums about the ends of the Universe. These were, 'does the Universe have a beginning and an end in time or is it eternal?' and 'does the Universe have an edge or is it infinite?' Neither finite boundaries nor infinite boundaries were satisfactory. The Hartle and Hawking model, based on quantum cosmology, concluded that the Universe is finite but unbounded, avoiding the problems raised by endless cause and effect.

Could quantum theory also help to resolve our understanding about consciousness and how it works? The physicist and mathematician Roger Penrose says in his book *The Emperor's New Mind,*

'I argue the phenomenon of consciousness cannot be accommodated within the framework of present-day physical theory'.

He also refutes the notion that consciousness can be generated within computers or that artificial intelligence (AI) can generate consciousness as 'the conscious aspects of our minds are not explicable in computational terms'.

The Missing Theory of Consciousness

Penrose believes that we should look to science for an explanation of consciousness rather than metaphysics, but at the moment science is too limited to explain consciousness. The task of scientists is to develop a scientific theory that is capable of explaining consciousness. He argues that the missing theory of consciousness is the same as the missing link between quantum theory and Einstein's theory of general relativity. The theory lies in the gap between the sub-atomic world of quantum physics and the macro world of classical physics.[1]

Currently there are two classes of physics, one for the macro world that explains things larger than atoms and one for the micro world that explains things smaller than atoms. Classical physics relates to the macro world and includes Newtonian physics and Einstein's theory of general relativity. These both provide a framework for explaining the force of gravity. Neither of these theories agree with each other, but the differences in most situations are negligible. For example, Newtonian physics explains why planets orbit the sun by basing this on the assumption that planets follow an elliptical orbital path around the sun. For most situations this gives sufficiently accurate measurements. Einstein's theory of general relativity also provides measurements for planets travelling around the sun, but is based on the principle that space and time are curved by the gravity from a massive object. Thus, instead of planets following a curved line in straight space, as in Newton's theory, the planets are following a straight line in curved space-time.

Observing a star during a solar eclipse, whose line of sight is close to the sun, can prove Einstein's theory. The solar eclipse allows the observer to see the star without its light being drowned out by the brighter light of the sun. The star is seen to shift slightly from where it is predicted to be. This is because the sun's gravity has bent space around the sun, so that the light coming from the star and passing through that bent space appears to have shifted. Although Einstein's theory of relativity is more accurate than Newton's laws, it is more complicated and, as Newton's laws are sufficiently accurate in most situations, they continue to be used. However in situations of very high gravity, such as near black holes or soon after the big bang, Newton's laws become inadequate and the theory of general relativity has to be used. Therefore the main classical theory for gravity is based on Einstein's theory of general relativity.[2]

Apart from the force of gravity there are three other forces of nature: electromagnetism, the strong nuclear force and the weak nuclear force. Whilst gravity is the weakest of the forces, it operates on large objects and over very long distances and applies to such things as apples, planets, stars and black holes. The other three forces are stronger than gravity and act on objects at or below the atomic level, such as protons, electrons, neutrons and quarks, and they act over very small distances.

The electromagnetic force interacts with electrically charged particles such as electrons and quarks. The force between a positively charged particle and a negatively charged particle is attractive, whilst the force between two positively charged particles is repulsive and the force between two negatively charged particles is also repulsive. This can be demonstrated using magnets. The electromagnetic attraction between negatively charged electrons and positively charged protons in the nucleus of an atom causes the electrons to orbit the nucleus. The strong nuclear force holds quarks together in the proton and the neutron and also holds the protons and neutrons together in the nucleus of an atom. The weak nuclear force is responsible for radioactivity.

These three forces of the micro-world are explained by quantum physics and not classical physics. The problem is that there are differences between the two types of physics which, whilst they are adequate for explaining their particular areas of the Universe, are not consistent with each other. What is missing is a single theory that explains everything. This is referred to as a Grand Unified Theory of everything or 'GUT'. Scientists have struggled considerably to search for a GUT, but at the time of writing, this still remains elusive.[3]

So the two theories, the classical theory of the macro world and the quantum theory of the micro world, remain inconsistent with each other. Classical theory is deterministic, so that every cause has an effect and vice versa. Thus we run into problems like does the Universe have a beginning and end in time or is it eternal? Deterministic classical theory says everything must have a cause, so something must have caused the big bang, which implies that something must have come before the big bang. But then you can go on infinitely looking for the predecessor of each cause.

Quantum theory is not deterministic, but is uncertain and we demonstrated in the previous chapter how this helped us out of the conundrum of whether the Universe has a beginning or end in time or whether it is eternal. In the Hartle and Hawking model, quantum theory predicts that the Universe is finite but unbounded.

Strange things happen at the quantum level that do not fit into the cause and effect framework that we are familiar with in classical physics. Sub-atomic things fluctuate between behaving like waves or behaving like particles. You cannot measure both their position and their momentum. According to Heisenberg's uncertainty principle, the more certain you are about one of these, the less certain you are about the other.[4] A sub-atomic particle can spontaneously disappear and re-appear somewhere else in the Universe. Reality starts to become nebulous at the quantum level and unreliable. It is no longer certain, but is subject to the laws of probabilities.

So scientists are still struggling to find a grand unified theory (GUT) of everything that will consistently explain all the forces of nature and reconcile the macro world with the micro-world. One theory suggests that at a very high energy, called a grand unification energy, the forces would have the same strength and could then be aspects of a single force. At this energy some of the sub-atomic particles, like quarks and electrons would also become the same particle. If scientists could understand how the forces behaved in this state, they could discover the unified theory. Unfortunately such energies are considerably greater than those that can currently be generated by particle accelerators like the Large Hadron Collider at CERN and the required energies are more at the scale of the energies that existed shortly after the big bang. So we are unable to create an experiment which provides the right conditions for testing this theory.[5]

Roger Penrose believes that when a grand unified theory is found, we will have an explanation of consciousness which cannot currently be explained by classical physics and certainly cannot be generated by systems that are used to create artificial intelligence (AI) in computers.

Consciousness expert, Stuart Hameroff, suggests that consciousness is a fundamental property of the Universe, like mass, charge or spin. Both he and Roger Penrose believe that consciousness exists at the lowest level of reality at the Planck scale, the level at which space-time geometry is no longer smooth but quantized or granular. They believe that these granules, or 'qualia', are embedded as patterns in this fundamental granularity of space-time geometry and that quantum computing occurs in protein structures called microtubules within the neurons of the brain. Stuart Hameroff says,

> *'I accept the fact that I am connected to the Universe and try to enjoy the interplay between the material world and the enlightened uncertainty of the quantum world. I became interested in the mystical Kabbalah which describes a world of materialistic strife and chaos, and another world of wisdom and enlightenment. According to the Kabbalah, consciousness 'dances on the edge' between the two worlds'.*[6]

The Manifestation of Spirit in the Material World

Other scientists, like the Hindu quantum physicist, Jay Lakhani, believe that we are approaching the problem of understanding consciousness the wrong way round. Lakhani believes that, instead of looking at matter as an explanation for consciousness, we should look at consciousness as an explanation for matter. Instead of looking at the material brain, with its neurons and synapses, as the area from which consciousness emerges, we should look at the brain as merely being the conduit for consciousness, which already exists at the quantum level, enabling it to come through into the material world. According to Lakhani 'spirit' is already out there.

It is the Hindu Brahman and we are all part of that spirit. We are all connected by it. The brain is not the creator of consciousness, but the switch that enables the spirit to come through us as individuals in the form of consciousness. We are not material beings living in a material world looking for spirituality, he argues, but we are spiritual beings on a material journey. Consciousness, he argues, is the manifestation of the spirit in the physical body.[7]

The material world that we see around us doesn't really exist as we see it. What we see is the manifestation of what is really there. For example, look at a material object such as a table and you see something solid. It appears to be hard and made of some material substance such as wood, metal or plastic. You touch it and you feel something robust that you can't pass your hand through. But the reality is that what you perceive as a hard, solid object is in fact mostly space with atoms spread out thinly within the space, held together by the electromagnetic force of repulsion between the electrons in the atoms. Then consider these atoms. They are made up of the sub-atomic particles, protons, electrons and neutrons, held together by the strong nuclear force, with vast amounts of empty space between them. Go down another level and these particles are made up of even smaller sub-atomic particles such as quarks, which have a mysterious and unreliable existence. What is really around us is a thin soup of sub-atomic particles which appear and disappear in an uncertain manner within vast fields of empty space, but the manifestation of that reality is the hard and solid material world which we experience at our material level of existence.

It is the same, Lakhani argues, for consciousness. The Hindu Vedantists would argue that the reality is Brahman, the universal spirit that exists all around us. The manifestation of this spirit in the material world is consciousness. This spirit manifests itself through the consciousness of the mind that is generated in the material brain, emerging into life, like electricity being generated when copper wire is spun around a magnet. This energy, which the Hindus call prana, flows throughout the Universe and through all living things. Animal bodies are said to have a system of nadis through which the prana flows, in the same way as blood flows through the body in the system of veins and arteries. In China this energy is called Chi or Qi and flows through the system of meridians. This system is used in acupuncture. In the Eastern traditions the mind, like the body, is a tool of the soul. The brain's ability to do all its functions, including operating the body, storing memories, thinking rationally and experiencing emotions, are all part of the toolbox of the mind. The soul uses these tools to do its work in the material world. This is similar to the dualist interactionist theory, which was first proposed by Socrates and Plato, whereby the body lived in the material world and the pysche lived in a separate non-material realm.

'Life is Brahman.
From life is born all creatures,
By life they grow, and to life they return.'
(The Taittirya Upanishad III 3.1)

But the spirit can lie dormant and conscious beings can live their material lives without ever flexing their spiritual muscle. Alternatively, the spirit can be developed and can flourish and grow, strengthening the connection with the spiritual realm. The Hindus believe that this is the union of the Atman (the individual spirit) with the Brahman (the universal spirit). Just as athletes can develop their muscles through physical exercise and people can develop their mental abilities through practising brain-stimulating exercises, so a person can develop their spirit through spiritual practice. This, the Hindus suggest, can be achieved by introspection through meditation or by prayer. Additionally, the Buddhists would suggest, it can be achieved by developing a compassionate mind and through the outward practice of altruism. This, they argue, is the next stage of spiritual evolution, it is the development from consciousness to higher-consciousness.

Emergence

If higher-consciousness can be attained it would be attained through the principle of *emergence*, whereby surprising properties appear at the level of the whole that cannot be understood through focusing on the parts alone.[8] It is a phenomenon whereby the whole is greater than the sum of the parts, but also where the nature of the entity formed by summing those parts cannot be predicted from an analysis of those parts independently, as it is entirely different in nature from the parts. In fact, the entity so formed becomes a system, where the parts interact with each other to form something entirely different.

Emergence appears throughout nature, starting from the most basic building blocks all the way up to what we experience as consciousness. The combination of up quarks and down quarks result in two forms of matter which have properties entirely unlike those of the quarks. These two forms of matter are protons and neutrons. When these protons and neutrons combine with electrons they create atoms which, again, have very different properties from their constituent protons and neutrons. Atoms combine through nuclear fusion in stars to form new atoms, each with entirely different properties from both their constituent sub-atomic particles and from each other. For example, at the same temperature some atoms can behave as gases, whilst others behave as liquids and yet others behave as solids. Some can form the building blocks of life whilst others are poisonous to life. They look and smell different and emit light in different parts of the spectrum. They combine in different ways with each other to form molecules, which also demonstrate entirely different properties from their constituent atoms and from each other. Compare the nature of water with carbon dioxide, for example.

At every stage we see the emergence of something which, not only possesses completely different properties from its constituent parts, but whose properties could not have been predicted from the properties of its constituent parts. The behaviour and appearance of water, for example, is totally different from that of the hydrogen and oxygen atoms that make it up. By looking at hydrogen and oxygen alone, who could predict that their combination would result in a substance with the properties of water? This effect gets even more impressive when molecules combine to form proteins and then amino acids and eventually DNA. Who could predict the emergence of cells and simple plants and animals with all their complexities from these ingredients?

Finally, the highest level of emergence of which science is aware, is consciousness itself. Somehow, from the workings of the synapses and neurons within the brain, consciousness emerges. Some would argue that these brain structures cause the emergence of consciousness. Others, like Lakhani, would argue that the brain structures create the switch through which an existing consciousness, that is a fundamental property of the Universe, can break through at the material level of the Universe. Either way something has emerged that could never be predicted from a cold autopsy of an animal brain.

Just because consciousness is the highest level of emergence that we can observe, does it therefore follow that consciousness is the highest level of emergence that can exist? Naturally from our perspective, as conscious beings, this is the highest level of emergence that we experience in our everyday lives. But it does not necessarily follow that our place in the hierarchy of emergence should be one of sitting at the top looking down. This would be a rather arrogant perspective. Perhaps there are further stages of emergence that we, at our mortal level, have not begun to imagine. Does this mean some sort of transcendence beyond the material world or a life after death? Is it the experience of the mystics? Is it enlightenment? If so, it cannot be our minds, as we currently experience them that make this transcendence, as they are created in the hardware of our brains. All our thoughts and memories are stored in the physical matter of our brains which die when we die, marking the end of those thoughts and memories.

If such a transcendence were possible, something entirely new would have to emerge, something not of the material world. Perhaps it would be something in the quantum world, or perhaps something from an even deeper level of being to which the quantum world was a bridge. Perhaps our view that the world in which we live is normal and such other world is strange, is a misconception based on our limited experience of this world, of which we are familiar. Perhaps the fundamental level of being, from which the Universe itself emerged, is normal and our Universe is the aberration! Ours may be one of many universes in a multiverse which just happened to evolve in the way it did, that made life possible for conscious minds, but in no way represents what is typical.

The writers of the Upanishads would argue that they have glimpsed a higher stage of emergence through their journeys into the depths of their minds and their consciousness to arrive at higher-consciousness. Buddha would suggest that he had glimpsed this state by meditating on compassion and Mahavira would suggest that this state could be experienced by the practice of ahimsa. The methods they used to achieve such glimpses of enlightenment will be the subject of our next chapter.

Morphic Fields of and Fields of Compassion

The biologist and author, Rupert Sheldrake, has proposed the theory of *morphic fields*, which suggests that there is a wholeness in self-organising systems that depends on a field for that system, which organises it. The morphic field gives each whole its characteristic properties that make it more than the sum of its parts.

For example, in plants and animals, genes have the instructions for building amino acids, proteins and DNA, but they do not have the instructions for their form. These details are held in the *morphogenetic field*, which is the type of morphic field that pertains to genetics. Other types of morphic field include crystal and molecular morphic fields, which determine the formation of crystalline structures within crystals as they grow. Behavioural and mental morphic fields determine memes and social systems.

Morphic fields, like the other fields of physics, are regions of influence in space-time, located within and around the systems they organise. They work probabilistically and impose order on an otherwise undefined system by guiding it to goals or end-points, called *chreodes*.

Systems in morphic fields contain other sub-systems which also have morphic fields, resulting in a hierarchy of morphic fields nested in other morphic fields, resulting in a *holarchy*.

Morphic fields evolve and are not fixed like the eternal equations in a transcendent Platonic Realm. Their structure depends on what has occurred before and they have a sort of memory for past patterns which they repeat and develop. The more the pattern is repeated, the stronger it becomes, although the element of probability allows the morphic field to change creatively and adapt. Activity patterns are transferred form one system to a new one by *morphic resonance* which influences the new system to repeat the pattern in the morphic field for its type of system. Such morphic resonance passes through space-time without limitation by distance.

The non-locality and non-separability of morphic fields are similar to those in quantum physics and may therefore be linked to quantum physics. Parts of a quantum system that have been connected together in the past retain an instantaneous connection even when very far apart. For example, two photons, moving in opposite directions from the atom which emitted them, retain an immediate non-local connection, such that, if the polarisation of one is measured, the other will instantaneously have the opposite polarisation. The two parts of the same system are separated in space but are linked by a quantum field which does not exist in our three-dimensional space but in a multi-dimensional space.[9]

It should be stressed that, unlike other fields in physics, such as gravitational fields and electro-magnetic fields, the existence of morphic fields have not been proven. Currently they are based on speculation which is based on observations made from the behaviour of self-organising systems in nature, but which should provide interesting and important investigation.

In her book *Fields of Compassion* Judy Cannato suggests that just such a morphic field is developing now, here on Earth and she calls it a *field of compassion*. This is our consciousness developing to a higher level. It is the development of the compassionate mind. She argues that we must develop this morphic field of compassion if we are to survive as a species and not destroy ourselves. The more we act with compassion, the stronger the field of compassion will grow and the easier it will be for others to develop within this field. This, she proposes, is the next stage of evolution for the Universe, to develop not only conscious life, but a conscious life which is compassionate.[10]

19

HIGHER CONSCIOUSNESS

'Therefore, realise with a still mind
your own true nature,
which is the one pure, undivided consciousness
underlying the restless mind
which is composed of
the whole Universe in all its diversity.'

The Tripura Rahasya

In the previous chapter we saw how self-organising systems emerged from other systems: how sub-atomic particles emerged into atoms, which emerged into simple molecules, which emerged into complex molecules, which emerged into life and from that life consciousness developed. We suggested that from consciousness a higher state of consciousness might emerge and that it may be arrogant to assume that the level of consciousness we currently experience might be the highest level there is. In this chapter we examine the studies already undertaken into higher levels of consciousness.

There are three common states of normal consciousness; the conscious state of being awake, the subconscious dream-state and the unconscious state of dreamless sleep. These states are experienced by nearly all animals on a daily basis and are routine. However, according to experienced meditators and yogis there is a fourth state, which is rarely experienced by the average person and is only achieved by practising yogis and meditators. This is the super-conscious state, known as 'moksha', 'samadhi', 'nirvana' or 'enlightenment'. Achieving this state was the objective of the ancient art of yoga, which was practised in India and China for millennia and passed down through the generations by tradition.

There are several recorded methods of attaining this state, including yogic sleep, meditation, the power of Now and the power of compassion.

Yoga

Yoga was formalised in the Yoga Sutras in around 200 BCE by the forest sage Rishi Patanjali, who lived in northern India. He consolidated the earlier writings of the Vedic texts, particularly the Upanishads, but was also influenced by the more contemporary Jain and Buddhist teachings. Patanjali described the 'eight steps of yoga' in the *Yoga Sutras*, which formed the philosophical basis of Raja Yoga. The objective of working through the eight steps is to achieve the final state of 'samadhi', the super-conscious state.

The first two steps of Raja Yoga involve daily behaviour and are based on the ethical principles of Jain and Buddhist philosophy. The first step is moral behaviour (yamas) which relates to how to behave socially and is the same as the five ethical principles of Jainism. These are non-violence, honesty, chastity, not stealing and not coveting. The second step comprises observances (niyamas) which relate to how to behave personally and are austerity, purity, contentment, study and surrender of the ego.

The third and fourth steps comprise the physical yoga. The third step is the physical postures (asanas), which not only keep the practitioner fit, but help to relax the body to allow the mind to undergo the next stages. The fourth step involves the breathing exercises (pranayama) to control the vital energy or 'prana'.

The final four steps focus on controlling the mind to achieve the ultimate state of consciousness (samadhi) and are based on the philosophies recorded in the Upanishads. The fifth step is the withdrawal of the senses (pratyahara). We are constantly distracted by the external world through our senses but pratyahara frees us from these distractions so that we can focus the mind on what lies within. The sixth step is the concentration of the mind (dharana) which can be practised during asanas and pranayama and paves the way for the last two steps. The seventh step is meditation (dhyana) which requires a focused mind to lead to the eighth step, which is the super-conscious state (samadhi). This final state is enlightenment or nirvana or a state of absorption with the absolute. It is union with the divine cosmic spirit or Brahman.[1]

Measuring Levels of Consciousness

Each of the four levels of consciousness result in different brainwave patterns. At its most active level, when the brain is awake and fully conscious, beta waves are emitted at between 13 – 20 cycles per second (cps). In the conscious state the mind is fully connected to the outside world through the senses. In the dreaming sleep of the subconscious mind, theta waves are emitted at between 4 – 7 cps. Suppressed desires, fears, inhibitions and deep-seated impressions are actively expressed through the medium of the dream. At the most inactive level of deep, dreamless sleep only the unconscious mind remains. This is where instincts, drives and deeply buried experiences reside. Here delta waves are emitted at between 0 – 4 cps. This is the fundamental rhythm of the material Universe. In yoga this state is known as 'the night of Brahman' or the 'womb of creation' as consciousness and prana (vital energy) are said to withdraw from the body to return to the creative source. In the super-conscious state, which is a state of deep relaxation that lies on the border between being awake and asleep, alpha waves are emitted which range between 8 – 12 cps. The wavelengths of these alpha waves lie between the beta wavelengths of the awake state and the theta wavelengths of the dreaming sleep state. These brainwaves can be measured through the use of an electro-encephalograph (EEG) scan.

Brainwave patterns for different states of consciousness:

State of Consciousness	Wave Type	Number of Cycles Per Second - CPS
Awake	Beta	13 – 20 cps
Super-conscious	Alpha	8 – 12 cps
Dream sleep	Theta	4 – 7 cps
Dreamless sleep	Delta	0 – 4 cps

The alpha wave state is experienced very briefly when falling to sleep in the few moments between being awake and being asleep. This rarely lasts longer than three to five minutes which is not sufficiently long enough for any benefits to be gained. During this period there is a progressive release of muscular tensions and withdrawal of the senses in a fixed order, starting with the sense of smell, followed by the sense of taste, then sight, then touch and finally the sense of hearing. As this happens the mind is drawn deeper and deeper inwards.[2]

Yoga Nidra

Yogic sleep (known as yoga nidra) is the practice of maintaining this borderline state between consciousness and dream sleep over a longer period of time. This is also known as the hypnagogic state. In yoga nidra the practitioner isolates the brain and becomes introverted, while maintaining a degree of external awareness by listening to and mentally following a set of instructions. As hearing is the last of the senses to close down, this allows the practitioner to close down all the other senses to the outside world. During the practice of yoga nidra, periodic bursts of alpha waves are interspersed between alternating periods of beta and theta waves, as consciousness remains poised on the borderline between wakefulness and sleep, fluctuating between extroversion and introversion. By remaining aware and alert in this state a profound experience of relaxation occurs which, the yogis believe, is a doorway to higher levels of consciousness. The greatest level of relaxation occurs when the brain is experiencing alpha wave activity, so by maintaining the alpha state the mind gets more rest than it does by falling asleep and entering into the beta wave and theta wave states of dream sleep and dreamless sleep. It is also for this reason that yoga nidra is claimed to have a regenerative, and even healing, effect that is beneficial for many psychological and physical illnesses.

Yoga nidra enables the practitioner to experience the sleeping state while remaining consciously aware. The ultimate outcome is total harmony and integration between all levels of consciousness. By perfecting yoga nidra, the yogis suggest, the three main states of awareness can be transcended and a fourth state can be entered into. This state goes beyond individual consciousness and merges with the universal consciousness. Some describe this as the religious experience of God-realisation, but yogis describe this as the experience of the total mind. According to the yogis, the average person only experiences fragments of his total mind and therefore never taps the vast resources within him, so he never lives in complete harmony with himself. This results in suffering. Yoga nidra enables a person to tap the depths of their being and to discover their source.

In sleep we have little control over our dreams, but in yoga nidra we can control our dreams. Dreams in sleep are rarely remembered let alone interpreted, as consciousness is not engaged. In yoga nidra the conscious mind is present and alert and able to watch the dream and take control. The fourth conscious state can be attained where there is simultaneous awareness of the waking state, the dreaming state and the dreamless state. This has been recorded in the yogic texts for thousands of years and is known as *Turiya*. This state has also been more recently recorded in the laboratory by measuring the electro-physiological operation of the brain. There is an enhanced functioning of the neocortex and greater control over the limbic system, thus reducing the emotional part of the brain function, whilst sharpening the witnessing part of the brain. This experience, it is suggested, produces changes in the practitioner's personality during normal life, giving him greater control over his emotions and his destiny.[3]

Evidence of the fourth transcendental state of consciousness was recorded in 1977 at the Menniger Foundation in Kansas, under the direction of Dr Elmer Green, where researchers used EEG scans to record the brainwave activity of the experienced yogi Swami Rama during a yoga nidra session. He demonstrated the ability to enter various states of consciousness at will. First he entered the yoga nidra state for five minutes and produced 70% alpha waves, by imagining blue skies with the occasional cloud. Then he entered the dream sleep state for five minutes and produced theta waves before finally entering into the dreamless state and producing delta waves. He managed to remain fully aware throughout the whole exercise and could recall all the questions he had been asked during the experiment, even those he was asked whilst in the delta state of dreamless sleep.[4]

Yogis suggest that managing to remain aware whilst in the deepest state of delta wave sleep is the experience of the super-conscious state, where the conscious, subconscious and unconscious mind operate simultaneously. Previously only described in mystical or religious terms, modern psychologists, such as Carl Jung, have tried to demonstrate that this is a state of merging into the collective unconscious and that a universal mind, a single underlying matrix of consciousness exists. This universal mind can be realised by separating the barriers of the three distinct forms of awareness that are normally experienced through practices such as yoga nidra and meditation. The unknown unconscious mind of the individual is then illumined, revealing the entire super-conscious dimension and achieving samadhi or moksha. Carl Jung said,

> 'In addition to our immediate consciousness, which is of a thoroughly personal nature and which we believe to be the only empirical psyche, there exists a second psychic system of a collective, universal, and impersonal nature, which is identical in all individuals. This collective unconscious does not develop individually but is inherited. It consists of pre-existent forms, the archetypes, which can only become conscious secondarily and which give definite form to certain psychic contents'.[5]

Meditation
In addition to practising yoga nidra to achieve the super-conscious state, yogis also practise meditation. While yoga nidra is practised in a state of deep relaxation, usually lying on the floor in the corpse position (shavasana), meditation requires concentration and sharp focus and is usually practised sitting upright, often in the lotus position (padmasana).

During meditation the mind concentrates on one thing, often the breath or a mantra or an image, and becomes more introverted as it disconnects the senses with the outside world and focuses on the object of its attention. Gradually everything else disappears and there is only the observed object and the observer. As the yogi goes even deeper the observer loses his self-awareness and the object and the observer merge into one. Eventually, as the meditator goes even deeper still, the object disappears and all that is left is the experience of 'Shoonya' or 'the dark night of the soul'. At this point samadhi, the eighth step of yoga, is experienced.

The metaphor of snowflakes has been used to describe the infinite expansion that is enlightenment. In the metaphor we are all like snowflakes. Each snowflake has its own unique crystalline formation that is never repeated anywhere in the whole of nature and each snowflake lives an individual existence, separate from every other snowflake. Like the snowflakes we are unique individuals, each living our lives separately from all the other living beings. But if snowflakes could think as they fall into the ocean, they might think, 'This is dreadful, I am going to die, I am going to be annihilated and never be a snowflake again'. But when they fall into the ocean they melt and become one with the ocean as water, for water is their true nature, though this was not apparent to them in their frozen form. This is a metaphor for death or enlightenment. It is an infinite expansion, for the snowflake was not just a drop of water, it was water. In the same way, we are all unique, separate conscious beings living our physical existence, unaware of our own true nature, which is the soul. This only becomes apparent on death or when we reach the super-conscious state and merge with the universal spirit. This is the Hindu belief of the individual soul, the Atman merging with the universal spirit, Brahman. We are not just individual spirits, we are all part of the universal spirit.[6]

The Buddha taught that people should not take what he had said as the truth until they had experimented for themselves. Enlightenment could only be discovered through the experience of it, not through learning. It is up to everyone to practise the methods for themselves and discover the truths through their own experience. Likewise, I would say to the reader, read about the various methods, but to understand them they must be practised and experienced. The advice given by the Zen Buddhists of Japan was that the methods described are just the maps to guide you, they are not the land. Use the maps to discover the land, but do not mistake them for the land itself.

Zen Buddhism emerged in around 500 AD when Boddidharma brought Buddhism from China to Japan. By that time Buddhism had been around for about a thousand years. Like most spiritual philosophies a large volume of scriptures had built up over time and there were huge volumes of texts about Buddhism that could be 'learned'. The Zen Buddhists recommended that this vast amount of 'knowledge' should be ignored and that the Zen practitioners should get back to the basic teachings of the Buddha. Zen masters placed emphasis on *'Satori'* which means a flash of insight or a moment of 'no-mind' and 'total presence'. The whole essence of Zen consists of a total awareness of being in the Now. The great Zen master Rinzai would ask, 'What, at this moment, is lacking?' which was a powerful question, known as a *koan*, that did not require an answer on the level of the mind, but was designed to take the attention deeply into the Now.

The Power of Now
In his book *The Power of Now,* Eckhart Tolle recognises the transformative power of living in the moment by being totally present and not living in the world of worry in the mind. The mind, he argues, is constantly making a noise that disturbs ones peace by incessant thinking. It dwells on the past and worries about the future, creating negative emotions that rise up in us and cause suffering. The mind he suggests should be used by us as a tool to enable us to survive in the world, but more often than not, the mind uses us by constantly thinking, worrying, getting caught up in negative emotions and causing suffering. 'The mind in itself is not dysfunctional,' Tolle says, 'It is a wonderful tool. Dysfunction sets in when you seek yourself in it and mistake it for who you are. It then becomes the egoic mind and takes over your whole life'.[7]

We can end this suffering simply by living in the now, by focusing on what is happening immediately and by being totally present. 'In the Now, in the absence of time, all your problems dissolve. Suffering needs time; it cannot survive in the Now,' says Tolle.[8] Eternity is not endless time, but is no time. There is no future or past, there were just other present times and the only present time that should concern us is the current one. 'Life is now,' Tolle says, 'There never was a time when your life was not now, nor will there ever be'.[9] There is no complicated or mysterious practice of meditation that takes years to develop. As soon as you realise that it is pointless to relive the past and feel anger or guilt, or to worry about the future, and just stop thinking and instead, experience the present, you enter that timeless world of pure being. You stop existing and start to live. It is a place of total peace and happiness. Tolle says that everyone has the ability to achieve this state, but they don't access it because their mind is making too much noise and they can't break out of the inherited collective mind patterns that have kept humans in bondage to suffering for eons. In fact, Tolle argues, thinking has become a disease. People believe they are their mind, but this is a delusion. When Descartes had said 'I think, therefore I am' he made the most fundamental mistake by equating thinking with being. Thinking actually impedes being. Tolle suggests that you should start observing your thinking. As soon as you start watching the thinker a higher level of consciousness is activated in the watcher.

The Now, Tolle argues, is the key to the spiritual dimension. It is a quantum leap in the evolution of consciousness, the awakening of consciousness from the dream of matter and form. It is the ending of time. Great spiritual masters recognised this. Jesus said 'Take no thought for tomorrow, for tomorrow shall take thought for the things for itself.' The Now is also central to the teaching of Sufism, the mystical branch of Islam, and Sufis have a saying, 'The Sufi is the son of time present.' Rumi, a great Sufi teacher said, 'Past and future veil God from our sight; burn up both of them with fire.' Meister Eckhart, a thirteenth century spiritual teacher said, 'Time is what keeps the light from reaching us. There is no greater obstacle to God than time'.[10]

The Practice of Compassion

Thus there have been many recorded practices for the development from consciousness to super-consciousness, including yogic sleep, meditation and the power of Now. But Buddhists also meditate on universal compassion. The Buddha had practised the traditional yogic methods of enlightenment and had found them to be unsuitable for him, as he found that their transcendental effects wore off after he came out of the meditation. Therefore he went away to try to discover his own method for achieving enlightenment and discovered this through meditating on compassion for all living things. What mattered to him was experience, not knowledge, and that experience was based on meditating on compassion and practising compassion towards all sentient beings. Mahavira had made the same discovery. For them their portal to the super-conscious state was the experience and practice of compassion to all living beings. They identified the causes of suffering and found that release from suffering was through giving up the ego, letting go of negative emotions and practising compassionate living. Their study of suffering will be the subject of the next chapter and the methods they proposed for alleviating suffering and developing a compassionate mind will be investigated in the chapter after that.

PART 5

DEVELOPING COMPASSION

20

SUFFERING
VERSUS INNER PEACE

'All of life is suffering.'
Buddha – The first Noble Truth

'Fear is the path to the dark side.
Fear leads to anger,
Anger leads to hate,
Hate leads to suffering.'

Yoda – Star Wars

One of the by-products of the development of the animal brain and nervous system is that it has the potential for suffering, both in terms of the physical pain experienced through the nervous system and the psychological pain experienced in the mind. The Buddha recognised this and defined it as the first noble truth, which stated that all of life is suffering. He discovered this on his first excursion from the palace where he experienced the four sights of a sick man, an old man, a dead man and a holy man. The second noble truth defined the causes of suffering, the third noble truth identified that there was a cure for suffering and the fourth noble truth explained the cure. The circle of Buddhist concern for the suffering of others encompasses all sentient beings, as reinforced in the daily meditations:

'Enthused by wisdom and compassion
Today in the Buddha's presence
I generate the mind for full awakening
For the benefit of all sentient beings.

The Jains also extend their concern for the suffering of others to all living beings through the principle of ahimsa. But in the world beyond the eastern spiritual traditions there has been much disagreement about how far this circle of moral concern for suffering should extend. Some believe that it should only include the human species while others, like the Hindus, the Taoists, the Jains and the Buddhists, believe that it should extend to all sentient beings. Those who believe that our moral concern should exclude animals base that belief either on the opinion that animals suffer but that their suffering does not matter, as they are only animals, or on the opinion that animals are incapable of suffering. In order to determine what suffering is and what species are capable of suffering we need to look at the research.

Studies into Suffering
There has been considerable scientific research into how far animal brains have developed and whether animals suffer. Since most animals have shared the largest part of the brain's evolutionary history with us, we should expect that animals would have much in common with us and share similar experiences of suffering. Unfortunately, as regards whether animals can suffer, there has been little consistency in the research results, although all researchers claim to support their findings with scientific evidence. The results of their research vary from suggesting that only humans are conscious and are therefore the only animal that suffers, to suggesting that all animals suffer.

At the time of the millenium the Universities Federation for Animal Welfare (UFAW) held a symposium on 'Consciousness, Cognition and Animal Welfare' at the Zoological Society in London from which it compiled a book consisting of a collection of editorial articles and abstracts on the subject of animal suffering. The articles were so varied in opinion as to whether animals suffer or not, the book concluded that deciding which species are sentient and determining the range of phenomena to which sentience applies, still remain difficult judgements. It stated that 'the papers provide an insight into the scale and very challenging nature of these questions' and 'raises hopes of major breakthroughs before long'.[1] So why are scientists so divided in their opinions on the subject of animal sentience and the ability of animals to suffer?

Animal Physiology and Physical Suffering

The debate over whether animals suffer physically or not revolves around the physiology of the central nervous system, which includes both the brain and the spinal chord. Those researchers that suggest that animals do not physically suffer, refer to reflex responses to stimulation and the ability of the brain to undertake unconscious decisions. Reflex responses occur in the spinal chord and the brain is only informed of the response afterwards. For example, burning your hand on the stove sends a signal from the sensory neurons in the hand, up the nerves in the arm to inter-neurons in the spine, which send the instruction back to the hand to remove itself from the hot stove immediately. The brain is then informed of the decision afterwards, as the inter-neurons in the spine send a second signal up the nerve to the brain. At this point the brain consciously acknowledges the pain and feels it. This enables motor neurons in the brain to instruct the body to take some further remedial action, such as running the burned area under cold water and applying medication if required. Such high-speed reflex actions would have had important survival value and would have been positively selected for.

In addition to reflex actions the brain also undertakes a large number of unconscious activities, such as respiration and regulating the body's mechanisms. Learned activities such as walking or driving can be taken over by the sub-conscious mind, as to continue to operate such activities consciously would be very slow and cumbersome. In some circumstances it has been demonstrated that certain behavioural activities can occur without conscious awareness. For example some brain-damaged individuals suffer from blind-sight where they cannot consciously see a given object, but when asked questions about the object they are able to describe it. The seeing has occurred in the brain and the patient has been able to report on it, but he has had no conscious awareness of seeing the object. In another example, human paraplegics have been able to demonstrate clear withdrawal responses from painful stimuli without consciously feeling any pain.[2]

Some scientists suggest that because the body can perform reflex actions, undertake unconscious bodily functions, perform some actions subconsciously and respond to some events without conscious awareness, it is not necessary to assume that all animals are consciously aware or feel pain. Such an argument would require pain to be experienced in the very highest regions of the neocortex, which most animals have not fully developed. This would mean that the conscious experience of pain would have developed very late in evolutionary history. The argument ignores the fact that reflex actions are followed by a signal to the conscious brain and it also ignores the fact that the patients with blind-sight and paraplegics are examples of a failure in the evolved system, not examples of the normal functioning of the system. The suggestion that animal behaviour can be explained by reflex actions and unconscious processes, which by-pass the need for sentience or to feel pain has certainly not been proven. Surely, until it has been proven, given the negative impact of pain, all beings with a brain and a nervous system should be given the benefit of the doubt.

One of the most thorough scientific investigations into certain classes of species' ability to feel pain was conducted by Victoria Braithwaite, who demonstrates this in her book '*Do fish Feel Pain?*' She shows that fish have a nervous system, which not only results in nociceptive responses to painful stimuli, but also creates conscious awareness of pain. She describes nociception as the *unconscious* recognition by the nervous system that damage is occurring somewhere, and pain as the *conscious* sensation that whatever is damaged is hurting. She proves that it is pain, not just nociception, that fish experience. She explains that, although modern day fish have not evolved a limbic system and a neocortex around their brains, which are associated with the higher brain activity of mammals, similar structures to those contained in these brain parts have evolved in the forebrain of the fish. Whereas the hippocampus and amygdala reside in the limbic system in mammals, Braithwaite points out that in fish these structures appear in their forebrains. Thus, she concludes that fish are capable of experiencing the feeling of pain and are therefore capable of suffering.[3]

Not only do fish have the capacity to experience suffering, but they also demonstrate an ability to use long term memory and to solve simple logic problems. Some of the cognitive functions that we associate with the neocortex of the brain have developed in the forebrains of fish. They can navigate and learn mazes and work collaboratively, as is demonstrated by the eel and the grouper who hunt together using each other's different specialisms.[4]

Victoria Braithwaite asks the question of where to draw the line with regards to animal welfare concerns and she examines other people's work on invertebrates such cephalopods, including octopus and squid, and crustacea, including crabs, lobsters, prawns and barnacles. This work concludes that they too experience more than nociception and she argues that their position serves to strengthen the position of fish, which she concludes should be grouped on the same side as other vertebrates. She states 'I conclude that they therefore have the mental capacity to feel pain...I see no logical reason why we should not extend to fish the same welfare considerations that we currently extend to birds and mammals'.[5]

Mental Suffering

Pain resulting from physical injury is only one form of painful experience. Other painful experiences include psychological pain such as boredom, anxiety, grief, heartbreak, unhappiness and depression. Such states are what the Buddhists call mental suffering. Apparently these are very common in human beings and it is claimed that such mental suffering has reached epidemic proportions in the modern world, as we seek a more materialistic lifestyle and develop unlimited material needs that can never be satisfied.[6] The more complex our minds become, the more they are capable of running out of control.

Buddhists are only too aware of the dangers of the uncontrolled mind. An unchecked mind, they believe, is the root of suffering. In order to prevent suffering and be happy, the Buddhists believe one has to control the mind. They suggest that an uncontrolled mind can get caught up in all sorts of egotistical manias that lead to desires and passions that unsettle a person's equanimity. An uncontrolled mind can worry about the future and cling on to things from the past, turning them over and over and exaggerating them and persecuting itself with blown up imaginings of how things really were or might be, sometimes developing into paranoia.[7] Negative emotions such as jealousy, hatred and greed, the Buddhists suggest, develop in such an uncontrolled mind.

Attempts to find liberation from such suffering by seeking short term pleasures such as a good meal, sex, the acquisition of some desired object or intoxication, rarely have a lasting effect and usually result in the suffering returning again shortly afterwards.[8]

Buddhists see the ego as being the root of all negative mental afflictions. It is the part of our minds that identifies itself as being separate from everything else because it is programmed by natural selection to strive for itself through the mechanism of survival of the fittest. It drives the emotions of selfishness, greed, jealousy and hate, which lead to unhappiness and mental suffering. Buddhists see the elimination of the ego as key to reducing mental suffering and finding inner peace.

Overcoming Suffering and Finding Peace
The Buddhists have developed various meditation techniques to control the mind to permanently end such suffering and create a state of peace and equanimity at one level. At the next level the experienced meditator seeks to enter the super-conscious state of enlightenment, through generating feelings of compassion for all living things.

The first state of the peaceful mind requires us to stop worrying about the past and the future. It requires us to be in the present moment, in the here and now.[9] The function of worrying about the future and thinking about the past lies in the frontal lobes of the neocortex. The more developed the frontal lobes, the more our ability to worry and create a state of anxiety and suffering for ourselves. We could deduce that, as the frontal lobes of humans are more developed than those of most other species, humans suffer more from this form of anxiety than do other species. Although it can also be said that other animals, which also have highly developed frontal lobes, also have the capacity to worry and suffer. These, in particular, include elephants, cetaceans and other apes. Another objective of the meditator is to suppress the ego, believed to be the source of all our suffering. As we have seen, the sense of ego also resides in the frontal lobes of the neocortex.

The Buddhists focus on suppressing or eliminating those emotions and passions which have the potential to wreak havoc on our peace of mind. These we have seen are associated with the limbic system, an area also shared with other mammals. So through meditation, the Buddhists are systematically reducing the brain activity of those areas of the brain that are causing them the most distress, the emotional areas of the limbic system and the egotistical and anxious areas of the frontal lobes of the neocortex. This is known as 'stilling the mind'. What they discover on accomplishing this process is a clear, still mind capable of seeing things as they really are, in their true nature and not through the distorted perspective of our emotions. Buddhists often describe such a mind as being clear like a reflective mirror, or like the sun coming out as the clouds pass away. There is then the experience of the watcher. Buddhists often talk about being without judgement and just observing things as they really are in their true state. This, they claim, is the achievement of the Seer. The Zen teacher Ho-Shan said,

> *'Our Buddha nature is there from the very beginning. It is like the sun emerging from behind clouds. It is like a mirror that reflects perfectly when it is wiped clean ... and returned to its original clarity.'*

It is often thought that in order to achieve happiness, one must achieve the perfect life. The achievement of wealth, beauty, admiration from peers, a new house, car or job, could be seen to provide that perfect life. But such material things only provide transitory satisfaction, after which the cravings return to make us dissatisfied once again. Such external things provide pleasures that are short lived, but what we need is a lasting happiness that is more fundamental and less likely to be shaken by life's upsets. This, the Buddhists claim, can only be found internally, within our minds. By letting go of such cravings, the Buddhists suggest, we can start to find genuine inner peace.

But what about really difficult life situations, such as loss or bereavement? Everyone has traumas in their lives at some time or another and everyone experiences ongoing difficulties in their life situation, which threaten to undermine their equanimity. The Buddha suggested that we cannot always control our external situation but we can control our internal situation, by affecting the attitude we have towards life. We have all met individuals who seem to have everything but remain unhappy and bitter, whilst other individuals remain cheerful and optimistic through the most terrible traumas. The difference between the two is their different attitudes to life, their internal perspectives.[10]

There is a famous Buddhist story about *Kisagotami*, a poor woman who was not treated with much respect by her husband's family with whom she had to live. This made her very unhappy. But then she bore a son and they treated her differently, with kindness and respect and her life situation improved. But then the son grew sick and suddenly died. Kisagotami was distraught. Not only was she heartbroken at the loss of her son, but her position of honour and respect within her family was lost. Desperate, she carried her son's dead body from door to door asking for medicine, but people just ridiculed her for asking for medicine for the dead. Eventually she came upon a kind man who knew of the Buddha and sent her to see him. When she found the Buddha and explained her situation to him, he advised her to bring him some grains of mustard from every household in which no-one had ever died. Kisagotami was delighted to be taken seriously and set about calling on the local households. At each house the person who answered her explained that someone had died in their home and told her their tragic stories. Gradually Kisagotami felt sorry for them and shared in their suffering, until her own suffering diminished in relation to theirs. She realised that all life dies, that everything is impermanent and that everyone shares in this suffering. So she took her son's body and cremated it. Then she returned to Buddha and became one of his followers.[11]

Is the ability to undertake this mental transformation purely a human one? If it is, it could be argued that very few humans even start the process of achieving inner peace, let alone achieve super-conscious mental states attained through meditating on compassion. Is it a process that requires a bigger, better brain than other animals or is a bigger, better brain potentially an impediment? We have seen that most of the problems of the ego and negative afflictions, such as worry and stress, are located in the frontal lobes of the neocortex, which would suggest that those animals with larger neocortices are more likely to suffer negative afflictions than those animals with smaller neocortices. Maybe our bigger frontal lobes inhibit our ability to achieve peace and a serene state of mind. How often, if one meditates, does one struggle to stop thinking about the past and worrying about the future? Have you ever noticed a cat sitting in a meditative position with a serene expression on his face, appearing not to have a worry on his mind? Can the cat have a deeper and more meaningful meditation than you? Maybe our brains have made us lose something in the process of development. Whilst a bigger brain serves as an excellent analytical tool, maybe its skilfulness in asking questions about the future and considering the consequences of situations also impedes our ability to achieve a peaceful state of mind. Maybe we humans actually have to work harder than the other animals to reduce our mental suffering and find a lasting inner peace that sustains through all of life's adversities.

Having achieved the first state of stilling the mind, reducing mental suffering and finding inner peace, by suppressing the ego with all its negative emotions and attachments, Buddhists suggest we can progress to the next step of achieving bliss. This requires stimulating the positive emotions of loving kindness or compassion. By focusing his thoughts on compassion, the Buddhist strives to create the experience of limitless love to finally attain the higher conscious state.[12]

21

DEVELOPING COMPASSION

'Until he extends the circle of his compassion
to all living things,
man will not himself find peace.'

Albert Schweitzer – The Philosophy of Civilisation

'We can all feel a natural spark of sympathy
for the sufferings of others.
I believe we need to catch that spark
and fan it into a fire
of rational and universal compassion.'

Dr Richard D. Ryder – The Political Animal

We have seen in previous chapters that Buddhists regard the practice of compassion as the portal to achieving the higher-conscious state, known as enlightenment and that this can be undertaken when a person has stilled the mind, eliminating the ego and all negative emotions. But what is compassion? Compassion is the emotional response to empathy, which leads to the desire to alleviate the suffering of others. Empathy is the capacity to recognise and share the feelings of others. Do some people have a greater propensity for empathy and compassion than others and can compassion be cultivated? Is compassion just a human trait or is it shared by other animals? What is its spiritual dimension?

Compassion and Evolution
In chapter thirteen we discovered that evolution made us essentially selfish, as we needed to compete in order to survive. In

particular, our genes are selfish because they need to compete with other genes in order to be passed down through the generations of their survival machines to continue with their potentially eternal life. But part of the evolutionary selfish survival plan included parental care and co-operation with other members of one's own social group. The offspring of parents who cared for them were more likely to survive than the offspring of parents who didn't care for them. The surviving offspring of those parents who cared for them were more likely to carry the caring genes of their parents and hand them on. Hence, by the principle of natural selection, those who carried the caring gene were more likely to survive and to evolve into animals who cared themselves. Furthermore, humans and other animals had to work together in groups and co-operate for their survival. So those who cared for their family or for their neighbours and friends and co-operated with them were also more likely to survive than those who didn't co-operate. Thus the selfish desire for survival resulted in parental care and co-operative behaviour with others inside your social in-group.

But caring for your nearest and dearest is not the same as compassion. Compassion may start with caring for your family and those closest to you, but compassion is about a wider altruism. It is about caring for people outside of your immediate circle of family and friends, sometimes at a significant cost to yourself. In order to achieve this we have to over-ride the selfish nature of our genes with our brains and consciously cultivate compassion. Compassion would include caring about strangers, such as people and animals in distant countries who you have never met. Humans certainly show their compassion when there are famines, droughts or wars, as is demonstrated by the amount of aid money they donate to individuals they have never known.

Compassion would also be about caring for those who do you harm and loving your enemy. Buddhists practice meditations on compassion for their enemies and there have been inspiring stories of Buddhist monks who have been imprisoned and tortured for many years and come out of prison with no feeling of hostility towards their captors. Many Tibetan monks, imprisoned during the invasion of Tibet by China, have said that their deepest fear during that time was that they would lose their compassion for their captors.

The Old Testament said 'Love thy Neighbour', but Jesus extended this to 'Love thy Enemy.' In the parable of the Good Samaritan, even though the Samaritans were enemies to the Jews, it was a Samaritan who had stopped and helped the Jewish man who had been beaten and left for dead by the side of the road. Other Jews, a priest and a Levite, had passed by on the other side of the road.[1] Jesus himself gave up his life to share his insights on compassion with others.

So while there is a sound evolutionary explanation as to why animals show concern for their nearest and dearest, how do we explain the compassion we feel for others – for strangers and for enemies? If we see a kitten drowning in a river our natural instinct is to go and rescue it without hesitating. We don't stop to think 'What benefit will it be to me to rescue this kitten?' or 'What reward will I get?', we just get on and rescue it, for its own sake. We cannot bear to think of it suffering. This is because of two things. Firstly we all want to be happy and avoid suffering.[2] This is only natural. The second thing is that basically we want others to be happy and avoid suffering too. We do this because we have empathy with them. Empathy is the capacity to recognise and share the feelings of others and, as we have seen, this ability is a function of the mirror cells of the brain. Compassion is the emotional response to empathy, which leads to the desire to alleviate the suffering of others. We are capable of mentally putting ourselves in their shoes and understanding what it would feel like to be in their position. Empathy is the root of compassion.

Everyone experiences different degrees of compassion. Only a minority of people feel no compassion at all and these are usually psychopaths or autistic people. Others experience varying degrees of compassion. Some people are naturally highly sensitive and can be particularly squeamish and 'wouldn't hurt a fly'. Others are more disconnected. If they stopped and spent some time considering the situation they could feel compassion, but because they are in a hurry or have other pressing things on their mind, they tend to overlook the sufferings of others. So people experience differing levels of compassion based on both the level of their innate compassion and also on the nature of the moment.

For others compassion is developed through practice. There are many meditative techniques, in which the Buddhists, for example, are particularly experienced, for developing the mind. These help to suppress or work out negative emotions, such as anger or hate, and develop the positive emotion of compassion. Prayer is also a very powerful method of developing and focusing compassion.

Desensitisation to Compassion

Compassion can also be knocked out of people. This can be achieved by desensitising them. This was particularly noticeable in the concentration camps during World War two, where ordinary, decent human beings complied with the most awful atrocities. It is unbelievable that people could commit such acts, but the very fact that they did so must be a lesson for us all. It raises the possibility that we may not be immune from becoming desensitised ourselves.

So what are the factors that could help to desensitise us in such a powerful manner? The four most common factors are the effects of an authority figure, peer pressure, detachment and justification. All of these were relevant in the example of the concentration camps. Because the frontline perpetrators of the atrocities were taking their orders from above, from an authority figure, they felt that this somehow absolved them of their responsibility. The people who were giving the orders, on the other hand, were so far removed from the horrors themselves that they became detached from those horrors. They all worked with other people who were carrying out the same atrocities, so there was peer pressure. Both the people on the frontline and those giving the orders justified what they were doing by convincing themselves that it was for the good of the country or that the people they were torturing and exterminating were bad and somehow deserved it.

An example of the effects of an authority figure, which illustrates these tendencies, is the famous 1960s Milgram Experiment by the social psychologist Stanley Milgram. In this experiment a scientist in a white coat asked the participants to administer an electric shock to a human subject with a heart condition every time they failed to answer a question correctly. The participants were unaware that the human subject was an actor and there was no real shock. Even when the person supposedly receiving the shock was heard to scream in agony and plead for them to cease, the participants, although disturbed by what they were doing, continued for a long time before they stopped, simply because they were being given an instruction by an authority figure. 65 per cent of participants went all the way with the experiment, administering the highest possible shock. In an article *The Perils of Obedience* Milgram summarised his experiment and said, 'Ordinary people simply doing their jobs, and without any particular hostility on their part, can become agents in a terrible destructive process. Moreover, even when the destructive effects of their work become patently clear, and they are asked to carry out actions incompatible with fundamental standards of morality, relatively few people have the resources needed to resist authority.'[3]

So compassion is something much greater than our evolutionary requirement to care for our nearest and dearest, as it is far more altruistic than that. It is innate in varying degrees in all animals and it can be nurtured or diminished depending on our experiences and our own efforts. So how do we nurture compassion? Upbringing has a very important role to play in how our compassion for others develops. Children who are cared for and treated with respect and compassion are usually far more likely to understand compassion and transmit it than children who are deprived of love or are neglected or abused. This seems common sense. Also children who are brought up with pets develop greater compassion for animals than those who are not brought up with pets. But there are, on the other hand, always examples of people who have suffered a hard childhood, who grow up to show considerable compassion to others. Some do very positive things and go out of their way to help those who have suffered as they had done. This is because their suffering has resulted in great empathy for the plight of their fellow sufferers. Charles Dickens is an example. After a very hard childhood he went on to write books about such hardships, to bring them to the attention of those in society who could do something to change things. And, as a result, some change was achieved.

So compassion, whatever its innate degree within a person, is capable of further development. This can be either by nurture, due to the receiving of compassion and the teaching of compassion, or by the experience of hardships which enhance empathy with others. Whenever we experience hardships in life, we must value them as life's lessons, from which we learn and develop spiritually. Without such lessons we can never grow. Some say that we are here on 'Earth School', to learn through life's experiences, in order to develop and grow spiritually, so that we can live fully in the life beyond.

Developing Compassion

Given that we can't change the experiences of our childhood, what can we do to develop our compassion further now that we are adults? The first step is to be aware of the things that can work on us to reduce our compassion, the things that desensitise us, so that we can guard against them. Are we living in a system or a society that encourages us to be hard? Do our peers discourage compassion in us and require us to appear tough? Is there an authority figure in our lives that discourages our compassion? Do we find ways of justifying our lack of compassion? We would hope that none of us would participate in atrocities such as those that occurred in places like Auschwitz.

But do we come near it at any point in our lives? For example, do we know where the chicken in our sandwich comes from? Have we ever thought about it before? Was she a higher welfare chicken or did she have a short and miserable life in a cramped cage, cooped up with thousands of other miserable chickens who were unable to meet their welfare needs? Did she live a life without sufficient space to move, sitting in faeces and suffering from painful hockburn on her legs, often with broken limbs, unable to stretch her wings, stand up or display any natural behaviour? Was she finally carted away to be strung up upside down by her legs, while fully conscious and then dunked unceremoniously into an electric bath to be stunned before finally being killed? Can we logically condone this treatment of a fellow sentient being whilst displaying such horror at the atrocities of Auchswitz? Many will say that this is different because it is only a chicken. But what exactly is the difference? She can still feel all of these things. A Jain and a Buddhist would say that all animals are part of the wheel of life, that they all have Buddha potential.

So why should we discriminate against this particular form of life? The fact is, we have allowed ourselves to become desensitised to this cruelty. Why? Because many other people are also eating a sandwich with low welfare chicken in it, including our friends – peer pressure. We see it advertised – authority figure. We have always eaten low welfare chicken – detachment. It's only a chicken after all – justification. Why should we wait for legislation to come in to ban such atrocities? So the first thing we can do in order to develop our compassion is to examine ourselves and ensure that we are not causing harm to any other sentient being.

Ahimsa is the fundamental principle of Jainism and *Tsa'ar ba'alei chayim* is a fundamental principle of Judaism. Both believe that in order to develop compassion, one must refrain from harming any other sentient beings. How, they would ask, can any living being develop compassion and grow spiritually when he is harming another living being, whether directly through cruelty or indirectly through indifference? The Jains' circle of compassion did not end at humans, but encompassed all living things.

Non-harming is not limited to physical violence, but also to harm done through word and deed. A spiteful word can cause deep wounds, as can neglect. We have to be, what Buddhists call, 'mindful' in everything we say and do in order to avoid harming others. This brings us back to the Golden Rule – never do to others what you would not like to be done to yourself. And the ancient philosophies on compassion are very clear about who those 'Others' are – *All* sentient beings. There is no room for prejudices in universal compassion, no racism, no sexism, no ageism, no homophobia and no speciesism. Compassion is clearly signed up to the equality and diversity awareness agenda!

Extending the Circle of Compassion
Once we have achieved the first and most fundamental step of refraining from harming other sentient beings, how can we further develop our compassion?

In her book *Twelve Steps to a Compassionate Life* Karen Armstrong describes a process for extending your circle of compassion. She starts at the centre of the circle of compassion and works out a step at a time. She states that the person at the centre of the circle of compassion is You.[4] It is often easy to overlook yourself and think that compassion is about forgetting yourself and putting others first. Ultimately it is, but first you have to be content with yourself. You need peace of mind and equanimity. How can you care about others if you dislike yourself, feel uncomfortable with yourself and have no peace of mind? So be kind to yourself.

Armstrong suggests that once you are happy with yourself you can learn about empathy and mindfulness and can start to expand your circle of compassion out to your family and loved ones. Then you can expand that circle to your friends and then to others in your community and workplace that you like and get on with. After that you can expand that circle to those in your community with whom you find relationships more challenging. Next you can expand the circle to strangers and finally to your enemies. You can then apply the golden rule throughout your life by doing to others what you would want them to do to you.

Buddhists use the practice of 'the four immeasurable minds of love' to cultivate compassion. This makes the practitioner aware of the huge, expansive and immeasurable feeling that knows no hatred and directing it out to furthest corners of the world and not omitting a single creature from his radius of concern. Firstly, he evokes 'loving kindness' (*maitri*), including in his mind an attitude of friendship for everything and everyone. Secondly, he meditates on 'compassion' (*karuna*), desiring that all creatures be free of pain. Thirdly, he brings to mind 'pure joy' (*mudita*) which he desires to be shared with all creatures. Finally, he frees himself from all attachment by loving all sentient beings with 'even-mindedness' (*upeksha*). Thus Buddha understood that hatred, envy, spite and ingratitude shrink our horizons and limit our creativity. But the benevolent emotions of gratitude, compassion and altruism broaden our perspectives and break down the barriers we erect between ourselves and others, in the vain attempt to protect the insecure ego.[5]

In *Therevada* (narrow vehicle) Buddhism, the practitioner is content to meditate on compassion, but in *Mahayana* (great vehicle) Buddhism this is not enough. The meditator, having cultivated compassion in his mind, must go out into the world and help to alleviate the suffering of others. Such a person is known as a *Bodhisattva*. In Jainism such a person is known as a *Jina*, or one who helps others to cross the ford of suffering safely over to the other side. For yogis this is called Karma Yoga. In other faiths people who do this are called missionaries or aid workers.

The Charter for Compassion

In November 2009, the writer and religious historian, Karen Armstrong, launched the Charter for Compassion to bring together the major faiths to restore compassion to the heart of religious and moral life. The Charter was designed to counter the voices of hatred, intolerance and extremism and to work together for justice and peace. It is based on the Golden Rule and reads as follows:

> *The principle of compassion lies at the heart of all religious, ethical and spiritual traditions, calling us always to treat others as we wish to be treated ourselves. Compassion impels us to work tirelessly to alleviate the suffering of our fellow creatures, to dethrone ourselves from the centre of our world and put another there, and to honour the inviolable sanctity of every single human being*, treating everybody, without exception, with absolute justice, equity and respect.*
>
> *It is also necessary in both public life and private life to refrain consistently and empathetically from inflicting pain. To act or speak violently out of spite, chauvinism or self-interest, to impoverish, exploit or deny basic rights to anybody, and to incite hatred by denigrating others – even our enemies – is a denial of our common humanity.*
>
> *We acknowledge that we have failed to live compassionately and that some have even increased the sum of human* misery in the name of religion. We therefore call upon all men and women:*
>
> - *To restore compassion to the centre of morality and religion;*
> - *To return to the ancient principle that any interpretation of scripture that breeds violence, hatred, or disdain is illegitimate;*

- *To ensure that youth are given accurate and respectful information about other traditions, religions and cultures;*
- *To encourage a positive appreciation of cultural and religious diversity;*
- *To cultivate an informed empathy with the suffering of all human beings* – even those regarded as enemies.*

We urgently need to make compassion a clear, luminous and dynamic force in our polarised world. Rooted in a principled determination to transcend selfishness, compassion can break down political, dogmatic, ideological and religious boundaries. Born of our deep interdependence, compassion is essential to human* relationships and to a fulfilled humanity. It is the path to enlightenment, and indispensable to the creation of a just economy and a peaceful global community.[6]

I wholeheartedly support the spirit and the letter of the Charter, but with the amendment of the words 'human being' to 'sentient being' and 'human' to 'animal' (see * above). Speciesism has been the root of so much suffering in the world throughout history. We need to extend our compassion to all sentient beings with whom we share the Cosmos.

The Tibetan Zone of Ahimsa

In 1987 the Dalai Lama outlined a five-point peace plan, where the first point required Tibet to be turned into a Peace Zone. The Peace Zone would be demilitarised, divested of all nuclear weapons and hazardous waste and used to promote human rights. The Tibetan plateau would be transformed into the world's largest natural park or biosphere, where strict laws would protect wildlife, where exploitation of natural resources would be carefully regulated so as not to damage relevant ecosystems and a policy of sustainable development would be adopted in populated areas. National resources and policy would be directed towards the active promotion of peace and environmental protection. Organisations dedicated to the furtherance of peace and to the protection of all forms of life would find a hospitable home in Tibet. The peace zone would be called the '*Zone of Ahimsa*'.[7] What a beautiful dream! Sadly it has yet to materialise.

The Dalai Lama says that we cannot solve the problems of the world today by external disarmament alone. We need internal disarmament and that requires a compassionate state of mind.[8] If humans are to succeed in ensuring a future for the world, they must achieve the enlightened state and this requires the cultivation of and practice of compassion.

PART 6

CONCLUSION

22

COMPASSION –
THE KEY TO THE FUTURE

*'The religion of the future will be a belief
in a Creed of Kinship,
a charter of human and sub-human relations.'*
Henry Salt – 'The Creed of Kinship'

*'The Earth has not evolved solely for our benefit
and any changes we make to it are at our own risk.
This way of thinking makes clear that
we have no special human rights;
we are merely one of the partner species in the
great enterprise of Gaia.
We are creatures of Darwinian evolution,
a transient species with a limited lifespan,
as were all our numerous distant ancestors.'*

James Lovelock – 'The Vanishing Face of Gaia'

Five billion years from now our sun will run out of fuel and die. When the sun's central hydrogen has fused into helium, the remaining fuel will drift outwards to cooler surroundings. Then the sun's gravitational force will exceed the nuclear force that holds it up and the sun will collapse, causing the temperatures and pressures at its core to rise. This will cause a second round of fusion from the helium atoms to create carbon and oxygen, allowing the sun to rise up again like a phoenix and shine for a short while, with the last breaths of a dying star. When this fuel is spent, the sun will expand and cool and become a red giant, rapidly spreading out into the solar system, devouring Mercury and Venus and then consuming the Earth, before evaporating into space. Everything that existed in the solar system will be destroyed, maybe destined to become cosmic ash or perhaps destined to be recycled into a new generation star.[1] All that we will have done, all that we will have been, all that we will have achieved, as the culmination of twenty billion years of the Universe's evolution, will die with it. This puts us into perspective. But perhaps we will be clever and invent inter-stellar space travel so that we can plan our exodus from Earth before its destruction and travel to a new home orbiting a younger star. Maybe humans or some other life form of the future will be able to make an inter-stellar Ark and translocate all the species of the Earth and its accumulated wisdom to this new home to preserve their unique heritage.

But perhaps humans will not even survive for the lifetime of the sun. Maybe they will not even survive the next millenium. And as for the other species, perhaps they too will be extinct in the not-so-distant future. The Earth is our life-support system. It is our only home. Without it we have nowhere else to go. What is the point of speculating about travelling to Mars and colonising it when we are not even able to manage the planet upon which we have evolved and on which we are perfectly adapted? There is no other environment in our solar system to which we are so well attuned. Even if we develop brilliant technology that can transform other worlds, such as Mars or Europa, we would still not be able to create a place that we could really call home, where we could be comfortable and free in a natural environment. It would be a sterile place. Intelligent life would have to evolve all over again. So wouldn't it just be easier to preserve what we have got, to manage the Earth as positively as we can for future generations, not just for our own species, but for all species? We will never know whether our descendants, in whatever shape they may evolve into, will ever be able to create the technology required to escape the sun's death-throws. But surely the best we can do for them is to preserve our current environment and the riches that we already have on this jewel of a planet.

Saving the Planet

The Earth faces many risks. Some, such as the possible collision of an asteroid or large meteorite, are from space itself and may be out of our control. There have been plenty of these in the past. They were common during the solar system's infancy and the moon's unaltered surface reminds us of their effects. The meteorite crater in Arizona tells us that there have been a few significant impacts in recent geological history. Indeed, a large meteorite collision is the most popular explanation for the extinction of the dinosaurs, animals that dominated the Earth for over 200 million years, far longer than the reign of humans upon this planet. Then there are natural disasters caused by the Earth itself including earthquakes, tsunamis, volcanoes, floods, droughts and famines. These regularly occur causing thousands of deaths and horrendous suffering. If we humans focused our resources properly, we could intervene to reduce the suffering caused by such natural events. Even an incoming meteorite could be deflected with the right technology. But are we planning for such things? Where are the contingency plans? If we invested as much of our resources in such contingency planning and preventative systems as we did in weapons and war, most of these problems could be resolved. Instead, millions of humans die of unnecessary starvation when the Earth currently has the resources to feed them, and of unnecessary diseases when there are vaccines, preventative treatments and cures available but which are not distributed fairly. Thousands of people and animals die every year from drinking unclean water! Thousands of others die every year from war! What optimism is there for our ability to prevent the effects of natural disaster?

But not only are we, the human species, failing to mitigate the effects of natural disasters, we are creating our own disasters. Destruction of the environment is rife with deforestation, the creation of greenhouse gases and pollution. The tropical rain forests are the lungs of the Earth and without them we will suffocate and die. Deforestation is the equivalent of cutting out our own lungs! Species are becoming extinct at an unimaginable rate, largely where rain forests are being destroyed. These species are our heritage, they are the unique product of millions of years of evolution that will never be repeated again. But they are also part of the fabric of life on Earth, a unique part of the web of interdependencies that make life possible. Cut too many of the threads and the cloth will fall apart.

Gaia

According to the scientist James Lovelock, the Gaia theory suggests that the Earth is a living, self-sustaining system and whatever damage may be done to her, she will rebalance herself and bounce back. That is very comforting for the Earth, but in such a system the Earth is not dependent on humans or on any other individual species for her own survival. She does not even need the atmosphere that we depend on. Our current oxygen-rich atmosphere, that we need to breathe in order to stay alive, is only a recent development on Earth. For a large part of her early life the Earth's atmosphere was mostly made up of hydrogen but also included water, ammonia, methane and hydrogen sulphide, an atmosphere that would be poisonous to us. So the Gaia theory does not offer any comfort to the human species. We can make ourselves extinct and Gaia will ensure that her living system will endure, maybe evolving a new atmosphere with a new set of species. In order to maintain the current system, which is the only one in which we can survive, we have to maintain the balance of our current atmosphere. We need it, although Gaia does not.

According to James Lovelock in his book *The Vanishing Face of Gaia, a Final Warning*, the Earth is already heading to a hot state and we are not doing enough to prevent it. He criticises the amount of international meetings with their talks and treaties, which lack the action required to prevent catastrophe. He says,

> *'Gaia still moves step by step towards the hot state, one that will allow her to continue as the regulator, but where few of us will be alive to meet and talk.'*

He argues that it is not just about emitting carbon dioxide into the atmosphere or deforestation, but that there are too many animals acting as parasites on the planet. He says,

> *'It is not simply too much carbon dioxide in the air or the loss of biodiversity as the forests are cleared; the root*

*cause is too many people, their pets and their livestock –
more than the Earth can carry'.* He warns, '*No voluntary
human act can reduce our numbers fast enough even to
slow climate change. Merely by existing, people and their
dependent animals are responsible for more than ten times
the greenhouse gas emissions of all the airline travel in the
world.'*

He believes that humans and many other species are unlikely to
survive but that we must do all we can for those that could evolve
in the future. He says,

> '*Our goal now is to survive and to live in a way that gives
> evolution beyond us the best chance.'*

He argues that humans are an emerging intelligence who over-
estimate themselves and have a long way to go before they attain
the wisdom required to manage the planet successfully. Indeed, we
cannot even manage our economies. He says,

> '*It is hubris to think that we know how to save the Earth:
> our planet looks after itself. All that we can do is try to
> save ourselves.'*[2]

Sustainability of Resources

James Lovelock identifies the size of the human and animal
population as being the biggest threat to the stability of Gaia. Each
year we produce 70 billion animals globally for the meat and dairy
industry. Meat production is both a huge emitter of greenhouse
gases and the most inefficient means of using the limited land to
feed the population. In 2004 the charity 'Compassion In World
Farming' commissioned a report, written by Mark Gold, on the
global effects of eating meat, entitled *Eat Less Meat – It's Costing
the Earth* [3]. It was introduced and supported by Jonathan Porritt,
the former director of 'Friends of the Earth'. The report concluded
that it is imperative for humans to reduce their dependency on meat
eating on the grounds of sustainable use of resources,
environmental protection, human health and animal welfare. The
report argues that just as a growth in the human population puts a

strain on the Earth's resource, so too does the growth in the animal population. A spiralling farm animal population threatens the Earth's stability.

Farm animals use considerably more food calories than they produce in the form of meat, because livestock waste most of the energy and protein value of their feed in digestion and bodily maintenance. Growing crops for direct human consumption is far more efficient and puts less strain on limited land resources. Farm animals compete with humans for resources such as land and water. Lack of water is the greatest threat to yields of arable crops, making it vital to develop food production systems that minimise water reliance. Also, each calorie of meat takes more water to produce than a calorie of grain. According to the report, livestock herds account for 10 per cent of all greenhouse gases, including 25 per cent of methane emissions, which is the most potent greenhouse gas. Farm animals produce around thirteen billion tonnes of waste each year, including ammonia and nitrates which pollute the land, water and air. The excessive use of fertilisers and pesticides to produce crops to feed livestock add to this pollution. Direct environmental damage includes large-scale deforestation of rain forests to make way for land to raise beef for hamburgers and to grow soya to feed livestock. Over-grazing has led to desertification over vast areas of Africa. In his introduction to the report, Jonathan Porritt says,

> '*Do the sums objectively, and only one conclusion emerges: if all six billion of us were to live at the same level of material wellbeing that the world's richest one billion currently enjoy, then we'd need at least another three planet Earths to provide the resources and absorb the pollution and waste*'.

In 2009 Friends of the Earth and Compassion in World Farming commissioned a further report entitled *Eating the Planet* [4] which set out proposals for feeding a predicted world population of nine billion in 2050 in a sustainable way. They concluded that feeding the world in 2050 is possible without using the most intensive forms of animal and crop production or a massive expansion of land for farming. The report suggests that humane methods of farming animals can provide sufficient food to feed a growing world population and they recommend that providing sufficient food for all would be helped greatly if rich countries adopted healthier, lower meat-based diets and if food is distributed more equally. The report suggests that sufficient food can be provided in 2050 without further deforestation.

In 2010 the United Nations Environment Programme also commissioned a report entitled *Environmental Impacts of Consumption and Production: Priority Products and Materials* [5]. It states that,

> *'More than half of the world's crops are used to feed animals, not people. Land and water use, pollution with nitrogen and phosphorus, and greenhouse gas emissions from land use and fossil fuel use cause substantial environmental impacts. Animal products, both meat and dairy, in general require more resources and cause higher emissions than plant-based alternatives.'*

They too recommend that a sustainable future requires the consumption of less meat.

Farmageddon

In 2014, Philip Lymbery, CEO of Compassion in World Farming and Isabel Oakshott, Sunday Times political editor, published *Farmageddon – The True Cost of Cheap Meat*. They travelled the world visiting intensive farming sites and reported back on their discoveries. Their conclusions were frightening.

Billions of animals are suffering in factory farms. Two thirds of the 70 billion farm animals produced every year are factory farmed. Humans living near factory farms have their lives shortened by as much as a decade (e.g. heart disease, birth defects and childhood asthma). Tax payers' money is being squandered on factory and other farming (e.g. the Common Agricultural Policy (CAP) is nearly half the EU budget, and 30 billion dollars a year goes in subsidies to US farmers). Mega-piggeries, mega-dairies, battery reared beef and genetically engineered animals will soon be the norm (e.g. only eight per cent of farms in England today grow crops and rear more than one species of animal). Factory farms use half the world's antibiotics to fatten animals and keep them alive in unnatural and crowded conditions (80 per cent of antibiotics in the US are used on farms). This encourages superbugs such as MRSA that are resistant to antibiotics and are found in meat and milk. (In the EU 25,000 people now die every year from drug resistant micro-organisms). The labelling of some meats as 'corn-fed' or 'farm fresh' is meaningless in welfare or health terms. Factory farming pollutes the countryside leading to the disappearance of bees, butterflies, birds and useful insects. Scarce water is being used up by factory farming. Just producing one kilo of beef requires nearly ninety bath tubs of water. Factory farms also pollute water supplies with E. coli. Feeding animals grain often produces fatty meat that can be bad for human health (e.g. obesity, diabetes and heart disease). Four billion starving humans could be fed on the grain and soya now used worldwide to fatten animals for meat. Thousands of trees are felled annually to support the factory farming of meat. Bees need trees and so does clean air. Millions of tons of fish are sucked out of the sea and fed to factory farmed pigs and chicken each year, causing vast marine damage. Neglect and cruelty frequently occur in abattoirs around the world where many workers are paid by the numbers of animals slaughtered. Workers are sometimes drunk or on drugs. Alternative proteins, such as those from seaweed and 'test-tube' meat, can avoid cruelty altogether. For every six tons of plant protein, such as cereals, only one ton of animal protein is returned as meat. A third of the world's cereal harvest and 90 per cent of the world's soya are fed to industrially reared animals. About half our food (in Europe and the US) is wasted - enough to feed the world's human starving between three and seven times over. In the UK the equivalent of 50 million chickens, one and a half million pigs and 100,000 cattle are thrown away each year, often ending in landfill sites that are running out. Globally, enough food is currently produced to feed around eleven billion humans, rather than the current seven billion. Nearly a third of the earth's land surface is now devoted to rearing farm animals or growing their feed. Forests are cleared in order to grow cereals to feed industrially housed animals. Live animals are transported cruelly across the world in their hundreds of thousands each year.

The authors have demonstrated that the economics of meat eating is no less than international lunacy. What solutions do they recommend? Although Lymbery and Oakeshott do not insist on vegetarianism but they do say *eat less meat* and *do not waste food*. According to Lymbery and Oakeshott, animals, humans and environments will all benefit if we follow these two simple rules. They also suggest that far more, however, needs to be done by the governments of the world and by the United Nations itself.[6]

Preventing Armageddon
The human race also has bombs that could destroy everything on Earth many times over. But the most frightening concern of all is that humans have a trigger to ignite those bombs and it is a very volatile trigger. That trigger is human aggression. All through history humans have fought amongst themselves. There have always been wars. With each generation of technology the wars get bigger, escalating to the scale of the recent first and second world wars. Another world war would be Armageddon! My guess is that we humans will eventually destroy ourselves and will take most of the other species on the planet with us. The Earth will be sterile for a long time. But she will bounce back and other new species will develop and flourish. Maybe they will be like the dinosaurs again or perhaps there will be a new set of mammals. Sea creatures will flourish and there will be animals flying in the air once more, or in whatever other atmosphere develops. Gaia will bounce back. These creatures will have another five billion years to evolve and flourish before they too have to contemplate the technology required to leave Earth for a new home when the sun has used up all its fuel.

If we were to draw up a risk register for the Earth, that highlights the major risks we face, it could look something like this:

Earth – Risk Register

Risk	Effect	Prob	Impact	Total Risk
Nuclear War	Mass extinction of most species & long term environmental damage	Medium 2	High 3	High 6
Global Warming – due to too many people & animals, deforestation and GHG emissions	Mass extinction of most species & long term environmental damage	High 3	High 3	Very High 9
Large Scale Natural Disasters from Earth, e.g. large volcano, tsunamis, earthquakes	Mass extinction of some species and long term environmental damage	Low 1	High 3	Medium 3
Large Meteor Strike	Mass extinction of most species & long term environmental damage	Low 1	High 3	Medium 3

Note: The total risk is the 'probability' of the risk multiplied by the 'impact' of the risk, where, for probability and impact, low is assigned the value 1, medium is assigned the value 2 and high is assigned the value 3. The assignment of these values is subjective.

Maybe we could survive this, but it would require enormous effort. We could destroy all our weapons of mass-destruction, but we would still have the knowledge of how to redevelop them. We could stop damaging the environment and live sustainably. This would mean that we would have to immediately refrain from emitting greenhouse gases and immediately cease deforestation and reverse it. But most importantly of all, we would have to reduce our numbers by cutting back on the human population, currently standing at seven billion, and we would have to stop livestock farming, or dramatically reduce the number of animals for meat eating.

Internal Disarmament

But even if we could make these changes and did make them, how could we be sure that we didn't slip back into our old bad habits? It is not enough to change on the outside. We need to change on the inside as well. We need to suppress our egos and our negative emotions such as fear, anger, hate and greed. Western civilisation has become an ego-driven, greedy society that has resulted in a huge gulf growing between the rich and the poor and between the powerful and the helpless. Recently, many of the world's economies have collapsed because of greed, but there are still plenty of rich individuals who continue to amass wealth, while others have seen their jobs, pensions and life savings evaporate. Where are the philanthropists today? This financial imbalance comes on top of the existing division between the wealth of the Western world and the poverty of the Third world. In the Third world millions already die of hunger and disease, while in the West, millions struggle with obesity and its related ailments, costing taxpayers billions of dollars in healthcare. As the world population continues to expand to a total beyond seven billion people, these problems will only be exacerbated. Only by letting go of our greed and sharing the world's resources and managing them well with wise stewardship can we hope for a sustainable future. As Gandhi once said,

> *'Earth provides enough to satisfy every man's needs, but not every man's greed.'*

We need to adopt Ernst Schumacher's economics of *Small is Beautiful*.[7]

I believe that we need to cultivate positive emotions such as compassion and behave with altruism. We should extend the circle of compassion out from our nearest and dearest to include all sentient beings. Most of all we need to practice ahimsa. As Gandhi said,

> *'Be the change you want to see in the world'.*

It is not enough for us to disarm externally, we must also disarm internally. The fourteenth Dalai Lama writes in his book *Ancient Wisdom, Modern World,*

> *'If, as individuals, we disarm ourselves internally – through disciplining our negative thoughts and emotions and cultivating positive qualities – we create the conditions for external disarmament. Indeed, genuine, lasting world peace will only be possible as a result of each of us making an effort internall.'*[8]

The Jain teacher, Satish Kumar says,

> *'Peace and disarmament are not possible without creating a whole culture of non-violence.'*[9]

We have a wonderful Compassion Project[10] founded by Karen Armstrong, which is an inspirational initiative and a positive way forward, but we must not limit that compassion to human beings. We should extend our compassion to include all our fellow sentient beings that share in universal consciousness with us. We must exercise our stewardship of this planet with wisdom and show kindness and respect to those who are weaker than us. We need to demonstrate altruism and positively go out of our way to offer them help and protect them. We need to practice the golden rule and do to them as we would want them to do to us.

A UN Declaration of Ahimsa
We require leadership from the United Nations. The world already has a Declaration of Human Rights. But this does not go far enough. We need a *'Declaration of Ahimsa'* to demonstrate the commitment of all member states to the principle of non-violence to all sentient beings and the natural world. As Gandhi said,

> *'The greatness of a nation and its moral progress can be judged by the way its animals are treated'.*

But above all we need a change of heart. We have to evolve another stage beyond the level of the naked ape with all his aggression and competitive passions. We should develop our minds to become calm and altruistic. We must rediscover and understand the ancient wisdoms of the compassionate spiritual traditions. We come into this world with nothing but our spirit and we leave with nothing more. Surely the best thing we can do is not to waste time in short-term material gain, but to lead a mindful and skilful existence. We should live a life of non-violence and non-harming to others and to help to alleviate their suffering. We should overcome all human hubris and eliminate our prejudices, particularly speciesism, by which we unjustly dominate the weakest in our Society. Our goal should be to leave behind a benevolent legacy for the benefit of all sentient beings. Indeed the survival of our planet and all its species, including ourselves, depend on it. To use the words of Albert Einstein, let us truly

> *"widen our circle of compassion to embrace all living creatures and the whole of nature in its beauty"*.

Let us become the Compassionate Animal!

REFERENCES

1. The Compassionate Enlightenment
1. Benjamin Hoff, *The Tao of Pooh & The Te of Piglet*, (Methuen Books 1994) pp.185 – 190.
2. Genesis 2:7-25; 3:1-24.
3. Jennifer Isaacs, *Australian Dreaming: 40,000 years of Aboriginal History* (Lansdowne Press 1980).
4. Natubhai Shah, *Jainism The World of conquerors – vol 2* (Sussex Academic Press 1998) pp.34 –39.
5. Karen Armstrong, *The Great Transformation* (Atlantic Books 2007) pp. xii - xviii.
6. Ibid pp 203 – 211.
7. Ibid pp 341 – 348.
8. Ibid pp 274 – 288.
9. Ibid pp 240 – 244.
10. Ibid p199.
11. Shab. 31a
12. Matthew 7:12.
13. Luke 20:45-46.

2. Brahman
1. Swami Vivekananda, Quoted by Willand Ariel Durant in *Our Oriental Heritage,* (Simon and Schuster, New York).
2. Karen Armstrong, *The Great Transformation* (Atlantic Books 2007) pp. 3 - 8.
3. Ibid pp 12 – 25.
4. Eknath Easwaran, *The Upanishads* (Nilgiri Press 2007) pp 13 - 22.
5. *The Bhagavad Gita* 18: 48-49.
6. Eknath Easwaran, *The Upanishads* (Nilgiri Press 2007) pp 22 - 47.

3. The Tao
1. Benjamin Hoff, *The Tao of Pooh & The Te of Piglet*, (Methuen Books 1994) pp.10 - 13.
2. Ibid pp.185 – 190.
3. Karen Armstrong, *The Great Transformation* (Atlantic Books 2007) pp. 341.
4. Laotse, *Tao Te Ching*, chapter 15.

4. Buddha
1. Karen Armstrong, *The Great Transformation* (Atlantic Books 2007) pp. 274 - 277.

2. Clive Erricker, *Buddhism* (Hodder & Stoughton 1995) pp 35 – 59.
3. Karen Armstrong, *The Great Transformation* (Atlantic Books 2007) pp. 277 - 288.
4. Clive Erricker, *Buddhism* (Hodder & Stoughton 1995) pp 61 – 72.
5. The Dalai Lama, *The Many Ways to Nirvana* (Hodder & Stoughton 2005) p27.

5. The Jain Tirthankars
1. Karen Armstrong, *The Great Transformation* (Atlantic Books 2007) pp. 240 - 244.
2. Satish Kumar, *You Are Therefore I Am* (Green Books 2010) pp. 62 – 65.
3. Jeffrey D Long, *Jainism An Introduction* (I.B. Tauris & Co 2009) pp 10.
4. Natubhai Shah, *Jainism The World of conquerors – vol 2* (Sussex Academic Press 1998) pp.34 –39.
5. Jeffrey D Long, *Jainism An Introduction* (I.B. Tauris & Co 2009) pp 117 - 118.
6. Ibid pp 15 – 22.
7. Ibid pp 13 – 15.
8. Satish Kumar, *You Are Therefore I Am* (Green Books 2010) pp. 53 – 54.
9. Ibid pp 58 – 59.
10. Ibid p 54.

6. The Greek Philosophers
1. Attributed by Ovid in *The Metamorphoses.*
2. Karen Armstrong, *The Great Transformation* (Atlantic Books 2007) pp. 313 - 314.
3. Ibid p188.
4. Ibid pp 257 – 265.
5. Ibid pp 314 –325.
6. Paul Davies, *The Mind of God* (Penguin Books 1992) pp 223 –232.
7. Roger Penrose, *The Emperor's New Mind* (Oxford University Press 1999) pp 550 – 552.
8. Karen Armstrong, *The Great Transformation* (Atlantic Books 2007) pp. 325 - 330.
9. Richard D Ryder, *The Political Animal* (McFarland & Co 1998) pp 8–14.

7. The Peaceable Kingdom of Monotheism

1. Karen Armstrong, *The Great Transformation* (Atlantic Books 2007) pp. 38 - 48.
2. Ibid pp 3 – 7.
3. Richard Schwartz, *Judaism and Vegetarianism* (New York: Lantern, 2001) p15.
4. Matthew 7:12
5. Rev Andrew Linzey, *Animal Gospel* (Westminster 2005) pp 1 – 3.
6. Ibid p 53.
7. Deborah Jones, *The School of Compassion*, (Gracewing, 2009) p134.
8. Karen Armstrong, *The Great Transformation* (Atlantic Books 2007) pp. 8 - 12.

9. The Perennial Philosophy of Saints and Mystics

1. F.C. Happold, *Mysticism: A Study and an Anthology* (Penguin Books 1963) p 20.
2. Ibid p 21.
3. Ibid pp 29-30.
4. Ibid p 34.
5. Ibid p 37.
6. Ibid pp 40-45.
7. Quoted by Richard D Ryder, *Animal Revolution: Changing Attitudes Towards Speciesism*, (Blackwell 1989).
8. Freda Le Pla, *The Ark* no. 244, p 40.
9. Julie Hopkins, *The Ark* no. 288, *Holy Hermits and Their Creature Companions* p 6.
10. Dr Deborah Jones, *The School of Compassion* (Gracewing 2009) pp 66 – 73.
11. Quoted in *The Life* by Bonaventura.
12. Dr Deborah Jones, *The School of Compassion* (Gracewing 2009) pp 73– 75.

10. The Rise of Speciesism

1. Saint Augustine, *The City of God*, trans. Marcus Dods (Massachusetts: Hendrickson Publishers Inc., 2009) pp 24-25.
2. Saint Augustine, *De Moribus Ecclesiae Catholicae et de Moribus Manichaeorum*, 2.17.59.
3. Thomas Aquinas, *Summa Contra Gentiles*.
4. Alan Butler, *Lives of Saints*, Bernard Bangley 2005, p 22.
5. Richard D Ryder, *The Political Animal* (McFarland & Co 1998) pp 14 – 19.

6. Richard D Ryder, *Speciesism, Painism and Happiness* (Imprint Academic 2011) p 40.
7. Richard D Ryder, *The Political Animal* (McFarland & Co 1998) p 51.
8. Richard D Ryder, *Speciesism, Painism and Happiness* (Imprint Academic 2011) pp 62 - 88.
9. Satish Kumar, *You Are, Therefore I Am* (Green Books 2010) pp 120 – 121.
10. Satish Kumar, *Resurgence Magazine*, (March/April 2012 edition, no. 271) p1.
11. Richard D Ryder, *The Political Animal* (McFarland & Co 1998) p 126.

11. Philanthropy and the Humane Movement
1. Aeschylus, *Prometheus Bound: Text & Commentary* (Cambridge 1983).
2. McCully, George, *Philanthropy Reconsidered, A Catalogue for Philanthropy Publication* (Boston 2008).
3. World Council of Churches, *Friends (Quakers)*, (www.oikumene.org/en/member-churches/church-families/friends-quakers.html).
4. Richard D Ryder, *The Political Animal* (McFarland & Co 1998) pp 19 - 20.
5. Ibid pp 20 – 23.
6. Ibid pp 23 – 25.
7. Jon Wynne-Tyson, *The Extended Circle* (Centaur Press 1985) p 386.
8. M.K. Ghandi, *An Autobigraphy or The Story of My Experiments with Truth* (Penguin Books 1982) pp 291 – 292.

12. Compassionate Geniuses
1. Jon Wynne-Tyson, *The Extended Circle* (Centaur Press 1985) pp 260 – 261.
2. Ibid pp 131 –232.
3. Ibid pp 248 –249.
4. Ibid pp 65 – 66.
5. Ibid p 220.
6. Ibid p 7.
7. Ibid p 184.
8. Ibid p 388.
9. Ibid pp 250 – 252.
10. Ibid p 62.
11. Ibid pp 371 – 373.
12. Ibid pp 375 – 376.

13. Ibid pp 382 – 383.
14. Ibid p 75.
15. Ibid p 76.
16. Ibid pp112 – 113.
17. Ibid pp 323 – 330.
18. Ibid pp 91 – 92.
19. Ibid pp 313 – 316.
20. Ibid p135 – 136.
21. Ibid pp 311 – 312.
22. Ibid p 200.
23. Carl Sagan, *The Dragons of Eden* (Hodder & Stoughon 1979) p 121.
24. Ibid p 120.

13. The Evolution of the Universe, Consciousness and Compassion

1. Carl Sagan, *The Dragons of Eden* (Hodder & Stoughon 1979) pp 13 – 17.
2. Carl Sagan, *Cosmos* (Macdonald Futura 1980) pp 218 – 233.
3. Prof. Brian Cox, *Wonders of the Universe* (Harper Collins 2011) pp 122 – 123.
4. Carl Sagan, *Cosmos* (Macdonald Futura 1980) p 233.
5. Prof. Brian Cox, *Wonders of the Universe* (Harper Collins 2011) p 135.
6. Carl Sagan, *Cosmos* (Macdonald Futura 1980) pp 287 – 289.
7. Richard Dawkins, *The Selfish Gene* (Oxford University Press 2006) pp 19 - 20.
8. Ibid p 7.
9. Ibid p 59.
10. www.raw-food-health.net/NumberOf Vegetarians.html
11. Vegetarian Times Magazine, *Vegetarianism in America study 1* (2008).
12. Mintel Survey (2006).
13. European Vegetarian Union.

14. Brain Evolution & Structure

1. Carl Sagan, *The Dragons of Eden* (Hodder & Stoughon 1979) pp 23 - 24.
2. Ibid pp 51 – 69.
3. Rita Carter, Mapping the Mind (Phoenix 2010) p 34.
4. Victoria Braithwaite, *Do Fish Feel Pain?* (Oxford University Press 2010) pp 96 – 103.
5. Carl Sagan, *The Dragons of Eden* (Hodder & Stoughon 1979) p 198.
6. Ibid pp 69 –79.

7. Rita Carter, *Mapping the Mind* (Phoenix 2010) p 231 - 232.
8. Ibid pp 30 – 31.
9. Eric R. Kandel, James H. Schwarz & Thomas M. Jessell, *Principles of Neural Science* (New York 2,000).
10. Rita Carter, *Mapping the Mind* (Phoenix 2010) pp 48 – 58.
11. Carl Sagan, *The Dragons of Eden* (Hodder & Stoughon 1979) p155 – 185.
12. Ibid pp 83 – 92.
13. Charles Darwin, *The Descent of Man.*

15. The Minds of Animals
1. Carl Sagan *Dragons of Eden* (Hodder & Stoughon 1979) pp 109 - 112
2. Ibid p108
3. Ibid p 121.
4. Ibid pp 107 – 124.
5. Marc Bekoff *The Animal Manifesto*, Resurgence Magazine March/April 2012 no 271, p35.
6. Jonathan Balcombe *Second Nature: The Inner Lives of Animals,* (Macmillan, 2010) p 105.
7. Ibid pp 106-115.
8. Ibid p 51
9. Ibid p 48
10. Ibid p 47
11. Ibid pp 55 - 56
12. Ibid p 54
13. Ibid p 55
14. Lisa Rogak, *One Big Happy Family: Heartwaming Tales of Animals Caring for One Another*, (New York: St Martin's Griffin, 2013).
15. David Ferris, *Elephant Art*, Resurgence Magazine no. 271, pp 54-55.
16. Neil R. Storey *Animals in The First World War*, (Shire Publications, 2014) pp 41-42.
17. Jonathan Balcombe *Second Nature: The Inner Lives of Animals,* (Macmillan, 2010) pp 23-24.
18. Rupert Sheldrake *Dogs That Know When Their Owners Are Coming Home: The Unexplained Powers of Animals*

16. Studies in Consciousness
1. Susan Blackmore, *Conversations on Consciousness* (Oxford University Press 2005) pp 1 – 2.
2. Max Velmans, *Understanding Consciousness* (Routledge 2009) pp 11 – 30.

3. Susan Blackmore, *Conversations on Consciousness* (Oxford University Press 2005) pp 104 – 105, Richard Gregory 'Life is full of gaps'.
4. UFAW, Consciousness, Cognition and Animal Welfare (UFAW 2001) pp 36 – 37, B J Baars 'There are no known differences in brain mechanisms of consciousness between humans and other mammals.'
5. UFAW, Consciousness, Cognition and Animal Welfare (UFAW 2001) pp 46 – 59, B Bermond 'A Neuropsychological and Evolutionary Approach to Animal Consciousness.'
6. Rita Carter, *Mapping the Mind* (Phoenix 2010) p313 - 315.
7. Max Velmans, *Understanding Consciousness* (Routledge 2009) pp 82 – 86.
8. Carl Sagan, *The Dragons of Eden* (Hodder & Stoughon 1979) pp 206 - 211.
9. Max Velmans, *Understanding Consciousness* (Routledge 2009) pp 86 – 117.
10. Ibid pp 206 – 231.
11. Susan Blackmore, *Conversations on Consciousness* (Oxford University Press 2005) pp 36 – 49, David Chalmers 'I'm conscious, he's just a zombie'.
12. Susan Blackmore, *Conversations on Consciousness* (Oxford University Press 2005) pp 115 – 124, Stuart Hameroff 'Consciousness is quantum coherence in the microtubules.'
13. Max Velmans, *Understanding Consciousness* (Routledge 2009) pp 327 – 351.

17. The Mystery at the End of the Universe

1. Stephen Hawking, *A Brief History of Time* (Bantam Press 1989) p 1.
2. Prof. Brian Cox, *Wonders of the Universe* (Harper Collins 2011) pp 66 – 71.
3. Carl Sagan, *Cosmos* (Macdonald Futura 1980) pp 253 – 257.
4. Stephen Hawking, *A Brief History of Time* (Bantam Press 1989) pp 45 - 46.
5. Prof. Brian Cox, *Wonders of the Universe* (Harper Collins) pp 228 - 239.
6. Carl Sagan, *Cosmos* (Macdonald Futura 1980) pp 259 – 260.
7. Rob Alder, The Many Faces of the Universe (New Scientist, Nov 2011) pp 43 – 47.
8. Carl Sagan, *Cosmos* (Macdonald Futura 1980) p 258.
9. Ibid p 259.
10. Peter Atkins, *On Being* (Oxford University Press 2011) pp13 – 17.

11. Stephen Hawking, *A Brief History of Time* (Bantam Press 1989) pp 54 - 61.
12. Carl Sagan, *Cosmos* (Macdonald Futura 1980) pp 253 -256.
13. Paul Davies, *The Mind of God* (Penguin Books 1992) pp 61 – 69.
14. Stephen Hawking, *A Brief History of Time* (Bantam Press 1989) p 136.

18. Quantum Theory and Consciousness
1. Roger Penrose, *The Emperor's New Mind* (Oxford University Press 1999) pp xv – xxiii.
2. Stephen Hawking, *A Brief History of Time* (Bantam Press 1989) pp 29 -34.
3. Ibid pp 63 – 79.
4. Ibib pp 53 – 61.
5. Ibid pp 74 – 75.
6. Susan Blackmore, *Conversations on Consciousness* (Oxford University Press 2005) pp 115 – 124, Stuart Hameroff 'Consciousness is quantum coherence in the microtubules.'
7. Jay Lakhani, *www.hinduacademy.org*
8. Stephan Harding, *Animate Earth* (Green Books 2006) p38.
9. Rupert Sheldrake, *Dogs That Know When Their Owners Are Coming Home*, (Arrow Books, 1999), Appendix C: Morphic Fields.
10. Judy Cannato, *Fields of Compassion*, (Sorin Books 2010)

19. Higher Consciousness
1. B.K.S. Iyengar, *Light on Yoga* (Harper Collins 2001) pp 12 – 31.
2. Swami Satyananda Saraswati, *Yoga Nidra* (Yoga Publications Trust 2008) pp 170 – 172.
3. Ibid pp 172 – 176.
4. Ibid pp 176 – 178.
5. Carl Jung, *The Archetypes and the Collective Unconscious* (London 1996) p 43.
6. Susan Blackmore, *Conversations on Consciousness* (Oxford University Press 2005) p146, Stephen LaBerge 'Lucid Dreaming is a Metaphor for Enlightenment.'
7. Eckhart Tolle, *The Power of Now* (Hodder and Stoughton 2005) p 40.
8. Ibid p 43.
9. Ibid p 41.
10. Ibid pp 42 –44.

20. Suffering versus Inner Peace

1. UFAW, *Consciousness, Cognition and Animal Welfare* (UFAW 2001) p1.
2. Ibid pp 41 – 46, L. Weiskrantz.
3. Victoria Braithwaite, *Do Fish Feel Pain?* (Oxford University Press 2010) pp 96 – 103.
4. Ibid pp 106 – 113.
5. Ibid pp 112 – 113.
6. The Dalai Lama, *Ancient Wisdom, Modern World* (Little, Brown & Co 1999) pp 5 – 11.
7. Matthieu Ricard, *Happiness* (Atlantic Books 2006) pp 80 – 96.
8. Matthieu Ricard, *Happiness* (Atlantic Books 2006) pp 97 –107.
9. Eckhart Tolle, *The Power of Now* (Hodder & Stoughton) pp 39 – 58.
10. The Dalai Lama, *Ancient Wisdom, Modern World* (Little, Brown & Co 1999) pp 52 – 66.
11. Clive Erricker, *Buddhism* (Hodder & Stoughton 1995) p 13.
12. The Dalai Lama, *Ancient Wisdom, Modern World* (Little, Brown & Co 1999) pp 131 – 139.

21. Developing Compassion

1. Luke 10:27-37.
2. The Dalai Lama, *The Art of Happiness* (Hodder & Stoughton 1999) pp 3 –5.
3. Stanley Milgram, Obedience to Authority; An Experimental View (Harper Collins 1974).
4. Karen Armstrong, *Twelve Steps to a Compassionate Life* (The Bodley Head 2011) pp 67 – 81.
5. Ibid p 34.
6. Karen Armstrong, *Twelve Steps to a Compassionate Life* (The Bodley Head 2011) pp 3 - 5.
7. The Dalai Lama, *Freedom in Exile* (Abacus 1998) pp 273 – 275.
8. The Dalai Lama, *Ancient Wisdom, Modern World* (Little, Brown & Co 1999) pp 193 – 194.

22. Compassion – The Key to the Future

1. Prof. Brian Cox, *Wonders of the Universe* (Harper Collins) pp 232 – 233.
2. James Lovelock, *The Vanishing Face of Gaia, A Final Warning* (Allen Lane 2009) pp 1 – 22.
3. Mark Gold, *Eat Less Meat* (www.ciwf.org.uk/eatlessmeat/).
4. CIWF, *Eating the Planet* (www.ciwf.org.uk/resources).

5. United Nations, *Environmental Impacts of Consumption and Production: Priority Products and Materials* (www.ciwf.org.uk/resources).

6. Philip Lymbery and Isabel Oakeshott, *Farmageddon, the True Cost of Eating Cheap Meat*, (Bloomsbury Publishing, 2014).

7. E.F. Schumacher, *Small is Beautiful: A Study of Economics as if People Mattered* (Vintage Books).

8. The Dalai Lama, *Ancient Wisdom, Modern World* (Little, Brown & Co 1999) pp 193 – 194.

9. Satish Kumar, *You Are, Therefore I Am* (Green Books 2010) p120.

10. Karen Armstrong, *The Charter for Compassion* (www.charterforcompassion.org).

INDEX